The Refuge

The Refuge

My Journey to the Safe House
for Battered Women

JENNY SMITH

**SIMON &
SCHUSTER**

London · New York · Sydney · Toronto · New Delhi

A CBS COMPANY

This edition published in Great Britain by Simon & Schuster UK Ltd, 2014
A CBS COMPANY

1 3 5 7 9 10 8 6 4 2

Simon & Schuster UK Ltd
1st Floor
222 Gray's Inn Road
London WC1X 8HB

www.simonandschuster.co.uk

Simon & Schuster Australia
Sydney

Simon & Schuster India
New Delhi

A CIP catalogue record for this book is available from the British Library.

ISBN (Paperback): 978-1-47112-948-3
ISBN (Ebook): 978-1-47112-949-0

Typeset by Hewer Text UK Ltd, Edinburgh
Printed in the UK by CPI Group UK Ltd, Croydon, CR0 4YY

While this book gives a faithful account of the author's experiences,
some names and details have been changed to protect the privacy
of the individuals involved.

My heartfelt thanks to my mum, dad and
family for not judging me.

Contents

Prologue

'Your mam's cooked.'

As I trudged up the hill to home with the fierce Derbyshire sleet driving horizontally into my face, I hugged my scratchy old overcoat closer round my body. Here in the Dales, the cold of winter seeped through your clothes and into your very bones.

The lights of our terraced house twinkled out across the rain-spattered fields like a beacon guiding me home. But my hands were like blocks of ice and, with every step I took, I could feel my feet prickling with chilblains.

Come on, Jenny Pickering. Stop being such a girl. Not long now and you'll be warming yourself by the fire.

Just then the front door flung open and an imposing figure with shoulders that soared into the heavens blocked the doorway. He seemed almost as big as the house itself.

My dad.

'Gerra move on, Jennifer,' he bellowed, his booming voice

sending a blackbird chattering up into the grey skies. 'Your mam's cooked.'

Were there three words in the English language more eagerly anticipated?

As he ushered me inside, the most incredible smell floated up to meet me. In the grip of winter's sub-zero temperatures, my mam's Sunday roast could always be relied on to melt the hardest of hearts.

Light, life and laughter spilled out from the kitchen as my three older brothers squabbled over who was going to get first dibs on the mouth-watering feast.

If it's to be believed that women show their love through their cooking, then my mam must have loved us very much. A giant rib of beef on a trivet was sizzling in the black-leaded range, with a whole tray of Yorkshire pudding rising nicely beneath it, while on the other shelf a tin of crisp roast potatoes were browning to a turn. A thick pat of home-made salted butter melted over a mountain of piping hot red cabbage.

Gravy as thick as treacle made with meat juices and cornflour bubbled on the stove and, behind that, a pudding sealed with one of my mam's stockings steamed away nicely, ready to ooze out strawberry jam and be smothered in a lake of home-made vanilla custard. It wasn't a meal. It was a masterpiece.

Beside the range, a coal fire crackled merrily in the grate and I could feel its warmth in my bones as I took my place next to my brothers.

There, in the midst of all this, stood my mam, calmly preparing a feast fit for a king as easily as if she were boiling an egg.

If home is where the heart is, then the heart of my home was my mother. Gladys Pickering or Higginbottom as she was before marriage to my father, was a housewife to her very core. Her lifeblood pulsed through every floorboard and joist in the house.

She had an affinity with our little home in the miners' village of Hasland that flowed from the soft brown hair on her head to the tips of her lace-up boots.

Watching her now, piling our plates high with slices of succulent pink beef, the faintest trace of flour smeared on her flushed faced, I loved her for her efforts.

There hadn't been a time in living memory when I'd not come home to find Mam busy stirring something on the stove, mopping the floor, ringing clothes out on her vast tabletop mangle or vigorously pounding clothes in the dolly tub.

If it wasn't housework, then she'd be busy pickling onions, stirring huge pots of boiling jam on the stove or darning clothes. Her house was spotlessly clean and her four kids always immaculately turned out.

Mam was typical of the women of her generation. Cooking, cleaning and having babies took up most of their lives, but by 'eck they had backbone. Gladys Pickering, Mrs Riggot, old Mrs Partridge and all the other indomitable women of our pit village lived a life that most young women today simply couldn't hack, working non-stop from dusk till dawn.

Each and every one had a fierce pride over the cleanliness of their house. The street might not have had two pennies to rub together but, by God, your doorstep better be sparkling and your windows gleaming.

Most of the women in the village were, to use the local vernacular, as rough as a bear's arse. I'm not saying we were better than them, but my mam was a bit more refined than that. She and Dad bought us magical books like *Treasure Island* and *Robin Hood*. As well as the power of reading, they also instilled in us decent values.

'Do unto others as you would have done to you' was a virtue both my parents lived by. Those virtues sat hand in hand with the values of strength, honesty, being kind to animals and cleanliness.

Because of this we grew up with a strong sense of family pride and respect for authority. But, mainly, Mam was just a good old-fashioned grafter. Even when she was sat down, her hands were just a blur of clacking knitting needles. She never rested. Ever.

The only time she did stop was to grab me and fold me into her pinny for a hug.

'Come here, girlie, and give your mam a cuddle,' she'd say in a voice like thick, creamy porridge.

It wasn't just the house she put effort into.

After a night of sleeping on metal rollers, her brown hair fell in soft waves about her face and her lips always bore the faintest flush of cherry-red lipstick. A cuddle with Mam left you smelling of lavender or Lily of the Valley. She would never dream of wearing curlers under a headscarf during the day or letting her stockings slip down her legs.

There's a saying about redoubtable Derbyshire ladies: *Derbyshire born, Derbyshire bred, strong int arm and weak int head.*

Mostly I think this just refers unkindly to their battle-weary faces and stout figures, rather than their intelligence, as most of the women I knew were sharp as steel. These women weren't just homemakers, they were the heartbeat of the community.

But my mam was different to the other women on the street. She was special.

At last, when the final dish was placed on the large wooden kitchen table, she stood back to admire her handiwork, her soft features finally relaxing.

'Dig in then,' she smiled.

'Aye,' laughed my dad, in his far broader Derbyshire accent. 'Eat thee snap.'

We didn't need telling twice.

Seconds later, it was every man for himself as my brothers piled into lunch. A flicker of a smile crossed Mam's weary face as the room was filled with the sounds of scraping cutlery and happy sighs.

And by the time the last trace of pudding had been licked from the bowl, it was harder to tell who was happier.

Mam's green eyes shone with love as she let out a long, contented sigh and folded her arms over her ample bosom.

'Have you had sufficient, Jenny love?' she asked in her soft voice, worried just in case the vast quantities of good food I'd devoured hadn't filled the hole. I laughed. It was the same question she asked after every meal.

'Give over, woman,' laughed Dad. 'Happen she's had plenty. Now, Jennifer lass, atha gonna brew up?'

I was so stuffed I felt my limbs were melting into the floor, but I obliged.

'That's the ticket, Jennifer,' he grinned. My dad always called me by my full name, unlike Mam, which automatically made me a target of fun for my brothers.

'Yeah, *Jennifer*,' teased my older brother Howard. 'Let it mash.'

'Shurrup or ahl belt thee one,' I warned.

'If it's owt to do wi' thee, ahl tell thee,' my dad shot back, quick as a flash.

A blissfully happy afternoon of cards, jokes and a reading of *Treasure Island* by the fire followed, with leftover Yorkshire pudding spread with jam and washed down with mugs of strong, sweet tea.

As darkness fell over the Dales, Dad dragged the old tin bath in from the small backyard and my brothers and I had our weekly scrub down with carbolic soap in front of the fire.

Screams of laughter filled the smoky kitchen as we flicked soapy suds at each other in the flickering firelight.

A week's worth of grime and countryside debris soon turned the bathwater as black as a miner's boot, but what did we care?

Mam sat knitting by the fireside, a gentle smile playing over her handsome features.

In later life I often wondered what dark demons were chasing through her mind but, on that day and on so many days like it, I knew nothing but a warm, fuzzy contentment.

By the time bedtime rolled around, I could hardly keep my eyes open.

The fresh air of the Dales, combined with the warmth of the firelight, was having a hypnotic effect and my eyes were flickering open and shut.

'Come on, Jenny love,' chuckled Mam. 'Up the wooden hill to Bedfordshire.'

I was asleep before Mam had even tucked me in under my candlewick bedspread. Dreaming of tomorrow and a world of adventures just waiting to be had. The perfect end to the perfect day.

CHAPTER I

Cobbled Streets and Daring Feats

I was born Jennifer Pickering on 25 May 1946. I'm sixty-eight now, but my idyllic childhood remains etched onto my memory and I remember it as if it was yesterday.

I was born in Hoole Street, Hasland, an inconspicuous terraced street in an inconspicuous mining village some two miles south-east of the market town of Chesterfield.

Hasland is set in a sleepy, untouched valley and village life has remained unchanged for centuries; its seasons dictated by the gentle rhythms of farming and its fortunes swelled by coal-mining.

The cobbled streets were set against a backdrop of lush farmland, and the beauty of the rolling Dales was breathtaking.

The only thing to interrupt this gentle tableau was the strangely twisted spire of Chesterfield church that dominated the skyline. Rumour had it that the devil had twisted it and that every time a virgin walked past, it bent slightly more.

Apart from that, all was still and timeless beauty in our village. Unruffled, peaceful and tranquil, *for now* . . .

The youngest of four, with three older brothers, Michael, Howard and Philip, I was the only girl and Dad's coming-home present from the war.

My dad, Thomas Pickering, was a miner born and bred, like his dad and his dad before him.

One of eleven children, he was born and raised in Grassmoor, over the very mines he was sent to work in, aged fourteen, in 1930.

There were rumours that there was gypsy blood in the family; Dad had an uncle with red hair and one leg. But, ultimately, it wasn't to the endless road that Dad found himself drawn, but deep, deep down into the very bowels of the earth.

The gypsy wandering spirit was something that infected me, not Dad, and I often wonder if it was responsible for the turbulence and mayhem that enveloped me in later life.

My father was a creature of the earth and a more powerful man you'd be hard-pressed to find.

His gravelly voice was rich with warmth and love and he greeted everyone the same way.

'Aer th areet, duck?' he'd smile. That may sound daft, but that's how men greeted each other back then. And, make no mistake, men were men in the proper sense of the word. He had a face that looked like it had been carved from rock and if you misbehaved, you'd feel the cut of his hand across your backside.

I sometimes think it wasn't muscle and bone holding my powerful dad up but coal.

The soft, green rolling hills and coal mines they hid flowed through his blood and being a miner was virtually imprinted in his DNA.

Coal ruled supreme in our communities. Men made their living from mining it, it heated our homes and it put food on the table.

'We don't eat chips,' my dad always said. 'We eat coal.'

It's almost impossible for us to imagine today what it would have been like for my dad, just a 14-year-old lad when he started. The conditions were atrocious. Mine shafts were hundreds of feet beneath the surface and temperatures at the bottom could soar to sixty degrees.

There were no cutting machines when Dad started. Dynamite, heavy pickaxes and sheer brute force were required to carve out the rich seams of coal from the earth.

It was dangerous work. People were regularly crushed to death when a tunnel they were working in collapsed on top of them. The cages that took them down sometimes plummeted without warning and explosions were commonplace.

Coal came with a high human price attached to it back then. Risking life and limb to crawl into the inky darkness of this strange underworld sounds like the nearest thing to hell I can think of.

And yet, not a single man went down those mines in fear. What held this fearless band of men together? One word. Community.

Chesterfield was the friendliest town on earth back then; the only place where you could stand at a bus stop and make a life-long friend.

The outbreak of the Second World War saw Dad pulled blinking from the gloom of the pits and propelled into a no less dangerous environment. Explosions of a different kind rocked his world. Sergeant Pickering, as he was then known, was wounded in action whilst serving with the Northamptonshire Regiment in North Africa and he also served in the D-Day landings.

The formidable spirit of the mining community must have served him well, as he and his comrades stormed the Normandy beaches that fateful day.

Growing up, I knew he had won the George Star for bravery and yet he never once breathed a word to us about the horrendous sights he must have witnessed.

The only way you'd ever knew he'd been out of the country was the presence of a pot of beautiful pink pearls he'd brought back from the Isle of Capri in Italy. They were Mam's pride and joy. The most beautiful things she owned, she'd had them made into a necklace.

'You'd never think something so beautiful could be so sturdy, would you?' she'd say, sighing. Those pearls must have felt like pure silk on her skin after a morning wringing sopping wet clothes through a mangle.

Apart from the pearls and a medal hidden in a drawer upstairs, the war was a forgotten element of Dad's life.

The only thing he ever said to me later in life was: 'Never mind what atrocities the Germans committed, what about what we did?' which shows the true mark of an intelligent man. He was honest to a fault and he had an inner core made of steel.

But when it came to me, his youngest child and only

daughter, he had a heart as soft as butter. And when he swung me high onto his shoulders and strode down our road, I felt ten-foot tall. I was as proud of him as he was of me.

He was the backbone of our family. He was never too busy to play games with his kids and teach us how to do things the right way, and I basked in his attention.

From mending shoes like a proper cobbler, to growing perfect rows of carrots, fresh garden peas and rhubarb in the backyard, lovingly tending to his favourite roses or making toy tanks for my brothers, there was nothing my dad couldn't make or do.

And yet, despite these pastimes that today would be considered so feminine, he was a proper northern bloke in one respect.

'I love you, Dad,' I grinned, throwing my arms around him one evening as he tucked me into bed.

'Aye,' he replied awkwardly. Sensing I'd got under his skin, I couldn't resist. 'I said, I love you, Dad,' I repeated cheekily again.

'Aye . . . Aye, I heard thee,' he replied gruffly. 'Nuff said.'

As the door closed and I heard his boots clomping down the stairs, I smiled to myself. He may have survived years down the pits and braved the German army, but he couldn't quite bring himself to say something as soppy as that. Miners never talked slushy, see, but I knew the old bugger loved me.

Perhaps it was this intense love from my mother and father that gave me confidence out of the home.

Money might have been scarce, but we had love, laughter and adventures by the bucketload. Every day was filled with magic and promise.

It was out there in the endless green fields and wild bluebell woods that my imagination could really burst into life.

Just as Mum was a housewife to her core and Dad was a miner born and bred, I was a tomboy. After three galloping lads, I think they hoped I'd be their perfect girl, happy to sit in and play with dollies. But why should I sit in and play with boring dolls when there were rivers to wade through, trees and gas lamps to climb and brothers to beat up?

Indoors was for sissies. I wanted to be outside where the action was, up to my neck in grime, mud and white-knuckle adventures.

Children in the 1940s and 1950s had a freedom that today's children can sadly never hope to recapture. We didn't have a big back garden; we didn't need one. The fields, barns, valleys and rivers were our playground.

Mam and Dad never worried about me. Why would they? Crime was pretty much non-existent where we lived.

Virtually as soon as I could walk, I was haring up the street and round the park in hot pursuit of my elder brothers, desperate to be included in their exciting games.

And by the age of five, I lived in my roller-skates, where I could usually be found whooping and clinging to the back of one of my brothers' speeding bikes as I clattered down our steep, cobbled street at top speed in a jaw-dropping, thrilling ride.

Perhaps that's why I came home one day to find Mam proudly clutching a little pink dolls' pram.

'Thanks,' I said hesitantly. 'It's er . . . nice?'

A dolls pram!

What the 'eck was I going to do with that? It wasn't long before the answer came to me.

An almighty crash outside our three-bedroom terrace one morning was followed by a hoarse shout and the rumble of a lorry reversing.

'Coal delivery,' yelled a man with a fag welded to his lips and hands as black as tar.

'Jennifer, Howard, Michael and Philip,' Dad boomed from the yard. 'Fetch us that coal in and drop some down to the Blacks, will yer?'

Suddenly a light bulb went on in my head.

'Aye, Dad,' I yelled back, pushing my dolls' pram as I headed out of the door.

Because Dad was a miner, he, like all miners in the village, got a commissionary (a perk) coal delivery every month. It was dumped on the road outside and us kids were told to bring it out back, into the coal shed in the yard.

Dad always looked out for everyone. Neighbourhood spirit you might call it nowadays but, back then, no one thought anything of helping out needy people in the area.

We, like most people, lived just above the breadline, but the iron glove of poverty still lingers in my memory. Newspaper used as a tablecloth and then cut into squares was used as toilet paper. Shoes were lined with oilcloth or patched up with cardboard.

A man used to come clattering up the street with a horse and cart on a Sunday morning to empty the outside lavs. The bog was basically a tin container covered with a flat piece of wood with a hole in it. You'd freeze your bum off in the depths of winter. How on earth would kids today cope with that?

It was generally felt that the poorest people on our street were a family called the Blacks, who lived at the end of Hoole Street. Old Mrs Black had a missing tooth and greasy grey hair. But that was the least of her problems. She had nine kids to clothe and feed and her husband had no job. The kids were always dressed in raggedy old hand-me-down skirts and trousers until there was virtually nothing left of them. Dad always made sure he sent down a sack of our extra coal for them.

On that cold, foggy morning, I carefully loaded the coal into my dolls' pram and set off down the street to the Blacks, where I promptly upended the coal out of the pram and onto the pavement outside their terrace.

What on earth this girl with platinum-blonde hair and a coal-smeared face must have looked like delivering coal in a little pink dolls' pram is anyone's business. A fallen angel, I dare say.

I only know Mam weren't best pleased when she clapped eyes on me.

'Jenny, love!' she gasped.

'What's tha' thinkin'?' Dad said, shaking his head.

'Yagreet pudding-head.'

Funnily enough, I didn't see much of the pram after that. Not that I cared. The fun was to be had out on the street anyway. All the kids played out front in one giant snotty whirl-wind of shouts, whoops and banter.

We bred mice and charged the neighbourhood a penny to see them. Other times we'd congregate at the bottom of Hoole Street, where there was an excellent fish and chip shop and you could buy a pennorth of fish bits, the delicious leftover bits of batter.

But way more exciting than fish bits was when Mrs Lee at number seventeen got the street's, probably the village's, first television set in 1952.

To a 6-year-old girl, it was an event so advanced and miraculous it was like watching a rocket blast off into space. Word spread up the street like wildfire.

Johnny from number eight ran up the hill, his little knock-knees pumping ten to the dozen.

'Mrs Lee's got one of them new televisions,' he blurted out, wiping his snotty nose on the edge of a crusty old cardigan.

'Tha'what?' I gasped.

'You heard me,' he said, his eyes as wide as gobstoppers.

'Gerron wi' thee,' I scoffed.

'No really,' he insisted. 'I saw it wiv me own eyes.'

Before long, a small army of kids had assembled outside number seventeen, our runny noses pressed up against the window, all desperate to get a glimpse at this new-fangled wizardry.

Balls were dropped, games of conkers abandoned mid-match, and an eerie silence descended over the cobbles.

Spotting she had an audience, Mrs Lee turned on the set with a proud flourish. Excitement rippled through the crowd as Muffin the Mule debuted before us. Every single one of us stood stock-still on the pavement, eyes growing wide with amazement at the spectacle before us.

The picture was a fuzzy pinky-grey and the sound tinny, but what a wonderful experience.

'*We want Muffin, Muffin the Mule,*' sang a shrill lady as she bashed away on a piano.

Meanwhile, a heavy string puppet of a mule clanked clumsily across the top of her piano. It wasn't the height of sophistication, but you could have heard a pin drop.

It was years before anyone else in the street could afford a set. In many ways it was a blessing, because it meant our childish games could continue on as before, blissfully uninterrupted by the march of time.

Sadly TV sets and computer consoles in every home means few kids know their neighbours any longer, much less play with them. Not so for the Hoole Street Gang. It was the littlest things that meant a lot down Hoole Street. A morning playing marbles and hopscotch out on the street would leave your hands rigid with cold.

But, as always, Mam had the answer.

'Get that inside yer,' she'd smile, slipping a warm, freshly baked meat and potato pie into our outstretched hands.

Did I mention my mam could bake like a dream?

Great British Bake Off? Don't make me laugh. Mam could have baked Mary Berry under the table.

There was nothing she couldn't turn her hand to.

Grazed knees could be soothed with a slice of her moist coconut cake. Bumps on the head would mysteriously disappear after a chunk of freshly baked white bread slathered with butter.

All manner of delicious, spicy, warm baking smells drifted out from the black-leaded range. The groans of delight that came out of that kitchen could be heard half a mile away.

But, sadly, those sounds weren't the only noises to drift out of our little home and up the street.

In many ways my idyllic childhood was the very best of

times. But life is full of light and shade, good times and bad, and hurtling our way was something so devastating that even my brave dad couldn't fix it.

Festering at the very heart of our family was a monster so cruel it destroyed each and every one of us in its own way, leaving us stunned and bewildered in its wake.

Little did I know as I fell out of trees and chased my brothers through the countryside, that my mam's life was infinitely less carefree. As she quietly pottered around her perfectly ordered kitchen, keeping the home and its inhabitants in perfect working order, her own mind was in turmoil.

I'd always sensed something wasn't quite right, no matter how hard my poor mam tried to hide it.

Growing up, I'd often heard raised voices between Mam and Dad. I could never quite make sense of what it was about, but Mam would suddenly go strange and start ranting at Dad.

My brothers and I never discussed Mam's strange moods and we also never invited friends from the street home. It remained an unspoken agreement. Children are more perceptive than adults give them credit for, and on a subconscious level we knew all was not well.

One morning, when I was aged about six, I remember her voice yelling out through the open window and down Hoole Street as I played out with my friends.

'You're having an affair, aren't you?' I heard her agitated voice ring out.

Then came Dad's reply, thick with frustration and despair. 'Don't talk daft, woman,' he yelled back. 'Course not.'

But Mam was just getting going and their words flew

about like bullets, back and forth they went, raging on and on. I had no idea what an affair was and why Mam was accusing Dad of it, but instinctively I knew Dad hadn't done anything wrong.

As their voices grew louder, I felt a deep pit of despair open up in my tummy. I wanted to cry and run. But where, and to whom? My brothers ignored it and carried on with what they were doing. Unlike the rest of the street . . .

Neighbours hanging their washing out in the yard, or chatting over the wall, stopped what they were doing and started nudging each other. Eyebrows raised the length and breadth of Hoole Street like a Mexican wave.

'She's off again,' I heard one neighbour mutter under her breath.

I issued a silent prayer. *Please stop.*

Just when I thought I could take it no longer, the door burst open and Dad stormed out.

Every housewife in the street glared at poor Dad, some obviously believing whatever it was Mam had just accused him of.

Poor Dad. Misery and confusion was etched over his proud face. He glared at everyone, then pointed to me, our Michael, Howard and Philip.

'Go and play in t'bloody ginnel,' he bellowed, pointing at the small alley that linked our house to next door.

After that, the rows and tension increased as Mam's 'episodes' ebbed and flowed.

When a dark mood came upon her, it could last up to four days, then there might be nothing for weeks. But my young brain, with its pathways still forming, grew anxious and confused, constantly braced in a state of readiness to run and hide when she launched her anger at Dad.

Her rages were never aimed at us kids, only poor Dad. And when they came, my brothers and I took cover. Flattening ourselves in the gas cupboard or under our beds, as the monster in her head unleashed its fury.

And yet . . . despite this, there was normality and fun amongst the madness. A mixture of magic and mundanity that weaved together to make childhood sparkle that much more.

Saturday morning trips to the bustling market in Chesterfield with Mam, Dad mixing water and ground ginger in a jam jar until it spontaneously bubbled and erupted into life. A ginger beer plant he called it. A supernatural feat, my brothers and I called it.

We even had a street party in 1953 to celebrate the queen's coronation. What a day to treasure!

As a nation celebrated the crowning of our new queen, Hoole Street hung out the flags. I loved it.

The street was transformed from an ordinary road of drab terraces to a brightly coloured, glittering spectacle. A sea of Union Jack flags and red, white and blue bunting flapped from every gas lamp and house window. All the kids were presented with a commemorative mug and spoon and the gasps from this put Muffin the Mule in the shade.

As the queen got ready for her new life and smart new address at Buckingham Palace, we also prepared for a new start.

Shortly after the coronation in 1953, when I was seven years old, the Pickering family moved to 15, Lee Road in the new-built Hady Estate, about a mile up the road from Hasland.

Our new four-bedroom home wasn't quite Buckingham Palace, but it felt like it to me. We had, joy of joys, an indoor toilet and an actual bath, signalling the end of baths in an old tin tub by the fire. Better still, I even had my own bedroom.

The estate was built on the side of a sloping hill and at the bottom ran a river, its inky swirling waters stained black with coal from the pits, and beyond that wide-open swathes of countryside stretched as far as the eye could see. Verdant green fields were dotted with old stone farmhouses and bluebell woods.

Dad started sowing the seeds of a new vegetable patch in the back garden and Mam set about cleaning down her already clean kitchen, complete with a new gas oven.

Optimism and hope blossomed. Perhaps this fresh start would see an end to whatever demons plagued Mam?

I was still far too young to get a sense of what 'it' was that tormented my poor mam, but whatever 'it' was, I hoped it would stay put, locked in the chilly old outhouse in the yard at Hoole Street.

This amazing new dream house would be a place to enjoy the rest of my childhood and put down roots. Wouldn't it?

CHAPTER 2

The Runaway

It wasn't long before me and my brothers had made friends with the other kids on the estate. There was a gang of about fifteen of us, all miners' kids, or the Hady gang as we called ourselves.

My mates: Aileen, Sandra and Christine, and my elder brothers' mates; big lads with impressive names like Roy Gold, Ernie Budd and Ronnie Egbert, ruled the estate.

For a tomboy, the lure of whatever it was the big boys were doing was hard to resist. And so we roamed the countryside in one big, feral pack. Dressed in our mam's best knitted jumpers and brown leather sandals, we were the children of our time and upbringing – tough, fearless and determined to find trouble out there in the countryside.

And what countryside to explore! Ditches to poke about in, bell mines and slag heaps to scale, and cowsheds from which to launch an ambush on an unsuspecting lad.

We were a small, tight-knit community and, like every

community, we had our unique way of communicating. Bravado and the heights of daring were the currency in which we traded. Each and every one of us wanted to be the king or queen of the estate and to earn that title you had to be prepared to go the extra mile. I had to match those lads, daring deed for deed.

Whether it be speeding from the top of the estate to the bottom inside a rickety old pram as it thundered down the hill, or clinging to the edge of a cardboard box as it hurtled down the side of a steep grassy railway embankment, I'd use any opportunity to beat the boys at their own game. God may have made me a girl but, by heck, I had more balls than Ronnie and Roy put together.

In 1956, when I was a 10-year-old tomboy rampaging through the countryside, Elvis Presley's 'Heartbreak Hotel' was tearing up the charts and the Clean Air Act had just been passed in parliament in response to London's Great Smog of 1952. Petrol was rationed, thanks to the Suez Crisis and double yellow lines were introduced for the first time. But I was oblivious to any of these life-changing events. Traffic and rock 'n' roll stars belonged to another world.

Each day brought an amazing new discovery – like the time we ventured up a thickly wooded lane and stumbled upon a family of hillbillies.

The cottage was hidden from sight and located at the end of a forbidding, thickly wooded lane. Feeling like the intrepid explorers we were, we picked our way through the churned-up mud. As we turned the corner of the lane, the Hady kids gasped as one.

Before us stood a ramshackle cottage. You'd have thought it deserted but for the thin trickle of pale smoke curling out the crooked chimneypot.

'You go and knock,' Howard hissed, pushing me forward.

'Gerroff,' I cried. 'I aint going in there.'

Then I spotted it – piled up in front of the cracked windows, box upon box of boiled sweets. Fear or no fear, the temptation was too much.

'Anyone coming wiv me?' I whispered.

Shoving the door, it fell open with a creak and we gingerly pushed our way in. Our eyes went out on stalks. It was like taking a step back in time to a bygone era.

There, in the smoky gloom, sat a family seated round a big wooden table eating from a giant pot of stew. This rag-tag bunch was dressed in strange overalls and barely had a tooth between them. These queer folk obviously lived outside of society, not gypsies but definitely outsiders, scratching a living from the land and poaching pheasants for the pot.

This family and their way of life fascinated me, and although I didn't really register it at the time, it showed me that families come in all shapes and sizes. Living outside the accepted norm wasn't really the way of things in the 1950s. Both magazines and TV were full of features on how to be the perfect housewife. Men went out to work in bowler hats and pin-stripe suits and 'terribly nice' ladies kept their 2.5 children squeaky clean while they ran their new Hoover round their suburban home.

Except real life wasn't like that. Housewives were just as likely to suffer from mental illness as families were to live outside society in the woods. No one talked about it, that's all.

The father of the family eyed me suspiciously.

'Next time knock, won't ya,' he said in a gravelly voice. 'This is a proper shop, thee knows.'

It was all I could do not to burst out laughing. I was fairly sure this 'shop' wasn't registered on any lists at Chesterfield Council.

Thanks to the new estate, pretty soon the hillbillies' family 'shop' was doing a roaring trade. Mr Hillbilly had a somewhat relaxed attitude to the supplying of nicotine to children and let us Hady kids buy Woodbine and Senior Service fags individually for 2d a pop.

We'd take our brown paper bags of sweets and fags and head to the stream at the bottom of the estate. Next to the stream was a huge tree with a rope swing attached. A big frayed knot had been tied to the bottom and the braver boys clung precariously to it as they soared fearlessly over the freezing, coal-stained waters swirling below.

'Bet you can't swing over, Jen,' shouted our Philip.

'Bet I could,' I sniffed back.

'Tha' cudn't knock skin off a rice pudding,' he teased.

Standing up, I purposefully ground my cigarette out on the muddy bank and hitched my skirt up into my knickers.

'Just watch me,' I said, all full of swagger.

Leaping onto the rope, I launched myself into the sky with a battle cry.

'Geronimo!' I whooped, as I soared over the river.

As the rope swung back and forth, more and more kids mounted, clinging to whatever bit of rope they could find.

By the time the twelfth kid had boarded the rope, my face

was ground into it so tightly I could actually hear it creaking.

'Gerrof,' I croaked. 'I think it's gonna—'

Too late. My words were lost on the wind as we hurtled into the river in one huge, seething mass of flailing limbs.

'. . . snap.'

The smack of thirteen grubby kids hitting the water could have been heard down in the mines.

By the time Philip and our Howard delivered me back home, I was helpless with laughter.

But, seconds later, the laughter abruptly stopped.

I could hear the screams before I even opened the front door.

'Cover up the wireless,' shouted Mam's wild voice. 'They're watching us.'

Once inside, my brothers and I cowered by the door. The room was thick with tension and, instinctively, we flattened ourselves against the wall.

Mam was screaming, her beautiful features twisted in terror. Her eyes were rolling about in her head and she was throwing her arms around wildly as Dad looked on.

'Who's watching us?' he asked helplessly, his voice cloaked with despair and confusion.

'Them,' she yelled back, jabbing a finger in the direction of our new TV set.

'They listen to us over the airwaves and ont' wireless. We've got to cover it up.'

With that she threw a tea towel over the set as she glared around the room.

Dad ripped it off.

'What voices, Gladys? Tell me who, I want to help,' he urged.

But she ignored him. I stared at Mam in horrified fascination. She was there, but not really there.

'Don't thee sick me,' she chanted, over and over.

I looked around the room, baffled, but there was no one else there. And what the hell did 'don't thee sick me' mean anyway?

Fear thundered in my chest as we edged our way round the kitchen.

'Go to your rooms,' Dad yelled when he spotted us.

Upstairs, I watched my brothers shut their bedroom door, then I did the same, flinging myself on the bed and burying my head under the pillow.

But it didn't block out Mam's tirade. Her voice grew louder with hysterical fear.

'They're there,' she insisted. 'They're always watching me.'

Her cries were so real, so convincing, I even started to wonder myself. Maybe she's right. Maybe it's us who couldn't see and hear it?

But even as a bewildered 10-year-old, I knew that wasn't right. The voices weren't in the room; they were in my poor mam's head.

Just who were these voices plaguing Mam? And when they were done with her, would they come for me too? Fear sliced through me. Was I next? Oh please God, no, what if the voices came for me too! It was like being in a nightmare you couldn't wake from.

'Leave my mam alone,' I whimpered.

But no one answered, except the tormented screams of my mother raging with her unseen enemy.

All thoughts of the childish pursuits of the day were long forgotten as Mam's bewildered cries rang out long into the night. The next morning, exhausted, I timidly pushed open the kitchen door and gasped in horror at the sight that greeted me.

Mam had her head in the oven. When she pulled it out, her face was etched with fear. She barely even looked like my mam any more. She looked like a woman possessed.

'I just want them to stop. Leave me alone,' she pleaded. And then louder, 'Don't thee sick me.'

Tears blurring my eyes, I ran to the door and down the hill past the rope swing as fast as I could. Fields flashed past in a blur of green as I raced along, just trying to put distance between me and home. I didn't stop running until I reached the very furthest wood.

Only there, out in the still and calm of the countryside, did I start to feel my heart rate return to normal.

Except nothing would ever be normal again.

Seeking solace from the gentle rustling of the wind through the trees, I tried to get to grips with what I'd seen and heard. But no matter how many times I tried to reason it out, I couldn't make sense of it.

I knew Mam was ill. Seriously so. But her illness was invisible. Outwardly there were no physical signs of anything wrong, but the things she said, the things she did . . . what did it all mean?

As a kid I had no idea that Mam was suffering from schizophrenia.

And that was precisely the problem – no one did. Not my dad, nor our relatives, who, scared by the issue, stayed away. Not even our local GP, whose medical knowledge didn't run to serious mental health problems.

Precious little was known by precious few about mental health back in the 1950s. Today, in 2014, people can function in society, but back then sufferers were locked up in gloomy institutions and sedated in bed. So it was left to my poor dad to struggle on alone with a problem that was way bigger than he was.

The only people that supported him and still visited him after Mam got sick was her brother, our Uncle Graham and his wife, our Auntie Dorothy. But, apart from that, he had nowhere to turn for help or advice.

Ten hours a day down the mines, the German army, the D-Day landings; these were all fears he could face head on. But his own wife's mind was a minefield he could never even begin to tackle.

And the worst thing of all was how so many doubted him. No one came out and said it, but every time Mam accused him of having an affair, neighbours believed her.

Throw enough mud and it'll stick and even the doctor doubted him.

Sadly, after that, Mam's illness got worse and as I entered my pre-pubescent years, major milestones were increasingly marked with her episodes. It was always there, always present – the black dog in the room.

We soldiered on, never questioning her, even when she began to dress downstairs so 'they' couldn't see her dressing upstairs, ignoring it when she broke off in mid-conversation to shout at some unheard voice.

Of course there were still idyllic times; roasting potatoes over an open fire on bonfire night, huddled round the fire until the last embers had died down.

But, like a fire that had taken hold in her mind, the madness was creeping up on Mam, devouring her thoughts until it was always there.

Only once did I dare ask her: 'Who are they, Mam?'

Her voice, so laden with sadness, took my breath away. 'They're always watching,' she whispered.

Mam's illness ate away at us like a cancer, picking at our souls and sanity until it threatened to devour us.

Increasingly I sought solace in the countryside.

I'd often walk for miles, sometimes covering the whole length of a railway line. I'd find myself wondering, what would it be like if I just kept walking? Followed that track to its final destination? My heart was gripped by such despair that, increasingly, one word kept popping into my shattered brain.

Run.

My brothers were fast growing up. By the time I reached thirteen, handsome Philip was fourteen and courting a local lass called Mary. Howard was seventeen, courting, and had joined Dad down the pits, and our Michael was eighteen and had already escaped into the army.

With one gone and the other two not far behind, I could see them slipping away from me, moving out, leaving me alone at home. The terror just sliced through me. I couldn't be left on my own, I just couldn't.

I was in that strange place straddling childhood and puberty, and my fears raged through me like wildfire. Nothing made sense any more. I felt loved, yet unloved.

I should have been chatting up the boys like Sandra and Christine, applying for jobs in factories and shops, preparing for a life of marriage, babies and respectability.

But I felt different to them.

I'd heard tell of this new motorway that had opened, the M1. Britain's first full-length motorway, a mighty road that thundered through the country connecting north to south. In my wildest fantasies a seed planted in my head and started to grow.

If only . . .

The urge to run wasn't a conscious thought, but a subconscious desire, an urge that took hold under my skin, growing and multiplying like a virus.

After one long walk, I came home to the now familiar sound of trauma. But this particular episode was worse than all the rest. Dad's usually placid face was twisted in utter torment.

Inside, images came to me like snapshots.

Dad's hands squeezed round Mam's neck. Mam's precious necklace snapping. Pink pearls bouncing over the floor.

And, in the midst of it, Mam's voice, possessed, as she spat one wild accusation after another at Dad.

Fresh tears glittered in my Dad's eyes and I knew Mam's voices had finally got to him.

'Dad!' I gasped.

He spotted me and his hands sprang from Mam's neck.

'Jennifer! I . . . I . . .' he gasped.

The awful stillness in the room turned my heart over. The

fragile dream of a normal life that I had clung to had just died. Mam's necklace had broken, the one she always said was so sturdy. Her pearls were lost for ever . . .

One dark evening just after Christmas, 1959, a 13-year-old girl walked out of her home, bound for London town. She held nothing in her hands. All she possessed was the coat on her back and a few bob in her pocket.

As residents of the Hady estate enjoyed their new presents, she stealthily crept away under the cover of darkness and headed to the bus stop.

That girl was me, and to this day I have no idea what was going through my head. All I knew was that Christmas I felt a strong, primal urge propelling my body southwards in the direction of London. The M1 was like an artery to the pulsing heart of Britain. Wanderlust drove me, but fate was directing me.

At the end of the M1 was a seething, throbbing, metropolis, but to a teenage runaway in the final days of the 1950s the streets of London weren't paved with gold. Far from it. Little did I know what unimaginable horrors were awaiting me there.

I managed to hitch a lift in a Spangers meat lorry bound for Smithfield meat market, and promptly fell asleep.

As I innocently dozed and we hurtled closer to London, the irony of travelling there in a meat wagon was entirely lost on me that day but, tragically, all too soon I would understand *exactly* what it felt like to be treated like a piece of meat.

But then, on that strange December day, I had hopes, dreams and aspirations to find a better life for myself.

Unfortunately, I didn't have much in the way of an actual plan and when the lorry swung in through the gates of Smithfield meat market, I realised I didn't have the faintest clue what I was going to do next.

It was midnight when we finally arrived. The rattling cold took my breath away when I opened the lorry door and jumped down onto the bloodstained tarmac. It was a hell of a wake-up call.

Instantly, my senses were assaulted. The stench of congealed blood and fresh meat drifted up my nostrils and I nearly gagged.

A hanging rail of pig carcasses seemed to loom up out of the darkness and I jumped back to avoid getting mown down.

'Watch yerself, gel,' shouted a cheery man in bloodstained white overalls as he bowled past.

The market was alive with deafening noise, pungent smells and glistening carcasses. Lorries pulled in and out and disappeared into a warren of mysterious underground tunnels, ruddy-faced men in chainmail gloves and bloodstained aprons called out cheery greetings to each other in strange voices I barely recognised, their cockney voices bouncing off the soaring Victorian ceiling.

'Get a load of the rack on that,' laughed one trader as he looked me up and down.

I shifted uncomfortably. Suddenly I felt very far from home. This was a man's world, not a place for a 13-year-old girl.

Dodging cartloads of meat, I scurried to the exit.

The earlier excitement of the day had all but deserted me. Now I just felt bone-tired. I was a kid who wanted a cuddle from her mam.

What had I done?

Soon the lights of the market were behind me and I was swallowed up by the inky darkness. And, just like that, I was sucked into the underbelly of London, another anonymous statistic. Officially homeless.

As I trailed the cold, deserted streets, the shouts of the market traders growing fainter, I felt like a ghost. I quickly came to realise, as I walked past late-night cab offices and tea stands with groups of men starting the night shift huddled over a brew and a fag, that I might as well have been a ghost. No one batted an eyelid at the sight of a young girl pounding the streets that late, not like they would have done in Chesterfield. They stared straight through me. I was invisible. Nameless. A nobody in a city of millions.

But I didn't care. All I could think about was how cold I was. I had a thin coat, but no hat, gloves or scarf and the cold was seeping under my coat and into my marrow.

Every car that swept past showered me with a fine spray of icy water and, all too soon, I couldn't even feel my face.

Most people think they know what cold feels like but, trust me, until you've spent a winter's night out in the cold, exposed and underdressed, you have no idea.

It started as a prickling in my fingers and toes and soon my whole body was a searing mass of ice-cold pain.

I walked and walked, the only sound my hollow footsteps pounding off the pavement and my sharp, jagged breath coming in rasps.

My breath hung like smoke in the freezing night air and the cold made me feel like I was losing my mind but, above all, my heart was pounding. A sickening feeling of dread clawed at my chest with every mile walked.

I thought of Mam, brewing up by the stove, Dad resting his boots by the coal fire while he gently supped a beer.

No. No. No.

Angrily I shook my head. That life didn't exist any more. Mam's voices had seen to that.

Now the hustle and bustle of the night market was behind me, a different London revealed itself. Massive dark churches festooned with Gothic architecture and grotesque gargoyles stared down solemnly at me, and huge Victorian buildings soared into the dark sky. Everything was big in London and I felt as tiny as a church mouse in comparison. It was murky and unwelcoming but I trudged through the streets regardless, at one point finding myself on the Embankment, gazing into the dark waters of the Thames.

It was the early hours and the city slept, tucked up in warm, cosy beds, while a teenage runaway tiptoed past, unseen and unheard.

Soon the vast warehouses gave way to leafy, affluent squares and glittering white hotels, flanked with stone lions and liveried doormen. This was the smart London I'd read about and seen on Mrs Lee's TV set.

Light spilled out from the hotel windows and, if I peered up through the wrought-iron railings, I could make out the outline of a few post-Christmas stragglers, nursing a brandy in a warm, convivial haze.

But at street level it was rough. Tramps huddled in doorways, trying to find shelter and litter was piled up in cobbled back alleyways. Stray dogs picked over scavenged bones and foxes slunk past me.

The trees cast eerie, flickering shadows over the pavements and the howling wind occasionally lifted up a bin lid and sent it slamming down with a crash behind me. At that moment I have never felt so alone, or terrified, in my whole life.

I'd done something so awful, so terrible, and I could never turn back. Of course now I see that, of course, I could have; my parents would have happily carved off a leg to have me home safe and sound but, back then, as a frightened 13-year-old, I couldn't see a way back home.

Finally, three hours later, at about 3 a.m., out of my mind with exhaustion and hunger, I found a church doorway, huddled up in the foetal position and fell into a fitful sleep.

Four hours later, the chiming of church bells woke me with a start. Cold exploded through my chest and every bit of my body throbbed. It was morning and London was slowly coming to life.

Genteel peace and prosperity prevailed in the West End, served by a dependable working class.

Porters stood out back, wearily smoking, getting ready to start a new day's shift, and delivery men made their rounds

Just then the smell of frying bacon drifted out from the back of a hotel and my mouth watered.

What I wouldn't have done for one of Mam's famous breakfasts; her creamy scrambled eggs, a couple of links of sausages and crispy bacon, washed down with a mug of hot, sweet tea.

I could almost hear her soft voice in my head.

'*Have you had sufficient, Jenny love?*'

Half-starved, my brain scrambled to make sense of its

surroundings. It was the last days of December, I knew that much, and notices on street signs announced this to be the city of London.

I needed food and drink. Desperately. As I wandered in search of a tea stand, warmly dressed families walked briskly past me, all bundled up against the cold.

I scanned their faces in vain, waiting for a flicker of recognition, for someone to say, 'What's tha' thinkin, Jennifer, gerrin withee, duck, while I brew up.'

A vision of my dad shaking his head popped into my head.

'T'wernt for yer brain you'd be smart, Jennifer Pickering. Whatever in the world were you thinking, now gerrin inside.'

Their voices grew distant, then faded into nothing. And when the faces swam back into focus, it wasn't warm Derbyshire folk staring back, but strangers. What's more, they were staring straight through me.

I hadn't dreamt it all and been whisked home like Dorothy in *The Wizard of Oz*. This wasn't fiction. This was real life. And it was brutal.

I spent the only money I had on a cup of tea and a buttered bun, which took the edge off my hunger, and found myself pulled in the direction of the West End.

There were no grim-faced housewives in curlers jostling for the pick of the best veg at the market here. As I wandered like a ghost on the periphery of life, blankly staring at passers-by and wondering where my next meal was coming from, I realised that if I stood any real chance of survival here, I was going to have to wise up. That night, my second night on the streets, I did three things that would have been unimaginable just two weeks before. Activities that show just how quickly life on the streets changes you, how thin the veneer of so-called sophistication is. When put under the ultimate test – survival – we are just feral animals at our core.

Cold, filthy and pulsing with pain, when darkness fell again and Big Ben's chimes rang out over the city, I couldn't bear another night in a doorway.

Testing the door of a Ford Anglia, I wasn't surprised to find it unlocked. In the same way no one wore seatbelts in those days, no one locked their car doors either. Gratefully I crawled in, curled up on the back seat and fell asleep. It was still cold and uncomfortable, but it beat sleeping in a concrete doorway.

Waking as soon as light pierced the horizon, I crept like an alley-cat up the street and, glancing down, saw a fat cigarette butt lying discarded in the gutter. Without hesitating, I picked it up. Player's No. 6. Strong, but who cared? Cadging a light off a passer-by, I lit it and gratefully drew the nicotine deep into my lungs.

I didn't care what I looked like. It was a small fragment of comfort and the crackle of the burning tip spread some warmth into my frozen fingertips.

Staring at my hands, already ingrained black with dirt, I marvelled once again at how in such a short time the home comforts of a hot bath and a decent meal already seemed so far away. My old life belonged in another world now.

Later that day, with not a penny to my name, it dawned upon me that if I didn't beg for money or food I would starve. There may well have been soup kitchens set up for the homeless in London, but I sure as hell didn't know about them.

A lady was sitting with her two children on a park bench feeding pigeons. As I edged towards her, her eyes widened with alarm and she pulled her children in closer towards her.

'I'm sorry to bother you, but you couldn't spare any change so I could get a cup of tea, could you please?' I asked politely.

'Clear off,' she gasped, gathering her children and scurrying off through the park.

Too cold and too numb to feel embarrassment, I tried asking again, and again. Finally, a nice young bloke gave me a couple of bob. I could have wept. It wasn't much. Just enough to buy a sandwich and a cup of tea, but it meant I could eat.

Sleeping rough, breaking into cars, smoking discarded fag butts and begging – I was now officially homeless.

The hours turned to days as I wandered, drifting through the streets of London. Detached, I observed people go about their lives, watched their routines unfold, saw them greet friends, laugh, shop, row, kiss, hug, gossip . . .

Through steamy restaurant windows I saw couples share a meal. Hidden in the shadows, I heard passers-by argue, make plans, hurry to their destinations. All life was unfolding around me. My own life was turning on its axis.

I was living in a twilight world, drifting through the half-light. *Hoping, searching, surviving . . .*

For the most part no one spared me a second glance. I was nothing. Just a pair of bewildered eyes staring out from a grubby face. A street urchin who looked as if she'd been dragged out of the gutter. I expect most people thought I was from a rough East End family but no one ever took the time to talk to me, to find out why someone so young was on the streets.

I never knew what day of the week it was or even what time it was. As the days drifted past, I even began to lose sense of how long I'd been gone for.

I watched day turned to dusk, then back to dawn, seeking shelter and scraps of food wherever I could.

By day I pounded the endless pavements, trying to escape the hunger in my stomach and the pain in my heart. At night I sought shelter. One night, I walked down a broad, busy street when, all of a sudden, a strange thing happened. As I turned the corner into a large, sweeping square, I became aware of huge crowds of people.

Perfect strangers were embracing each other, red-faced and flushed with alcohol. They flung their arms around each other with gay abandon, sang, kissed and even did the hokey-cokey, whilst others formed conga lines, drunkenly weaving in and out of four vast bronze lions.

From somewhere up above boomed the chiming of a bell and over the shining curve of the Thames fireworks exploded.

Bong. Bong. Bong rang Big Ben.

The whole city seemed to be celebrating. Suddenly a light bulb went on in my head. *Of course.* It was New Year's Eve and I'd washed up in Trafalgar Square. It was now 1960. In four months' time I would turn fourteen.

Suddenly, a strange feeling of determination rose up inside me. Perhaps buoyed by the swell of good feeling from the crowd, I felt a glimmer of optimism tug at my heart. It wasn't much, but it was enough. Enough to make me see I couldn't keep drifting like this. I had to claw back some respectability. And, with that, my brain kicked in and feisty Jenny returned.

As soon as first light broke on 2 January, and after a couple of snatched hours' sleep in a car, I started walking. I knew just what I was looking for. Finally I spotted it. Even handier was that it was right next door to a public toilet.

I had a few pennies from begging, so I ducked into the loo. In them days you could buy a comb, soap and a flannel for just a few pence from a toilet attendant in most public lavatories.

Spending my last pence, I washed and scrubbed my face until I'd washed the grime of the streets off.

Next, I dragged a comb through my hair. My clothes were a crumpled mess, but at least I didn't smell any more. I was half-presentable.

Taking a deep breath, I made my way inside the grand entrance to the labour exchange in Seven Sisters Road, north London.

In my rush, I failed to see the newspaper hoarding outside announcing the *News of the World* headline: MISSING. With my photo plastered right underneath.

Had I seen this, I may have paused, read Mam's tearful plea for her only daughter to return home; taken in my dad's begging request for anyone with any information to get in touch and his concerns over the safety of his thirteen-year-old daughter out there by herself.

But I didn't see. I was utterly oblivious to this and to similar front pages of the *Derbyshire Times* back home that were covering my disappearance.

Likewise I had no idea, as I'd slept rough and begged, that poor Philip was tasked with visiting the police station in Chesterfield to see whether the body of a young girl in a police photo was his little sister.

When we are young, we are selfish. I like to think that had I known that, it might have pricked my conscience and I would have turned myself in.

But I didn't, and now I will never know. Instead, I took a deep breath and went to find myself a job.

CHAPTER 3

Confessions of a Teenage Runaway

I rang a little bell on the countertop and waited until an offi-cious-looking woman arrived and snapped, 'Name?'

'Rita Barlow and I'm eighteen,' I lied.

Rita Barlow was in fact a 13-year-old girl I went to school with, and I daresay she'd have been quite surprised to find herself on the books of a London labour exchange.

You didn't have to provide any ID in those days and, in 1960, work was plentiful. Within an hour, I had a new job.

Jenny Pickering was now the new sales assistant at Harts House Linens and Drapers in Seven Sisters.

My salary was to be two pound ten shillings a week and my hours of work 9 a.m. until 5 p.m.

With my new job I was able to secure myself lodgings at a nearby house. It was just a dingy little room with a shared toilet on the landing. No cooking facilities or 'owt, but it was a roof over my head and the rent was only thirty bob, or one pound ten shillings, a week. I thought I was the bee's knees.

The older women who worked there took me under their wing and, to my delight, I found I enjoyed my job. What's more, I was pretty good at it too.

'You've been down in the gutter but you've come up smelling of roses,' I congratulated myself.

Having a warm bed to sleep in, the company of friendly older women and a hot meal from a nearby cafe in my tummy each night was a godsend.

After my first week, I celebrated the monumental arrival of my first pay packet by treating myself to a huge meal at a local Turkish cafe on the Seven Sisters Road. No matter that there was barely enough left to cover my rent, every mouthful of that pie and chips tasted like sheer heaven.

Each day the radio crackled out music and the small draper's shop hummed with chatter and warmth. My memories of that time are crystallized in sound, wrapping me in a warm blanket of nostalgia.

Singing along to the Everly Brothers, I breathed in the comforting smell of crisp linen and beeswax from the polished wooden countertop.

The silken tones of an Elvis love song, the satisfying ping of the till, the shouts of the rag and bone merchants on the streets outside.

It was such a lovely place, a world away from the chaos of the streets.

Outside, the numerous cafes pulsed to the music of Elvis

Presley, Cliff Richard, the Shadows and the Drifters. The seeds of rock and roll had been born only a few years earlier. Every man wanted to look like Cliff or Elvis and every woman styled her hair in a bouffant to look like Jacqueline Kennedy. Me? I was just happy to have a roof over my head.

Without hunger and cold dominating my every waking thought, I started to grow in confidence and soon I went from sweeping up the scraps of linen from the floor to serving customers. I got my head down and did whatever was asked of me, making sure never to be late and to listen and learn whatever was shown to me.

There was nothing more satisfying than wrapping up strips of linen in waxy brown paper and cashing money in the heavy silver-coloured till.

'Thank you so much for your custom,' I always beamed brightly at customers as they left.

'Very good, Rita,' nodded the manageress approvingly. Mrs Braithwaite was an old-fashioned sort – very exacting on manners and etiquette. She was from a world where you showed nothing but the utmost respect to your superiors at all times.

'What year did you say you were born, Rita?' she asked.

Remembering always to add five years to my birth date, I replied quickly.

'1941, Mrs Braithwaite,' I smiled.

'Good, you have a bright future ahead of you here,' she replied.

I may have had too. I may well have gone on to get a manageress position in time, got myself a bigger room and put down roots but, thanks to a local scrap-dealer named Ted, I would never find out.

Ted and I met in the local Turkish cafe I went to. Being the chatty sort, he and I had soon got talking.

One afternoon, three months after I'd started working at Harts, I'd gone into the cafe for my tea. Spotting Ted at the next table, I grinned.

'Evening, Ted.'

'All right, *Rita*,' he grinned, winking at me.

Something about the way he had emphasized the name caused my tummy to turn over.

'Yeah, fine. You, Ted?' I replied as casually as I could. When you've lived on the streets, you can spot trouble a mile off.

'Now then,' he drawled. 'Wotcha really called?'

'I told you, Ted,' I replied, shifting nervously. 'My name's Rita.'

Ted roared with laughter. 'Pull the other one, gal, it's you, ain't it? You're that gal outta the newspapers.'

Panic washed over me. *Papers?* What the bloody hell was he on about?

'Nah, it's not me,' I lied.

By now, people in the cafe had stopped their conversations and were turning to stare. My heart quickened.

Stay calm.

Ted was just getting going.

'It's you ain't it, go on, admit it,' he pressed.

Calmly draining my tea, I shook my head, threw a few coins on the countertop and smiled as evenly as I could.

'You're mistaken, Ted,' I insisted.

45

But, minutes later, I was out of there and, as soon as I was out of sight round the corner, I started to run, my heart thundering in my chest.

They were looking for me.

Back in my room, tears blurred my eyes as I packed my bags. It didn't take long. I had pitifully few possessions.

I closed the door behind me, tiptoed down the stairs and out onto the Seven Sisters Road. It was April and a perfect spring evening in London, young people were milling everywhere, dolled up to the nines.

But I stared through the sea of painted faces and men all dressed up in their best suits as I scanned the streets, my eyes darting this way and that.

I half expected to see a squad car out there waiting, ready to bundle me in the back and take me to the nearest police station.

There wasn't, but I had been recognised, and I knew with certainty that it would only be a matter of time before they came knocking. The net was closing in.

I knew I had no choice to run that day, to leave behind my newfound security, but it was still agony leaving behind everything I had grown to love.

But I wasn't ready to go home; I couldn't face Mam's voices, not yet.

Unwittingly, with a few choice words, that scrap-dealer had altered the course of my life for ever.

I could get another job, sure, but it would only be a matter of time before I was spotted again.

Angry tears filled my eyes as I started to walk. By now I was on the verge of turning fourteen, or had already turned fourteen, not that I would have had a clue when my birthday was in any case or cared much about celebrating it. Homeless people don't celebrate birthdays, you see.

Without the security of a job and a roof over my head, I was fast running out of options and I'm deeply ashamed at the course my life took next. For the next five months I lived like a vagrant and I would be lying, or at least telling half-truths, if I didn't share with you what I did next.

Life on the streets is unsavoury, brutal, heartbreaking, and you do what you can to survive. I write this with tears in my eyes and a deep-rooted sense of guilt in my heart. But I owe it to my family to be one hundred per cent honest about my time as a teenage runaway.

In the first days of the new decade, all life went on as normal in London. By day, old Mrs Braithwaite faithfully opened up and served the finest linen and drapery from behind her polished counter, the traders at Smithfield were hard at work selling meat, and Ted on the Seven Sisters Road flogged scrap.

I hadn't eaten for days and my spirit was broken. I drifted constantly, always on the move, never stopping in one area of London for more than a few days. It didn't occur to me to find another job right away. I didn't yet have the logic of an adult. It felt as if my fate had been sealed – that I would always be rumbled if I tried to play it straight.

Waifs and strays are magnets to each other, and often I found myself huddled in a cluster of teenagers in the park, trying to fool each other with ridiculous stories, drinking, joking and bumming cigarettes. But behind the bravado, lank greasy hair and defiant, thrusting chins, all wore the same haunted expression in their eyes. These kids were just like me, no matter what lies we told each other. They were running from an unhappy home.

Any problem always stems back to the home, you see, be the problem abuse, violence or, like in Mam's case, illness. Homeless people are just trying to escape. Why else would you go to the hell that is the streets? It's because your home is so bad you have nowhere else to turn. So when you see young people begging on the streets, please think about the story behind those soulless eyes, consider what hell they are running from and spare them a quid or a cup of tea.

Where you get vulnerable girls, you find men willing to exploit them.[1] If you stayed with a group long enough, sure enough, some man with shifty eyes would appear out of the shadows, sniffing out the crop of youngsters. The line was always the same: 'All right, new girl, aint yer? Fancy some of this?' Then they'd thrust a small blue triangular pill under your nose. Drinamyl amphetamines or 'purple hearts', as they were known, were the drug of choice of British teenagers back in the early 1960s. These and later the highly

---

[1] In 2012, Barnardo's worked with 1,200 children and young people who had been sexually exploited, though the true number of victims is likely to be much higher. Younger victims than ever are being targeted. The average age of a victim has dropped from fifteen to thirteen, and Barnardo's have identified children as young as ten who have been subjected to sexual exploitation. (Source: Barnardo's.)

addictive sedative pill Mandrax were eaten like sweets amongst homeless people.

I daresay many of the girls I chatted with were addicts who had turned to prostitution to fund their addiction, but that was a road I was never going down. I have never and would never consider taking drugs. The minute I was offered drugs, I was off. It was hard enough keeping your wits about you, even more so if you were bombed-out of your head.

And so I never made friends. I kept on running.

I hitched lifts with lorry drivers, just for somewhere warm to sleep and some company. I must have travelled the length and breadth of the country just for a cup of tea and a sandwich. Hitchhiking, but with no destination.

One time I even caught myself staring out onto a choppy grey sea and discovered that I'd washed up in Portsmouth. Other times I'd ride the length of the Tube, from one side of London and back again, just to keep warm. Instinct told me to keep moving. No wonder today, fifty-three years on, my feet still ache and I've got osteoarthritis in my back.

But no matter how many miles I covered, my unhappiness followed like a black cloud, the memory of my poor mam driving me ever onwards.

I slept in doorways, parks and unlocked cars at night. I washed my knickers and face with a scrap of soap in public toilets by day and begged for food. My feet were calloused and covered in sores. When I had a period I would use rolled-up toilet paper. I owned nothing. Not a single possession in the world. I was filthy, exhausted and starving.

Fourteen-year-old 'Rita Barlow' was a nowhere girl, living

outside society. Life washed over me and I was oblivious to this amazing wave of culture and pop exploding on the streets around me. I was just intent on living that day and surviving. But I was also tired by now, so desperately, desperately tired.

I wanted to curl up in a ball and die.

And that's when, at my absolute lowest, I met Pete. I hadn't eaten for three days when I approached him in Finsbury Park one summer evening.

It was one of those glorious evenings where London looks its best. The park was dappled with a hazy evening sunshine. Couples and families sat around, lazing on blankets. The sun was about to dip down behind the rooftops. I was so hungry. I was desperate to eat before another night fell without food in my stomach.

My clothes hung off me and my cheeks were so sunken you could see the outlines of the bones beneath. I wasn't a pretty sight, and I must have smelt rotten. Which is why what happened next makes it even harder for me to fathom.

He was a young guy in his thirties, I guessed, reading a copy of the evening paper.

'Excuse me, sir, I've had my bag stolen,' I said, trotting out a sob story. 'You couldn't spare a bob for a cup of tea?'

He looked me up and down and a broad smile spread over his face.

'I can do one better than that, darlin',' he winked. 'I'll buy you a meal. Pete's the name.'

He took my hand in his to shake and I winced at the sight of my dirty, cracked nails.

Then he was off, heading to the park gates.

I trotted behind him, suddenly quite conscious of my skinny bare legs.

He led me to a nearby bed and breakfast. It was a cheap, tatty place but I didn't care. I was just so relieved at the prospect of food.

Pete strode to the reception desk.

'We'll have a double room for the night please,' he said.

My eyes shot open in alarm. I thought I was just getting a meal. But Pete obviously had other plans.

'Let's eat first though, eh,' he smiled.

Suddenly it dawned on me what was expected of me after I'd eaten. Sat opposite him in the empty dining-room, my mind span out of control.

I could have got up and run like crazy from that B&B. But I was so hungry I felt like I could die. The garish patterned wallpaper seemed to close in on me but, as I stared back at Pete, I made a decision to stay.

It's hard to put into words how hungry I was that day, and how revolted I feel writing this now.

The shame has consumed me and I want to close my eyes and stop, but I must be truthful. Everything about it was seedy beyond words: the man ready to prey on a young girl's hunger for sex, the stale air in the room. Even the meal that was served to me wasn't worth the act it bought, but I had to eat. I had to survive.

I can't even remember the taste of that greasy sausage and chips, but I do remember the nasty taste it left in my mouth after.

As I climbed the cheap lino stairway behind him, I wanted to cry in despair. I wanted my mam. I wanted to be back in the sleepy cobbled streets of Derby, before it all went so dreadfully wrong.

Once inside the stuffy room, I took a deep breath.

Get it over and done with.

I was good at blocking out my emotions; I'd done little else since I left home that Christmas five months previously, so it was second nature to me.

I may have been fourteen but, in my mind, I felt forty.

I peeled off my flimsy cheesecloth dress that I'd found in a rubbish bin a few days before, and slowly removed my pants and shoes. I stared in shame at my shoes. The soles were virtually hanging off the bottom and I kicked them under the bed before Pete saw.

Standing naked before him, I swallowed hard and then lay back on the bed. Now a young woman, I had developed breasts and hips, but the rest of me was scrawny, pale and covered in bruises.

Please let it be over quickly.

Pete's eyes seemed to glaze over as he stared at the naked 14-year-old lying before him and his breathing grew shallow.

Frantically he started undoing his trouser buttons and, as he fumbled in his haste, I squeezed my eyes shut. I couldn't bear to watch. I didn't want the image of his lust-fuelled face in my mind.

And then his rough hands were all over me, frantically pawing at my flesh, his hot, stale breath turning my stomach. The weight of his body crushed mine and, pinned underneath him, I realised in despair I was totally helpless.

He entered me roughly and I remembered as he did so, that it had all happened so quickly I hadn't even asked him to wear a johnny.

As he thrust against me, his breathing grew more ragged.

Summoning up every ounce of my willpower, I detached myself from my body. I took my brain out of that poky room and back to the wide-open fields of Chesterfield. I thought of flying free over the river on the rope swing and sitting in my favourite bluebell wood.

Finally, with a violent shudder, his body grew limp. It was over.

I had done what I had to do.

I did what thousands of homeless girls did, and are still having to do, in order to survive.

I never saw Pete again. We spent the night in that B&B and the next morning he went his way and I went mine, but that sordid episode will never, ever leave me. It marked my transition from naïve teenage runaway to a woman who would go on to be scarred by her past.

There were no consequences at the time. The damage would come later. But, as I walked through Finsbury Park, hot, angry tears trickled down my cheeks.

Sadly, after that, having sex with strange men in order to eat became commonplace. Over the next five months I couldn't tell you precisely how many times it happened. I'd have to do it anywhere, a B&B if I was lucky, in a park, up a back alley.

It's nothing short of a miracle I didn't become pregnant, catch a STI or get raped. How I didn't become a statistic, just another homeless corpse laid out on a mortuary block, I will never know. I don't know how many homeless girls there were in the 1960s, but it felt to me like there were hundreds.[2]

I wasn't alone, you see. I became aware of countless young girls doing exactly the same thing in order to eat, though I got the feeling I was definitely the youngest girl on the streets.

The early 1960s was a watershed era for teenage runaways. Waves of baby boomers were transitioning from childhood to adulthood. Previous generations had been fighting or enduring the war on the Home Front. Not so for this new, disillusioned 'youth' who were spilling out onto the streets. The generation born into the ruins of the Second World War were determined to do things their way and the generation gap was never larger than in the 1960s.

It's little wonder then that so many young girls found themselves homeless like me. And there was no shortage of men willing to take advantage and pay out for a burger – just a burger, mind, not even a bun, or a saveloy and chips. It was cheap, fast food and cheap, fast sex.

I became adept at cutting off my feelings and having sex on autopilot. I became utterly numb. But, increasingly, I found my mind wandering to home. My homesickness was overwhelming by now. How had my big adventure gone so wrong?

---

[2] Homelessness escalated throughout the 1960s and saw a boom of charities established, including Shelter in 1966 and Crisis in 1967. This followed in the wake of a 1966 gritty drama about homelessness called *Cathy Come Home*, directed by Ken Loach, which was watched by twelve million people. Today, an estimated 80,000 young people a year experience homelessness in the UK. (Source: Centrepoint.)

When I'd travelled down to London, I'd been full of hope and optimism for the future. Now I was crawling with shame.

Mam had always taught me to be kind, tell the truth, be clean in my mind and in my body and show respect to everyone, no matter their social position. This was my moral foundation, so to behave the way I was doing was tearing me up inside.

No face stood out, but I was always aware of their bodies. Big, rough, hairy men's bodies that stank of cigarette smoke and sweat.

I used my body as a means to an end, for what else did I have? But every act chipped that bit further at my self-esteem. Perhaps that's why I fell prey to what happened later in life?

Finally, after eleven months on the street, I was on my last legs. Life looked hopeless.

I wanted to go home.

In all that time I had only committed one crime, unless you count the crimes I had committed against myself. In desperation, I had stolen a pint of milk off a doorstep.

Until one terrible night when I was accused of a crime I actually hadn't committed.

I'd got friendly with an Irish lad who lived with his brother near Highbury. We'd been chatting in his flat when his brother showed up and started ranting.

'I'll bloody kill you, you bitch,' he screamed.

'What are you talking about?' I gasped.

'You've stolen from me,' he ranted.

I barely had a chance to defend myself before he locked me in a bedroom.

I was imprisoned. Locked inside his bedroom for three hours, my heart hammering out of control.

Suddenly, something inside my head clicked. If I didn't go home, it was only a matter of time before a situation like this, or something similar, would see me dead, a nameless corpse at the age of fourteen. And, worst of all? I knew they would never be able to identify my body and I'd be buried in an unmarked grave.

Rita Nothing from Nowhere.

My family would never know what happened to me.

There and then, I made a decision. If I got out alive, I would find a way home.

Salvation came in the form of his brother, who took pity on me and unlocked the door.

'Run,' he hissed.

I didn't need telling twice.

It hadn't been a coffin, so a truck it was. And I knew just where to go, too.

Three lifts later, I arrived in the town of Aldershot, in Hampshire. It's known as the 'Home of the British Army', and that's exactly why I went there.

Deep down, I hoped my elder brother, Michael, who was in the Royal Army Service Corps, might be there. Of course it was like looking for a needle in a haystack but, subconsciously, knowing he might be there was a small crumb of comfort.

I scanned the face of every soldier that walked past me in the hope it might be our Michael, but my prayers remained unanswered.

When darkness fell, I climbed over a barbed-wire fence and bedded down near a bush.

A few hours later, the terrific crack of gunfire woke me. 'What the hell?' I gasped, sitting bolt upright.

A white flash of heat whizzed past my ear, followed by the pop and crump of explosions in the air. Suddenly it dawned on me. I'd bedded down in a military firing range.

'You bloody idiot,' I cursed, flattening myself on the cold earth and praying for dear life. I'd escaped London for safety, but with a troop of soldiers firing bullets at me, that hope was fast vanishing.

After a few hours, the zinging of bullets whizzing past seemed to grow faint.

'Thank God,' I murmured, staggering to my feet.

Eventually, I wandered to a nearby pub and tried to warm up while I worked out what to do next.

A girl my age sat down next to me.

Soon we were engrossed in conversation, merrily telling each other the biggest pack of lies you've ever heard about who we were.

'My name's Brenda Bolland,' she said. 'I'm eighteen.'

'I'm Rita, and I'm eighteen too.'

A hilarious conversation ensued in which questions were met with lies, or half-truths. And the laugh of it is that I knew she was telling me a whole heap of lies and she knew I was. It was almost a code of honour amongst runaways, a common understanding not to probe too deep.

No matter. I had a friend at last, and meeting Brenda was a turning point.

For it was she who gave me the courage to get home.

But, by God, she could tell some whoppers.

'Let's go to Scotland,' she announced. 'I've got a friend there who can get us some really well-paid jobs and put us up in a flat.'

'Nice one,' I said, not believing her for a moment.

So, just like that, we hitchhiked our way to Glasgow. It was cold, dark and the wind was whistling up Sauchiehall Street by the time the lorry dropped us off. My God, the state of us. Our shoes were virtually falling off our feet and our clothes were ripped to ribbons.

And, surprise, surprise, the mystery benefactor never materialized. We needed money and fast.

'Follow me,' I said, disappearing into a police station.

'We've been to the cinema and had our purses stolen,' I said to the desk sergeant.

'Is that right?' he replied, arching one eyebrow.

'Take this, there's a hostel up the road.'

He fished out a few bob from a tin under the counter and sent us out into the night.

The hostel was like somewhere the devil himself might bed down. Rows of iron bunks stretched out along a long, empty dorm room. It was for destitute drunks with nowhere else to go. The stench of meths hung in the air and the only sound was the soft groaning of a man on his last legs. The door clanked shut and a key turned behind us.

We were locked in.

Terrified, Brenda and I bedded down, but we didn't sleep a wink. Every so often a drunken man would stagger past and let rip with an explosion of indecipherable swear words.

'Move it, yer basturt weedgie,' yelled a man.

'Can we get out of here first thing?' Brenda's voice quivered from the bunk below.

The next morning, we were out as soon as the door was unlocked. We hitchhiked our way out of Glasgow as fast as we could.

But who were we kidding? Wherever we wound up would be no better than the hellhole we'd just left.

Later that day, we found ourselves sitting in a bleak roadside cafe somewhere near West Yorkshire.

Rain lashed the windows as Elvis Presley's number-one hit, 'It's Now Or Never' crackled out of the radio.

A limp plastic Christmas tree sat forlornly in the corner and it suddenly dawned on me it was December.

I'd been missing for nearly a year.

We were down to our last couple of bob and had managed to scrape enough together for a cup of tea to share. The bottom of my shoe had finally given up the ghost and cold water was soaking my frozen toes.

Enough.

'I've run away from home,' I blurted. 'I'm not really called Rita.'

Brenda's face crumpled in relief.

'I'm a runaway too,' she sobbed.

Before I knew it, her skinny arms were wrapped round me and we were sobbing together.

I didn't ask her why she'd run away. I didn't get a chance.

Because, at that moment, a police squad car pulled up outside, its blue lights blinking through the drizzly gloom. Everything happened so fast that I barely even got to say goodbye to Brenda.

I was driven to Chesterfield police station. Once there, a kind policewoman came and led me to a room.

'Your mam and dad are waiting outside,' she smiled.

I nearly collapsed on the spot. Terror pumped through me and suddenly I was a little girl again.

'I'm scared,' I cried. 'I don't want to see them.'

What if they rejected me?

Suddenly the door opened and Mam flew in.

The tears were streaming down her face as she opened her arms out to me. No recriminations, no shouting, no blame.

No words were needed as I fell into her arms and clung to her.

'Oh, Mam, I'm sorry,' I whimpered.

And then Dad was there, all three of us entwined in a bear hug as the policewoman gently closed the door behind her.

They hugged me so tight I could hear Dad's heart pounding through his chest.

'You've got a pulse, Jenny,' Mam croaked finally. 'And that's good enough for me.'

They never once told me about the months of suffering, the countless newspaper interviews they gave or the amount of bodies our Philip was forced to look at. Not to mention how my disappearance must have affected Mam's illness.

I could see the damage etched on their exhausted faces though. And I vowed there and then not to tell them about the lies, the death threats or sleeping with strangers for food. Some things are best left unsaid. It was enough of a miracle I was alive after my year on the streets.

'We're just happy to be taking you home, Jennifer,' smiled Dad.

But then came the bombshell.

'I'm afraid Jenny can't come home yet,' said the PC, re-entering the room. 'She's a minor under police protective custody and she's been missing for a year,' she explained. 'She's due in court in the morning.'

The chief magistrate at the Family Division of Chesterfield Magistrates Court was not unkind, but he didn't mince his words.

'Jennifer Pickering,' he said solemnly, 'we are committing you to an Approved School.'

In my whole year away I'd never committed a crime, but I'd been a naughty girl and I was going to be punished by the state.

CHAPTER 4

Teenage Bride with a Secret to Hide

For most people the idea of living in an Approved School full of troubled runaways would be nothing short of hell on earth, but for me it was my salvation. After my horrific year on the streets, being cosseted in safety, routine and discipline was just what I needed.

The all-female staff may have paraded outside our dorm rooms at night to stop any would-be runaways and, by God, you didn't dare step out of line, but through healthy doses of fresh air and plenty of decent, home-cooked English grub, the Approved School slowly brought me back to life.

It was a baptism of fire though. I still remember my first day in the common room and my encounter with top dog Sharon.

A girl who looked like a bulldog chewing a wasp loomed over me. She must only have been fifteen, but when she opened her mouth she sounded like Lily Savage.

'What's your name, like?' she'd growled in a thick Scouse accent.

'Jenny, but you can call me Jennifer,' I'd replied, refusing to be intimidated.

'You swear, Jennifer?' she'd challenged.

'Sometimes.' I'd shrugged, not flinching.

'Well, don't fucking start swearing in 'ere, Jennifer,' she'd snapped.

It was a hell of an introduction to Northenden Road Girls School in Sale, Cheshire.

I'm not sure whether they even have such a thing as an Approved School today, it would probably be a young offenders' institution or a children's home, but back when I joined the school in February 1961, it was like nowhere I'd ever been before.

Once I'd established my place in the pecking order, amongst the sixty other girls, we all rubbed along quite nicely and, in time, Sharon and I even became good friends.

The girls were in for all sorts of reasons, mainly running away from home like me, but also for stealing, truancy, violence and general delinquent behaviour.

Dormitory life was a revelation. I listened each night as snatched conversations drifted my way.

'Elvis would get it . . .' 'Nah, Cliff's more up my street.' 'No way! Elvis is the dog's bollocks.' 'Shurrup, you rotten sod, you know Elvis is gonna marry me.' 'In your dreams!'

After living with three older brothers, I'd never been in the company of just girls. It was an eye-opener. As was the heavy breathing, giggling and sounds of heavy petting coming from a corner of the dorm.

'Pamela and Mary,' shouted a voice. 'Put a sock in it.'

I went to sleep every night with my head spinning. As my time at the school passed, I came to see that lesbianism between the girls, if you could call it that, was rife. I don't think these confused girls had strong sexual persuasions that way. It was nothing to do with sex, in fact. But there was a human need in these girls for affection, even if it just came from a scrawny pair of arms around you in the middle of the night.

Besides, who was I to judge? After what I'd been forced to do on the streets, I knew by then that life was complicated. Who knew what backgrounds these girls had come from? No one ever asked, but I could see many were troubled and I wouldn't be at all surprised if many had been abused.

We were certainly a rough bunch though, and the teachers had their work cut out smoothing the rough edges. When we weren't smoking, fighting or making crude innuendos about what we'd like to do with Elvis, we were marched to church on a Sunday morning in a crocodile.

It wouldn't take long before some eagle-eyed girl would spot a fag butt, otherwise known as a dimp, bob down and scoop it up.

Church visits were always great for dimp-picking and often the whole line was singing in time to the march.

Dimp. Dimp. DIMP. DIMP. Our rowdy voices grew louder as we marched and cackled our way to church.

'Gals, please!' implored the deputy head. 'Some decorum.'

We'd quieten down, but as soon as we got back to the home we'd make for the nearest lav.

The thick tracing paper-like loo roll may have been murder

to wipe your bum on, but it weren't half good for emptying out the meagre strands of tobacco from our dimps and rolling into a makeshift fag.

No matter that it nearly blew your head off and left you gasping for breath.

Aside from learning how to improvise makeshift fags, I also learnt the more constructive skills of shorthand, typing and cookery. After thirteen months, the scruffy vagrant who used to sleep in cars and wash her knickers in the sink had been transformed into a confident, happy teenager. In fact, by the time I was released early for good behaviour, in March 1962, two months shy of my sixteenth birthday Mam and Dad barely recognised me.

On the day of my departure, the elegant headmistress, Mary McIntyre Brown, pulled me to one side.

'You have so much to give, Jenny,' she'd smiled.

Me? A scruffy, damaged tomboy with fag butts stuffed in her pocket and a dark past?

Her belief in me meant more than words and there and then a special magic weaved its way around my heart.

When women support other women, great things can be achieved, their kindness a powerful force for good. *A lesson I would never forget.*

Mam greeted me back at the home I had fled from two years previously in typical northern, understated style.

'Hello, Jenny, love,' she grinned as I walked into the kitchen. It was said almost as if I'd just popped out for a pint of milk from the shops, not fled under the cover of darkness more than two years previously.

'Would you like a cup of tea?' she asked, gently taking my bag from me.

But by the intensity of the hug she wrapped me in, I knew she felt the emotion of that moment every bit as much as me. Relief and love shone in her pale-green eyes.

Dad was less emotional.

'Na' then, Jennifer,' he boomed when he came back from the pits that evening. 'Thee's not sitting around on yer arse all day. Tha gonna gerra a job, or what?'

Three months later, I'd done one better than that, at least in my dad's eyes. I managed to bag myself a handsome fiancé *and* set a wedding date.

Sixteen seems like an incredibly early age to marry but, in the small pit village in which I was raised, it was entirely normal. Girls married before their bodies and minds had even developed and, what's more, they had often been planning and saving for it since they were knee high. All the girls off my estate, including Sandra and Christine, were either married or engaged. They were just blindly following a well-trodden path. I too thought that was what I wanted. I really believed it.

I really wanted to believe it.

Reg was as cocky and as handsome as they come.

From the moment I'd got chatting to him shortly after my sixteenth birthday, I was completely taken in.

He was twenty-one and had all the chat. His teeth shone almost as brightly as his blue Tonic suit. His slicked-back dark hair and the leather briefcase he carried just added to the air of cool respectability.

'A girl like you needs a fella like me to look after you,' he smiled silkily.

I don't mind admitting I was dazzled. Reg had a job in insurance and big plans for the future. We'd only been dating three months when I took him home to meet my family.

'A home almost as beautiful as your daughter, Mrs Pickering,' he oozed.

Perched on Mam's leather sofa in her good room, he set his sights on Dad.

'I work for an insurance company, Mr Pickering,' he went on. 'That's where the money is nowadays, not down the pits. I've got enough money saved for a semi-detached too,' he added.

'Have yer now?' Dad said.

As he talked, I noticed how out of place he looked in Mam's slightly faded good room. Everything about him dazzled just a little too brightly, like a peacock that had washed up in a mining town. Suddenly I realised everyone had stopped talking and was staring at me.

'Well, Jennifer,' probed Dad. 'Do you?'

Did I what?

'Does thee wanna marry him?' he asked.

Reg had just asked Dad for my hand in marriage! *Without even asking me first.*

Patting my beehive, I squirmed uncomfortably. Doubt nagged at me. I did love him. Didn't I? We'd only been seeing each other for three months. But if not this, then what? The options open to teenaged village girls weren't exactly leaping out at me. At least Reg was respectable.

'Yeah,' I said, lamely, thinking how tight the white stilettos Reg insisted I wear suddenly felt.

'Aye,' said Dad, holding out his hand for Reg to shake. 'Alreet then.'

The deal was done and we even opened a bottle of Babycham to celebrate. As Reg held court and chattered brightly about the insurance game, I noticed the smile never quite reached Mam's eyes. But when it came to the wedding dress she did me proud. She took me down the Co-op and bought me a beautiful satin ivory dress.

'A proper princess,' she wept, when she saw me in it.

To complete the look, I dyed my blonde hair raven black, as was the fashion of the time. It was so shiny it was almost navy-blue in places and I wore it piled high in a beehive, offset by heavy kohl eyeliner.

Dark hair to match the dark secrets in my head.

My head was still spinning when I walked down the aisle in October 1962, just five months after I turned sixteen.

A teenage bride, with a secret to hide.

I soon became adept at playing the dutiful wife. We moved into a semi-detached in Chesterfield and, to the outside world, I was the image of respectability.

Sex was just an act. I never once breathed a word of what had happened to me that year I went missing or the voices that drove me there. Not that Reg seemed interested in me or Mam's illness in any case. He wanted a good little wife. Always dressed in a twin-set, beehive set just so, and never without a coating of sugar-pink lipstick.

The perfect front.

I performed my wifely duties detached and through gritted teeth. I cooked and cleaned for him, and every time the tug of wanderlust whispered tantalisingly in my ear, I shook it clean out my head.

As I trod the cobbled streets of Derbyshire, admiring the blossoming baby bumps of my former school friends, and being the perfect wife, the world around me seemed to be changing at dizzying speed.

John F. Kennedy campaigned on behalf of the civil rights and the Beatles seemed to take over the world.

People were going places, achieving great breakthroughs and standing up for causes they believed in. I, meanwhile, was stuck stock-still in a failing marriage. What was my purpose in life?

Frustration thrummed in every single cell of my body. Life was so fragile. Didn't I owe it to myself to make the most of mine?

What was it Mary McIntyre Brown had said? *You have so much to give, Jenny.* So much, and yet not a clue where to start.

One weekend, when we'd been married for six months, I returned home to visit Mam and Dad. Dad was thrilled for me that I was finally respectable. It must have been a huge relief for him to see me married, but he couldn't hide the familiar tension that cloaked the house and I felt it wash over me the minute I stepped through the door.

By now all of us kids had moved out. Michael was in the army, Philip had married a lovely local girl called Mary and Howard was working and courting.

It was just Mam and Dad on their own now. At least, I

thought it was just them. Sickeningly, a familiar voice had also returned . . .

At the end of my weekend with them, I cornered Dad.

'Everything OK, Dad?' I asked, while Mam brewed up.

'Aye, course it is,' he snapped. 'Don't tek on so, Jennifer.'

I knew he was lying to protect me.

Outside the house and on medication Mam could just about hold it together, but inside the home it was a different matter. I watched her as she sat at the kitchen table sipping at her cup of tea.

Suddenly she moved the cup to hide her lips, but there was no mistaking the whispering noise coming from behind the cup.

Alarm bells rang.

'Mam, who you talking to?' I asked.

'No one, love,' she smiled brightly. 'Come and sit down and we'll get your wedding photos out for a little look.'

But a few minutes later, as we were chatting, another voice appeared. Louder and more terrifying, this voice wasn't my mam's and it seemed to have a grip on her as it bubbled without warning from her mouth.

'Don't thee sick me,' she shrieked, setting down her cup with a clatter.

Seconds later, the voice had vanished and confusion and shame flashed over her face.

'I'm sorry, love,' she babbled. 'Don't mind me, silly old Mam.'

She tried to laugh it off, but she wasn't fooling me. I could see she was absolutely terrified. A slow, creeping dread spread over me.

No. No. No. Not again.

'I'm just nipping to the loo, love,' she said.

'All right, Mam,' I said, stroking her arm as she walked past.

The mam that came out was not the one who went in. Her face was as pale as flour and her hands shook.

'They're even watching me in there,' she cried, jabbing a hand in the direction of the toilet.

'Who, Mam?' I yelled. 'Who?'

'Them buggers,' she shrieked. 'There's a crack between the skirting and the wall. They can see me.'

Hearing the commotion, Dad rushed in.

'I'll call the doctor,' he said. 'Jennifer, you gerroff home.'

Mam was growing wilder by the moment, her eyes rolling about in her head as she thrashed about. Dad did his best to try and contain her, but she was a strong, well-built woman, and it took every ounce of his effort just to keep his arms around her. Dad was a well-built man, sixteen stone in his miners' boots, but holding Mam was like containing a wild bull as she lurched about the kitchen, ricocheting from dresser to table.

'Mam, please,' I whimpered.

Suddenly her flying hand dislodged Dad's cap and it landed on the floor. Without his cap he looked suddenly older, more vulnerable.

An ancient pain was in his eyes. Mam had been ill for as long as I could remember. Total despair consumed me. I'd run from this, risked my life to escape it, spent a year in a state home protected from this, and yet nothing had changed.

'No, Dad,' I cried, fiercely. 'I want to stay and help you.'

'No, Jennifer,' he said. 'You can't help. Don't yer gerrit, no bugger can. Now just go. She don't want yer to see her like this. Go!'

Running from the house, blinded by my own tears, I realised he was right. There was nothing any of us could do. Back home, I wearily turned the key in the lock when I heard my neighbour call me over.

''Ere,' she said. 'Know what your Reg has been up to? He's had a girl there all weekend, you know, Jen.'

'Oh, has he indeed?' I stormed, feeling a rage mushroom inside my shattered brain.

As I sprinted from room to room, my anger exploded inside me. Every room stank of treachery.

The sink was piled high with unwashed dishes and the bedroom sheets were rumpled and unmade. I imagined their bodies intertwined, laughing, while I'd been watching my poor mam suffer. How dare he? We'd barely been married two minutes.

I expected Reg to put his usual spin on things but, when he returned home later that evening, he was blasé about the matter.

'It's all over, Jen,' he shrugged.

'You're not talking your way out of this one, Reg,' I fumed.

'Calm down, love,' he went on.

As I watched his mouth open and close, I zoned out. There was nothing worth listening to. Reg was a sweet-talking charmer. He'd dust glitter on everything until I doubted whether he even knew what the truth was any longer.

But I knew the truth. Our marriage was a sham, and in playing the happy, dutiful wife I was complicit in the deception.

Mam might have been losing her mind, but she still had enough good sense to know he was a wrong 'un.

In November 1963, after one year of marriage, I left Reg.

After another three years of bumming around I made a decision I know my family were bewildered by. In 1966, aged twenty, I returned to London.

Dark London with all its memories, ghosts, lies and strangers. The myriad of haunted back alleyways where I sold my soul swirling through my mind . . .

But the capital was whispering to me, summoning me back, and I was powerless to resist.

Besides, there was nothing for me in Chesterfield any more and, surely, this time I would conquer the demons of my past.

Surely, this time, I would find my destiny?

I didn't know what the future held, but it had to be brighter than my past. Had I known what a firestorm was coming my way, I might have hesitated.

CHAPTER 5

East End Survival

The year was 1966 and the place was 12 Evering Road, Stoke Newington, in the borough of Hackney in London's East End.

My new home.

It was just a bedsit in a sea of other bedsits, nothing to set it out as being remarkable from any other community. But pause long enough on the streets outside and you could almost smell it in the air. Trouble was brewing. A sea change was coming, and menace hung heavy over the rows and rows of drab terraced housing.

Up until now, old East End families had lived cheek by jowl, trying to repair the damage done to their communities by Hitler and face the daily uphill task of feeding their families.

Except now, in 1966, new communities were being born, establishing their foothold and trying and failing to live peacefully alongside each other.

Villains like the Krays lurked round every corner; wannabe

villains strutted the streets in Tonic or mohair suits and slicked-back hair, pirate radio stations operated secretly from attic rooms and clubs and snooker halls were fronts for protection rackets.

Not five minutes from my front door was the Krays' stronghold and club, The Regency. And everywhere the police prowled, eyes narrowed, ever on the alert for trouble, ears straining for the distant throb of a Rolling Stones track or a witness to bring down the Krays.

But they were always met with a wall of silence.

Because, as I quickly came to learn, living in the East End means that when trouble explodes: '*You see nothing, you hear nothing and you keep your trap shut.*'

Frustrated energy and the ever-present threat of violence reverberated through the streets.

And, thrown into the melting pot were waves of West Indian immigrants, settling down in and making their home in the streets of Hackney. It was an extraordinary time in an extraordinary place.

I'd got myself set up with a bedsit and a job assembling toy Matchbox cars on an assembly line at Lesney's Toy Factory in Hackney Wick in early 1967.

What a mind-numbingly boring job! I spent nine hours a day on a production line with hundreds of other East End women. It was my job to pick up the shell of a plastic car as it trundled past, press on a plastic base, then place it back on the line.

Car after car, hour after boring hour, forty-five hours a week for the princely sum of seven pounds a week, just enough to cover the cost of my rent, my fags and a bag of chips for tea. The only thing that livened it up was the Lesney Ladies, as they were known. What a bunch!

Lesney's had an enormous workforce of these formidable women; 5,500 of them streamed in daily.

From the minute they poured in through the doors onto the factory floor, the air was alive with the babble of raucous cockney voices.

Just as well I hadn't come from a sheltered background! The parlance was enough to make a docker blush. I'd barely sat down when a woman opposite me flung down her soldering iron in disgust and glared over the top of my head.

''Ere, Violet. I 'eard what you bin sayin' 'bout me and I ain't 'avin it.'

A distant voice bellowed back, 'Oh give it a rest, Ivy, you can't tell shit from clay.'

Ivy turned purple with rage. 'You wanna smack in the gob, do ya?' she screeched.

Sensing my dismay, the woman sitting next to me smiled and shook her head.

'You're new, aincha, love?' she chuckled. 'Ignore 'em.'

With that, she turned up the crackly transistor radio to drown out their voices. But even Dusty Springfield's sultry tones couldn't drown out the raging fishwives. It was a game of verbal ping-pong as insults flew back and forth across the factory floor like bullets.

'Come and 'ave a go then, Ivy, your old man has enough times,' Violet screeched back.

A vein throbbed on the side of Ivy's face and the radio went up a notch.

'I Just Don't Know What to Do with Myself' sang Dusty.

'Shut it, you old whore,' yelled Ivy, whilst welding a car component together. 'I might have the luck of nine blind bastards, but I ain't as unlucky as your old man.'

'I hear yours gets lucky every Friday night down Hackney Marshes.'

On and on they raged, while everyone else cheerfully carried on working around them, tapping their feet and humming along to Dusty.

Over time I came to understand that these little dust-ups were just part and parcel of factory life. The routine mundanity of life was eased by a good old singsong from the radio that was permanently on or the constant flow of rude jokes.

Factory life might have been dull, but to these women it was in their blood. Many were third-generation workers, and women like Ivy and Violet were the backbone of their families. They worked because they had to and many had five or more kids who depended on their wages to eat. The older women had spent years battling grinding poverty, disease and over-crowded living conditions. Make no mistake, they were as tough as the pit wives from back home.

But they didn't hold grudges either and, to my amazement, at the end of my first day I saw Ivy and Violet bent double over a fag outside, tears of laughter streaming down their faces.

'So I says to 'im,' cackled Ivy, 'is it even in yet?'

After that I learnt to take the rows with a pinch of salt.

Many of these women were on first-name terms with the Krays and the twins' mother, and if they didn't know them they still spoke about them in hushed tones of respect. I overheard their whispered conversations and quickly learnt that, when it came to Ronnie and Reggie, you wouldn't last long if you bad-mouthed them.

'Lovely lads they are. Credit to their mother.'

To them, the Krays weren't criminals, they were a 'street-cleaning', law-enforcement agency in their own right.

Apparently, a man who mugged an old lady in the East End could expect to be put in a concrete overcoat if the brothers or any of their gang found them. They were the closest thing to Robin Hood these women had.

Sadly, the hundreds of West Indian immigrants flooding the streets of Hackney weren't spoken about in the same reverential tone as the Krays. The British Nationality Act of 1948, which gave all Commonwealth citizens free entry into Britain, started mass migration to the mother country. Ever since the *SS Empire Windrush* docked at Tilbury in Essex from Kingston, Jamaica, on 22 June 1948, and 492 West Indian immigrants set foot on our shores, hundreds more had followed in their footsteps. And now, in 1967, many of their number had chosen Hackney as their home, all searching for work and opportunities.

Instead, they found open hostility and a casual, insidious racism at every turn. Skilled jobs like those in the police force were totally closed to them, so many took low-paid work as labourers, cleaners or working on the buses as conductors. Only now, a backlash had begun in response to the high numbers of immigrants and racial tension was high.

'It ain't right, is it, Jenny?' the woman sat next to me on the factory line was fond of saying. 'Bloody coming over 'ere and nicking all our jobs. My Bobbie can't get a job now, you know. He's been looking for months.'

'That's funny 'cos every time I see 'im, he's down the Cat and Mutton,' shot back another woman.

I laughed along but, inside, I felt a nagging unease. I scarcely knew any black families. The only family I'd ever met were virtually the only Jamaican family in Chesterfield, the Johnsons, and they were lovely. Up north, people had treated them like they would any other family – with respect and courtesy unless proved otherwise.

But down here, in London, there seemed to be a simmering anger towards immigrants bubbling just beneath the surface. It riled me. To me we're all the same, two legs, two arms, a head and, hopefully, a brain. It's the heart and the generosity of spirit that count. But to these war-weary battle-axes, white was white and black was black and never should the two mix.

They weren't alone in their attitudes. On occasion, after work, myself and a few of the Lesney girls would pop to the pub for a drink. I was just pushing open the door of the pub when I saw it: 'No blacks, no dogs, no Irish', read a tatty handwritten notice pinned to the door of the Hackney boozer.

I read it in dismay.

One of the girls clocked my surprise. 'Too right,' she scowled. 'I wish all them black bastards would just piss off back to their own country. All these strange voices in the street. Where will it end?'

Her voice dripped with pure vitriol and she spat on the doorstep for good measure. Once inside, cradling a port and lemon, I couldn't resist. 'But what have they done to you?' I ventured.

She stared at me like I'd just told her the moon was made of cheese.

'Because it ain't right, is it?' she spluttered. 'They need to stick to their places and we stick to ours.'

She sniffed disdainfully. 'Besides, might catch summit off 'em if they come in here sitting on our seats. Don't have nuffin' to do wiv 'em.'

I said no more, what was the point?

On the way home, my walk took me past a black barber shop along the Lower Clapton Road. I gazed in interest through the steamed-up windows. Groups of men stood about laughing, drinking dark liquid from plastic cups and some were bopping about in time to some unheard music.

As I drew level with the doorway, a young black man not much older than me popped out for a cigarette. Relaxed and smiling, he leant back against the door frame and sparked up before carrying on bobbing his head in time to the music that now floated out the door.

He was dressed in tight polyester trousers, a Pringle jumper and a jaunty trilby, and looked so laid-back he was virtually horizontal. He fixed his gaze on me and the widest smile I'd ever seen flashed over his face.

''Allo dere,' he beamed in a friendly West Indian accent.

Like a rabbit caught in headlamps, I froze. I went to open my mouth, but nothing came out.

'*Don't have nuffin' to do wiv 'em,*' echoed the warning of the Lesney Lady.

The man looked amused.

'I said h-elllooo,' he repeated.

Suddenly I was running scared. My skinny legs seemed to take on a life of their own as the pavement flashed by in a blur.

The man's voice drifted after me as I ran. 'What I say?' he chuckled.

His laughter wasn't mocking, or nasty. He just seemed genuinely amused at the sight of my scrawny legs pumping up the Lower Clapton Road.

Once back inside my dingy bedsit, I sat down on the bed and scratched my head.

Why had I run? He was only being friendly.

But then everything about London was strange and edgy. Back in Chesterfield everything was so straightforward. Kids played out together on the streets. Doors didn't have signs on them. Most of them were permanently open. Everyone treated each other as equals. The community was warm and friendly.

But here women rowed for fun, communities lived on top of each other but were closed off, some doors were open and some were closed, depending on the colour of your skin.

Soon after this, I decided to return home to Chesterfield to pay Mam and Dad a visit. After the state of Mam on my last visit, I had an uneasy feeling that I shouldn't leave it too long before my next trip home.

My premonition had been right. When I returned to our little house on the Hady estate one weekend early in 1967, I was dismayed at the scene which greeted me.

Dad was sitting in the kitchen in the dark. I could just make out his outline in the gloom, his head in his hands, slouched over the table. The dying embers of a coal fire glowed in the hearth.

My heart turned to water. I flicked on the light and Dad didn't flinch.

'Dad,' I said gently. 'Where's Mam?'

Finally he turned to face me and the look of utter heartbreak on his face took the breath clean out of my body.

'Whatever's the matter, Dad?' I gasped.

'I'm sorry, Jennifer,' he said. 'She's gone.'

'Gone?' I repeated, confused.

'I've had your mam committed,' he replied.

I looked around the empty kitchen as if I half expected Mam to walk out of the shadows. I just couldn't compute this simple fact in my brain as I stared around the kitchen. This place was synonymous with Mam. The place where she'd toiled for so many years, always made sure we had 'sufficient', kept us warm, safe, read to us in, cuddled us in.

If I closed my eyes, I could still see her ladling out huge portions of jam roly-poly smothered in custard.

But when I opened them, the image vanished.

A mother is as central to a home as a stove to a kitchen and to not have her here hit me like a leaden hammer square in the chest. All that was left was memories and heartache.

And there, in the midst of this pain, was my father. A colossus of a man, five feet eleven inches of raw male pride crumbling in front of my very eyes.

He started to weep openly in front of me and I realised it was the first time I'd ever seen my father cry. He'd been holding it together for so many years and now, finally, he couldn't keep it in any longer.

For a while I said nothing, just waited until he was ready to tell me what had happened. Slowly, the story came out.

Apparently Mam had gone mad, one of her 'dos', as Dad called them. He had sent for the doctor and when he arrived, he'd finally seen her in full flow. My poor mam had been fighting as they forced her into a straitjacket and bundled her into the back of a waiting ambulance.

Curtains must have been twitching the length and breadth of the estate as she screamed at the top of her lungs, 'You're not taking me nowhere. This is where I live.'

Shaking his head at the memory, Dad winced.

'She's as strong as an ox,' he cried. 'She didn't want to go.'

Finally they had managed to force her in and slammed the door. A waiting medic had then swiftly sedated her. Just before he left, the doctor turned to my dad.

'I'm sorry I never believed you,' he'd said.

The effort of recounting the whole traumatic scene seemed to have swallowed Dad whole.

'So there you have it,' he croaked. 'A bloody mess and no mistake.'

He was a broken man.

My father had avoided being blown up in the trenches, shot to smithereens on D-Day, risked his life daily down in the mines, but it was having his beloved wife sectioned that had finally destroyed him.

The enemy at war and deep beneath the coalmines of Derbyshire was at least visible. When danger threatened him, he knew what form it would take. But this, *this illness*, was just an unfathomable monster that struck without warning. This was his toughest fight yet.

He gazed at me now, a look of utter bewilderment and pain etched on his face.

His soft voice, when it came, was just a whisper,

'Have I done the right thing, Jennifer?'

'Of course you have, Dad,' I cried. 'No one believed you for years, now they do. She's getting help.'

'Mebbe.' He smiled sadly.

'I know so,' I insisted.

And then, almost because I couldn't resist: 'Why didn't you ever just pack your bag and leave us?' Suddenly Dad found his strength and sat bolt upright, his proud chin thrust out.

'How could I?' he blazed. 'Leave a sick woman and four kids? Do you know what would have happened? You'd all have been taken into care and I couldn't do that.'

I said nothing more. Just stared at his strong, handsome face and marvelled at the man I felt proud to call Dad. I knew I always loved him, but now I respected him too. I found my real dad that day in the kitchen.

The next day, me, Dad and our Howard visited Mam in the ill-named 'The Haven', a mental institution near Derby.

'The Haven,' grumbled Dad. 'Who came up with that name?'

Howard and I hesitated on the doorstep.

'Any road,' Dad muttered, swinging the door open and ushering us inside. 'Let's do this.'

Mam was a shadow of herself. She was slumped over a grey

Formica-topped table in a visitors' room, staring blankly into the middle distance.

I tried to hide my shock at the sight of her. Her shiny, softly curled hair was now limp and unbrushed and, without her usual coating of Yardley lipstick, she looked utterly washed out. But worse was the realisation that she had clearly been drugged up to the eyeballs.

'Mam,' I cried, clutching her hands in mine.

'Hurry up and get better, Mam, and come home.'

She smiled at me vacantly. I wasn't sure if my words were even registering.

What drugs had they got her on? Stuff this. Getting up, I flung my arms around her.

'I love you, Mam.'

While Dad talked to the doctor, Howard and I both tried to focus on Mam. We didn't want to look at the faces of the other patients in this bleak place. It was a proper old-fashioned mental home: grey and gloomy with an unspeakable misery seeping from its white-tiled walls.

When it came to saying goodbye, there weren't really any words. I knew Dad hated leaving Mam there even more than I did, and I gripped his hand all the way out.

Back in Hackney, it wasn't long before Dad wrote:

Your mam's come home. She walked out the hospital and got the bus home. 'I've come home, I'm not stopping there. I live here,' she said. I had to call the hospital and they came out to get her. Bloody awful it were, sending her back to that place.

Gripping his letter, I stared at the four walls of my dingy bedsit, with its two-ring gas fire, tiny iron bedstead and the damp seeping up the faded walls.

This wasn't my purpose in life, surely? Or was it, *was this my destiny*?

My life was unravelling, spinning out of control again. Suddenly I crumpled the letter up and hurled it at the wall. 'My life's shit!' I yelled.

I heard the lady in the bedsit next door cough loudly and my head fell into my hands. I could top myself in here and the neighbours would just tell me to keep the noise down.

I had gone from the wide-open fields of Derbyshire to living in a box where I knew no one. Where was the sense of community, the warmth and camaraderie? Why did no one talk over the wall or exchange recipes? Where were the kids dashing in and out of each other's houses?

Back up north, where I belonged, that's where, and yet I couldn't bring myself to return. Something was keeping me here in these strange streets, some invisible force compelling me to stay in the East End. There was no tangible reason for living here, but the urge to stay was strangely overwhelming.

For days after, I walked about as if in a dream. Even the friendly black barber, who still insisted on smiling, I ignored as I walked past each morning on my way to work.

The murder of the Krays' associate, Jack 'The Hat' McVitie, in a basement flat at 97, Evering Road, just a few doors up from my bedsit didn't even really register. Their reign of fear may well have been coming to an end but, as usual, they were put on a pedestal. The girls at work were full of it.

'He had it coming,' muttered one through thin lips in the canteen at lunchtime. 'They lured 'im out The Regency and up to blonde Carol's flat on the pretence of a party,' crowed another.

'I 'eard they flushed his liver down the toilet,' said the canteen assistant clearing our table with relish. The woman opposite me stuffed a crab paste sandwich into her mouth with melancholy delight.

'His guts must have been spilling outta of him,' she cackled as she chewed.

Me? I carried on eating and said nothing. And later, with every car base I fitted, I felt waves of anger and irritation washing over me.

Lift, click, replace.

With every toy car I helped to assemble, I felt as if a little piece of my brain was sailing away from me down that production line.

The constant chatter of my co-workers that used to entertain me, now seemed to bore through my skull until I just wanted to scream. Little did I know it but, unable to cope any longer, my brain was shutting down, cell by cell. The pain of Mam's illness was just too much for my mind to cope with any longer. I was scrambled, exhausted and broken.

The next day at work I felt unreal – as if my body was there but my brain was floating somewhere else.

'Fag break, Jenny?' smiled the woman next to me at 11 a.m.

I said nothing. Just kept on fitting bases.

'Suit yourself,' she shrugged.

Suddenly, something fused in my brain. All hell broke loose.

'Arghhhhh,' I screamed, jumping to my feet and flinging my tray into the air.

Horrified faces froze and the world went into slow motion as dozens of tiny plastic cars rained down on the factory floor like confetti.

'She's gone bloody mad,' I heard a distant voice cry.

'NOOOOOOOO,' I raged as the foreman came pelting over and slammed the red button that stopped the conveyor belt.

And then I was on my hands and knees, sobbing and clawing at the concrete floor as if to find a way out of my wretched misery. Pure, undiluted anguish seeped out of me. The image of my mam, my lovely mam, in that hideous institution just refused to budge from my brain.

Gentle hands were placed round me, coaxing me to my feet.

'Come on, Jenny love,' said Ivy. Her kind smile never left her face. 'We all feel like doing that sometimes.'

And then I was being ushered out of the factory and escorted to the doctor.

'Breakdown,' diagnosed the GP without a shred of compassion. 'Take these, go home and rest.'

With that, he pressed a prescription into my hand. I read the shopping list of drugs.

Valium, nortriptyline, Librium . . .

And that was that. No counselling, no support, no compassion. Just sent off home on my own to my bedsit with enough drugs to sedate a bull.

Later, I sat and stared at the four walls of my poky room. As dusk fell and bruised the sky to a deep purple, then black, I sat motionless in the dark.

The next morning, some of the girls from the factory visited.

'They're keeping your job open, Jenny, so that's somefing, innit, love?' They beamed brightly.

I was grateful for their compassion but, aside from their visits, I was totally alone in the world.

Mam was in a mental home. Poor Dad was wracked with guilt. How could I tell him what had happened? He had enough on his plate just dealing with Mam.

And me. What did I have going for me?

I was twenty-one with nothing to my name but a troubled past. When danger came knocking, I ran to it. What did that say about me? I was a dark, disturbed soul with nothing to live for. Damaged goods . . .

And with that realization came another. Carefully, I lined up every bottle of medicine the GP had prescribed. Slowly and methodically, I drained each bottle, gulping back the liquid so fast it didn't even touch the sides.

When, at last, every bottle bar one was empty, I shuddered, the taste making me wince as hundreds of millimetres of seda- tives and antidepressants trickled down the back of my throat. And then I lay back on my bed and stared at the stain of damp that was slowly creeping its way across the ceiling.

Mercifully, my brain was starting to grow cloudy, my finger- tips fuzzy like the way you feel just before anaesthetic knocks you out. My eyelids started to flicker open and shut. Sweet release was imminent.

CHAPTER 6

The Power of Love

As the room swam back into view, I blinked. The tiny cupboard, the two-ring gas fire, the sea of jumbled rooftops out the window all homed into view.

I was alive.

Blinking groggily, I tried to sit up but just fell back in a wasted heap. As I lay there, I tried to make sense of my situation, but my brain was just so hazy. Nothing made sense.

But, finally, the fog cleared enough for me to be able to stand. Staggering a little, I made my way along the corridor to the shared toilet where I splashed cold water on my face.

Back in my room, my gaze fell on the medication bottles. All empty bar one. The realization was so strong it was like a wave of sea water smacking me clean in the face.

I had survived!

And, as crazy as this sounds, an enormous sense of relief flooded over me.

The Power of Love

Grabbing the only bottle of medication with any liquid left in it, I emptied it down the sink. There and then, I made a vow. Never again would I allow anyone to drug me senseless. I might have been mixed-up, but I wasn't stupid. From now on, I wasn't going to let anyone drug me like they had Mam.

My brain might have been sick, but it wasn't broken, and any decisions I took about my life from now on would be my own.

I had survived a year on the streets without touching drugs offered by dealers, so why had I let that doctor stuff me with drugs so he could get rid of a problem he couldn't cope with?

Stuff him. Stuff 'em all. I was alive and I bloody well intended to stay that way too.

Soon after, I returned to work and on my walk there I passed by the black barber's shop. As usual, the young man was hanging out by the door, smoking a cigarette. When he saw me, he cocked his head to one side.

'Why you never say hello to me, girl?' he asked.

For once I stopped. And this time, I didn't run.

'I don't know you,' I shrugged.

'Well,' he said slowly. 'You'll never get to know me if you don't stop and say hello, will you?'

Defiantly, I flashed him my cheekiest grin. 'All right then, hello! Jenny's the name.'

His face crumpled into a wide, white smile.

'Hiya, Jenny,' he laughed, sticking out his hand. 'My name's Gerald.'

His eyes sparkled with fun and, instinctively, I knew I could trust him. 'Right, now we acquainted, how do you feel about you and me going out sometime?'

'Why not?' I smiled back. 'When?'

'What's wrong with tonight?' he shrugged.

I couldn't see the problem. He seemed like a decent enough fella. The girls at work thought it was a problem though.

'Oh, Jenny,' one gasped when I told them. 'How could yer? Aint you worried?'

'About what?' I snapped back. 'That I might catch something?'

'Nah, I didn't mean that but . . . But, oh I don't know, it just ain't right, a black man and a white woman. Mixing, like. You'll get no end of grief.'

She was right about that. From the moment Gerald picked me up and we walked down the road in the direction of the Grange House in Stoke Newington, we were treated like a travelling freak show. The air crackled with hostility and disbelief.

'Black man's meat,' hissed an old woman as she drew level. And then, louder, from a passing car, 'Fuck off back to your own country!' Shortly followed by a low, menacing call from a boy on a bike: 'Nigger lover.'

I was horrified. Just what on earth was I doing that was so wrong exactly? For the first time I wasn't proud to be English. A deep disgust and shame flowed through my veins.

Gerald, on the other hand, was obviously used to being on the end of a daily truckload of abuse and just seemed to let the poisonous comments wash over him.

'Don't stress it, man,' he shrugged. 'It is what it is.'

Gerald was the perfect gentleman and, once inside the club, told me all about how he came to be in Hackney.

'I came here in 1960 from Jamaica,' he explained. 'My father worked on a sugar plantation from 7 a.m. until 5 p.m. six days a week. He earned three dollars a week; it was just one up from slavery.'

I nodded, intrigued by his roots. In many ways he and I were both strangers in this strange land.

After a few drinks at the club, Gerald turned to me.

'How's about I tek you to a real club?'

Warm from the glow of rum, I nodded as he led me from the club and, giggling, we ran down the road.

'Where we going?' I asked, my head spinning as we started to climb the steps of a normal-looking house.

'It's a shebeen, man,' he replied, rapping on the door.

The distant rumble of music seemed to throb from the very foundations of the terraced house.

'A sha-what?' I gasped.

'You'll see.' He grinned mysteriously.

The house might have looked ordinary from the outside but, once the door swung open, I was suddenly transported into a magical new world.

Although life was flat, grey and dangerous out on the mean streets of Hackney, inside this house it was colourful, alive, blazing with light, laughter, music and amazing new sounds, smells and flavours.

A shebeen was an illicit bar or club where alcohol was sold. But in Hackney in 1967 it was much more than just a place to buy booze. It was a safe haven where the newly settled West Indian community could meet, drink, dance, eat and talk, free from the prying eyes of bigots.

'It's a safe place for us to be, you know,' explained Gerald. 'It brings together the whole community, all dem dat belong together gather here.'

And with that he led me into the throbbing core of the shebeen.

My eyes went out on stalks. Black men and women of all ages danced to an up-tempo reggae track in a hot, happy, heaving crush. Their bodies were writhing, their hips undulating as they moved freely, loosely, dancing to the music as they laughed and let themselves go.

There was no dance floor, as such. Every spare inch of the house was a 'dance floor', as people grooved about on the stairs, crammed up against the wall or in alcoves.

As Gerald held my hand tightly and we weaved our way through the house, he greeted everyone by name.

'Wha'ppun' rude bwoy,' to the men and 'Wha'ppun' sistren,' he said in a deep Jamaican patois.

'You know everyone here,' I gasped.

'Mi bredrin fram yuuts?' he shrugged.

And then we were dancing. Gerald had his hand in the small of my back as we jigged and swayed in a small patch of floor that looked no bigger than a postage stamp.

The music was infectious, and soon my limbs relaxed into the vibe as the whole house seemed to move as one.

'What's this music?' I shouted over the noise.

'Blue Beat, reggae, ska and a lotta, lotta loving. Dat

wicked, nuh? Reggae give us joy, love, hope and freedom, you know.'

I laughed, suddenly feeling quite heady with happiness. There were a few other white faces, but hardly any, and yet, despite the barrage of abuse most of these people must have faced daily out on the streets from white people, no one showed me anything but kindness.

'I bloody love it here,' I shouted up at him.

Gerald laughed and tweaked my chin.

'Wa' mek you so sweet?'

By the time Gerald announced he had to be up for work in a few hours and we'd best go, I could barely be prised from the shebeen. After months of being out in the wilderness, I felt like I'd come home.

The poky bedsit, the drab grey streets, the mind-numbing factory floor all melted away. My world had just burst into Technicolor.

At the door I half expected to walk out onto a warm, moon-lit Jamaican beach with silver sands and whispering palms. Sadly it was just a terraced Hackney street shimmering under a soft but steady rain, but as dawn bled across the chimney-stacks I felt happier and more content than I'd felt in months. And with a tummy full of rice and peas and a head full of reggae, I floated home.

After that night, Gerald and I became good mates and every weekend he took me from party to club to shebeen. My suicide attempt became nothing but a distant nightmare as I partied, danced and feasted on delicious West Indian cooking.

Perhaps now a whole new world had opened up to me, a

world of music and community, of spice and warmth, my heart was now open to love too?

All I know was that the minute I set eyes on Lennox Ignatius Smith in October 1969, two years after I met Gerald, I was a gonner.

Lennox, or Lenny, as he was known, was a regular at the Grange House in Stoke Newington and no one would grow to hold my fragile heart in quite the same way he did.

When love strikes, it strikes without warning and it spears you straight through the heart, rendering you quite, quite vulnerable. Who knows the peculiar mix of alchemy that transforms two ordinary souls into lovers or what strange forces stir up such a whirlwind of emotion?

Not sweet, lovable Gerald, or even my first husband, Reg, that's for sure. But Lenny, a humble blender in a chemical factory, with not a single penny to his name.

No matter that he lived in a bedsit smaller than my own, or that I knew nothing about him or his past, or his home country of Guyana. *He was the man for me.*

Lenny with his mile-wide smile and boundless charisma was heating me up faster than a Scotch bonnet chilli. I'd become aware of him one night when I'd been dancing at the Grange House and I felt a body press up behind me.

I whirled round ready to give whoever it was trying it on a mouthful and found myself staring into the most beautiful pair of brown eyes I'd ever seen.

'You're a handsome bugger,' I blurted out.

His laugh was like nothing on earth. So dirty and explosive it could have carried over oceans.

'Well, hello to you too,' he laughed, those captivating eyes twinkling like stars.

That laugh was infectious and soon I was laughing along.

I'd love to tell you what we talked about, what music was playing the night we met and I fell in love for the first time, but I can't. Because all I remember is his intense physical presence, his intoxicating closeness and something else I couldn't quite put my finger on that was inexplicably drawing me to him.

Gazing into his strong handsome face it was almost as if the missing piece of the jigsaw had slotted into place.

Of course.

That insatiable, irrational urge to stay in the East End now made sense. It had all been leading to this moment in time. The primitive feeling in my gut, almost like a hand grabbing my intestines and pinning me to this postcode. I had the strangest feeling that I might just have met my soulmate.

And so I stayed rooted to his side, jigging in time to Jimmy Cliff, self-consciously flicking my hair like a silly teenage girl even though I was now a 23-year-old woman, and giggling too loudly at all his jokes.

We could hardly tear our eyes away from each other. That feeling of his broad, powerful body pressed against mine was addictive and sent delicious, tingling shock waves up my spine.

And at the end of that night I didn't let him kiss me, but I did when we met the night after, and the night after that . . .

As we tumbled headlong into love, Lenny never left my side for a moment.

The scent of spicy cooking and hormones, combined with the throb of reggae music reverberating up through the floorboards was having a truly intoxicating effect on us both. When we were together it was like there was no one else in the room.

I loved his attention. I loved the way that, despite having barely a penny to his name, he took real care over his appearance, always wearing beautifully pressed shirts and perfectly shined shoes.

I loved the way he was the life and soul and every room he walked into just burst into life. Mostly though, I just fell in love with him and that mystery spark that glowed within him. Wrapped in his strong, muscled arms, I felt cocooned from the outside world and safe for the first time. Even Mam's voices couldn't touch me there.

His arms were beautiful – like slabs of polished black marble. I'd never seen such perfect, even white teeth, and his smooth chest was so wide it seemed to fill the whole room.

When he kissed me, the air between us crackled. With his luscious lips pressed against mine, I lost all reason. The courtship between us was breathtakingly fast and intense. I stopped hanging out with Gerald. I just wanted to spend every single second of every single day with Lenny.

I'd stopped working at Lesney's by now and had a new job at Alba Radio in Old Street, soldering the resistors that went into the back of radios. I'd count down the seconds until I could clock off and race over to Lenny's tiny bedsit in the attic of a terraced house in Leswin Road, Stoke Newington, just round the corner from my own.

We'd only been dating six weeks when I was getting ready to go out one Friday night round his and I felt his body behind mine, his big hands encircling my waist. His warm breath on my neck sent my heart rate rocketing and the air between us immediately began to heat up.

'Oh, Jenny,' he moaned, running his fingers down my spine until my skin was trembling.

His brown eyes reflected back at me from the small cracked mirror over the sink. His gaze was so intense I felt as if he were searching my soul.

Without taking his eyes from mine, he peeled off my dress. The effect was electric and every nerve ending in my body tingled. Hot desire pooled in my tummy.

Suddenly he spun me round, gripped my face and planted a long, lingering kiss on my lips. It was so powerful I could barely breathe. Next he was tearing off the rest of my clothes and, before I knew it, we were in bed.

The intensity of his love-making took me by surprise, but I yielded to his touch and as his powerful body pinned me to the bed, his eyes still never left mine for a moment.

'Steady on,' I gasped. 'You'll bruise my lips.'

'You do something to me,' he groaned in his deep voice.

I didn't feel as if he were making love – more that I was being *consumed*, such was the passion with which he took me. Afterwards he tenderly wrapped his arms around me and we lay in silence, naked and bathed in a single shaft of moonlight that streamed through the tiny top-floor window. Something magical was brewing in that little attic room, weaving a spell over my heart.

I could have stayed in that room for days, just he and I. Safe. Loved. Protected. Away from judgemental eyes and poisonous comments.

We stayed that way all weekend, making love, laughing, never leaving the bedsit. We never even left to buy food, not that we could afford much anyway.

Instead we improvised, boiling eggs in the kettle and heating beans in a Pyrex dish over a two-bar electric fire.

Like Dad, Lenny never said he loved me but I knew he did. Anyone who was as possessive must have been in love. Surely?

But behind that cocksure persona there lay a vulnerability. Aside from a West Indian man called Noel and his family, who had unofficially adopted him and looked out for him, he had no one. All his family were back in Guyana. I knew his dad was a sugar plantation worker and, like so many others, Lenny had come here for a better life.

I never pushed him on his family or his past. I sensed he didn't like to talk about it, and he never asked me about mine for that matter. Lenny didn't seem to like to talk about the past full stop.

Instead he seemed intent on looking to the future and, at the end of the weekend, as I was getting dressed to go, he announced, 'You'll move in.'

I wasn't sure if it was a question or a statement, so I said nothing.

There was no need. For the next thing I knew, I'd been pulled into those powerful arms of his and we sealed our new living arrangements in the way Lenny liked best.

I don't even remember going home to collect my things. But I do remember the intense pride I felt in my man. I was twenty-three, he was two years older than me at twenty-five, and I felt that no one understood or could ever imagine what it felt like to feel the way I did.

I lived for the weekends. Going to Ridley Road market in Dalston on a Saturday morning was a ritual, almost a rite of passage, and no one wanted to miss it. It was as much a part of the scene as late-night shebeens.

Lenny always insisted on looking his best when he went out with me on his arm.

'Got to look sharp, Jenny,' he beamed, polishing his black shoes.

I loved that he took pride in his appearance and that he encouraged me to do the same.

'Wear this,' he ordered, holding out a smart navy-blue Mary Quant-style wool suit. I had to admit, by the time I wore it with a slick of red lipstick and dark eyes, I did look the business.

'Beautiful,' grinned Lenny. 'My princess.'

Clutching Lenny's hand and glowing at his praise, we set off in the direction of Dalston, along with swarms of other young men and women all heading to the same place.

Thanks to Lenny, Hackney no longer seemed like a strange, grey, alien place. In fact, it was the best place to be in the whole world right now. As was Ridley Road Market. It wasn't just a shopping trip. It was an experience not to be missed.

The first-ever black man had just been granted a pitch and Tim, as he was known, sold reggae, Blue Beat and ska records from a small stall virtually hovering off the floor from the thick throb of bass.

There was not a drop of racism in the market that I could see, and black and white faces mingled happily, their voices combining together in a deafening cacophony of noise. It was alive and throbbing.

The market was thick with characters. The stalls rung with the noise of cockney voices shouting their wares, their banter merging together in one loud humming noise. Each would try to outdo the man next to him with his patter and showmanship.

'Come on, ladies. Beautiful whelks, one paaand the lot,' cried the costermonger. 'Come and get 'em while they're luverly and fresh. Buy, buy, buy, I says bu-u-uy!'

A fella with a voice to shatter glass hollered, 'Hot spiced nuts, nuts, nuts! If one'll warm you, wha-at'll pound do, I says wha-a-a-at'll a pound do?'

The man next to him jumped on top of an upturned crate.

'A pack of gen-u-ine cashmere socks, like slipping yer foot in a bunny's arse.'

Peals of laughter rang out amongst the crowd of punters.

'Not ten, not five, but three paand the lot, I says, three paand the lot. Tenner they are down Marks and Sparks.'

Not to be outdone, a man over the other side picked up a load of crockery and started juggling it high in the air.

'Oi. Oi. Oi. Look at this lurverly dinner set, ladies,' he whooped, sending it flying up high over the stalls.

'Come and get em, all wiv a guarantee, folks.'

Seconds later, he deftly caught it all with a large plastic tray as it crashed down.

'Look at that, ladies, indestructible porcelain,' he hollered. 'Smash it over your old man's head and it won't even break. Lurverly.'

The watching housewives started to applaud.

Lenny seemed to feed off the energetic market patter and was on top form, exuding happiness and confidence. Casually he threw one arm around me and used the other to high-five people he knew.

People were drawn to Lenny like a magnet.

'Irie, man,' cried his mate, Noel, hanging out with some mates by a record stall. 'Here comes de big bout yah.'

'You know it,' beamed Lenny, as they bumped fists. 'I is large and in charge.'

After chatting, we went on our way, with a promise to meet at a party later.

'Mek sure you come nice up the dance, heh,' cried Noel after us.

'Man, I love it here,' grinned Lenny as we weaved our way through the stalls.

I could see why too. Everyone knew everyone and nothing was out of reach. Unlike Chesterfield market where I shopped with Mam as a kid for swedes and turnips, the stalls were groaning with all manner of exotic fruit and vegetables, from yams to green bananas. Housewives flirted with fishmongers for the best bit of cod while, nearby, a young black man bartered with a stallholder over a mohair suit.

'You look right handsome in that whistle,' the stallholder winked.

'Me knows,' he grinned. 'Me get 'nuff amount of lovin' in dis, crucial!'

I couldn't help but smile. No one had much money, but looking good was a badge of honour to the young men in the markets and shebeens. All life was gathered here and you could get anything from a whippet to a green coconut. All tastes and desires were catered for. Want a live chicken? No problem. A bit of weed? Just give the guy on the record stall a wink and make a puffing motion and within five minutes some would appear like magic from five stalls up.

Lenny had just been paid, so was loading up on yams.

'I'm going to cook you a meal that'll blow your mind, girl,' he grinned.

And then I spotted it. The most beautiful bottle-green velvet coat I'd ever seen. I tried it on and twirled round in front of a tiny mirror.

'A right tasty bit, darlin',' whistled the white market stall-holder.

Lenny slung a protective arm around my shoulder as I paid for it. I felt his body bristle, but I didn't mind, he was only staking his claim. It was only natural for a young man like Lenny to feel a prickle of jealousy.

Half an hour later, we walked home hand in hand, Lenny clutching his bag of yams and me my treasured velvet coat. I don't remember ever feeling happier.

Sadly there were also darker elements at play on the streets of Hackney that day. We were nearly home when a police car slowed down until it was level with us and then trailed alongside us. Four white policemen glared out at us as they drove ever so slowly, never letting their intense gaze leave Lenny.

I felt his hand tense in mine.

'Ignore 'em,' I muttered. 'They're probably checking out everyone.'

'Nah, dem scum are looking for anyone to have a bit of fun wit',' he growled.

'Stay cool,' I urged, yanking his hand and guiding him down a side street.

The panda car swung round the corner and trailed after us.

'Can't a man walk down the street in peace?' he muttered.

And then they were getting out. My heart quickened. Striding towards us, their chests puffed out, they glanced around the streets to check they were deserted.

In a flash, four of them circled round Lenny, crossing their arms, their eyes glittering with malice.

'Hello then, what we got here then, lads?' said one.

'I done nothing wrong, just walking home with my lady,' said Lenny, lifting both hands above his head.

Their eyes narrowed in disbelief as they shifted their attention from Lenny to me.

'What's a girl like you doing with him?' spat one.

Suddenly they were rough-housing Lenny, pushing him back against the wall. Their hands were everywhere, searching inside his coat, treading on his well-shined shoes, like parasites crawling all over him.

'Leave him alone,' I yelled. 'You can't do this!'

'Oh but we can, darling, and we will,' one gloated. 'Cos we don't need a warrant, see, in fact our next shift ain't starting for, ooh let me see . . .' He checked his watch with exaggerated drama. 'Ooh, a good hour, so we got time to give this gentleman a good going-over.'

He spat the word gentleman like it was a dirty word. They

pinned him to the wall and roughly frisked him, throwing anything they found on the pavement.

'What's this?' laughed one, rifling through Lenny's carrier bag. 'Monkey food, is it?'

He laughed and tossed it to his mate.

'Catch the wog food,' he called.

One by one, he tossed the yams Lenny had lovingly selected from the market onto the pavement.

I watched, dumbstruck, as yams bounced over the pavement and into the gutter. One of the officers whirled round, his black eyes narrowed in triumph.

'Stay outta trouble, you black bastard,' he warned, scrunching up the now-empty bag and thrusting it in Lenny's face.

'We're watching you, sonny.'

And then, almost as if an afterthought, he turned round, tilted his head back and spat violently in Lenny's face.

I watched in dismay as the trickle of spit made its way slowly down Lenny's cheek. And then they were gone, nonchalantly strolling back to the police car before booting a discarded yam over the road for good measure.

I saw the look of utter defeat in Lenny's eyes and a tight ball of anxiety formed in my gut. What would this do to his self-esteem? He would never say as much, but I knew they had stripped him of his dignity.

Hot, angry tears trickled down my face.

'How dare they?' I whispered at last.

Lenny's eyes blazed with a deep and terrifying anger. An anger I knew I could never reach.

His pride had been dented and in some way that had to alter

a man's soul. Storm clouds gathered in his face and a muscle in his cheek twitched.

'I've had worse,' he snapped, wiping the spit from his cheek. 'Now let's just get home.'

I said nothing. Just trailed behind him, mute with disbelief at what I had just witnessed, fear clawing at my heart.

CHAPTER 7

Love in a Cold Climate

In a strange way that incident bonded me even closer to Lenny. How could a human being treat another like that? In all my years I had never seen anything so vicious. *It was just me and Lenny against the world now.*

Unsurprisingly, it also altered the way I viewed the police. I'd always been brought up to treat authority with respect. Sadly, the atrocious racism and rough treatment I saw white policeman dish out to black men and women in Hackney in the 1960s chipped away at that belief.

I saw it on a daily basis: Lenny and his mates getting roughed up by a bored policeman. Gerald's sweet cousin, Marilyn, getting fifty factory doors slammed in her face before she finally got a job on the buses. And the countless other young men and women in Hackney who couldn't find work and were forced to claim UB40 (Unemployment Benefit, Form 40).

I didn't surprise me that, in just under a decade, in 1978, the

National Front would set up their headquarters in Great Eastern Street, Hackney, hoping to cash in on and exacerbate existing racial tension. And as for me and Lenny, a white woman with a black man? I may as well have walked down the street with a target painted on my forehead.

White skinheads cruising the streets in souped-up Ford Cortinas always spelt trouble.

'Slag, black man's meat, nigger lover,' shouted the more charitable tormentors. Everyone else just assumed I was a prostitute.

Unlike Gerald, Lenny couldn't let it wash over him, and on more than one occasion I saw a frightening flash of his hot temper rear its head.

'You want some?' he'd bellow.

'Cool it, Lenny,' I always urged. 'Empty vessels make the most noise.'

But, deep down, I couldn't blame him. His body was always on red alert for trouble. The only place he could relax was within the safety of our home. Which is why when, after being together three months, I leapt at the chance to move somewhere new.

We rented a bedsit in Shakespeare Walk, Hackney, and I set about the place with a domestic pride Mam would have been proud of. It wasn't much, a fifteen-square-foot box with a bed, a tiny cooker and a two-bar heater. But it was ours, mine and Lenny's. A safe haven away from the turbulence of Hackney's mean streets.

I was totally infatuated with this troubled, handsome young man and I set about feathering our nest with devotion.

I bought a pretty candlewick bedspread and ornaments from

the market, proudly washed the oven with soda crystals like I'd seen Mam do and even arranged little bowls of fresh flowers in chipped cups.

Between paydays we were often so skint all we could afford to eat was a plate of baked beans, heated in a dish over the two-bar electric fire.

'Dinner is served, madam,' Lenny would grin.

'Cooked with love,' I'd smile back.

Lenny was breathing new life into me and every day spent in his arms seemed to make the memory of my murky past grow ever more distant.

Sex with him was breathless, passionate and intense. After *that* year of faceless encounters down shadowy back alleys, I needed his strong presence in my life. No matter that he was a touch over the top, glaring at any man who showed an interest in me, at least it showed he cared . . . Didn't it?

And I owed him too. Lenny had brought my world alive by introducing me to his friends and the West Indian community. Thanks to him, my days were now never lonely; there were parties and shebeens every night and street markets in the day. Doors were never closed, not even to my white face. The whole area was alive with reggae music. Being into Blue Beat and ska was almost like having a religion and listening to this music put fire in my belly as well as West Indian bellies.

In Hackney, music was *culture*; it blossomed outside the system, nourishing friendships and unity.

It was a golden age. At parties everyone moved in unison, with passion and freedom. No matter that it was so hot you had to carry a hankie to wipe the sweat off your face, it didn't stop people from dressing up sharp.

Lenny always looked his best in these clubs, the smoke curling round his strong, handsome face making his black skin seem almost midnight blue. He was firmly at the centre of this warm and vibrant community. He had given me so much; it was no wonder I adored him.

I wanted him to come home from a day in a stinking East End chemical factory to the smell of fragrant, spicy cooking. More than anything, I wanted him to be proud of his home – and me.

We'd not been living together long when I decided to throw a dinner party and invited his mates, Vivienne and Derek, round to eat. I had the day off so, shrugging on my velvet coat, I headed down the market and bought all the ingredients needed for a proper Caribbean feast.

I was so busy smelling a mango in the way Lenny had shown me, to check it was ripe, that I didn't see Gerald until he loomed up behind me.

'Wha'ppun, sistren?' he grinned. 'Where that Lenny been hiding you, beautiful? Big party at the Grange House tonight, make sure you there?'

'All right, Gerald,' I laughed. 'I'll catch you later.'

At home, I tied on a pinny and set about cooking.

By the time Lenny came home with Vivienne and Derek, the place was perfect.

The bedsit was filled with the warm, rich smell of chicken cut through with chillies, limes and a special jerk marinade. Lenny nodded approvingly.

'Dig in,' I ordered our guests.

Derek tucked in with gusto and sliced into his chicken . . . and sliced. Soon he was virtually grunting with the effort of trying to saw into his chicken.

Why wasn't it falling off the bone like when Lenny cooked it?

'What's wrong?' I gasped.

'Well, it's a little, er, hard to cut, Jenny,' he ventured.

I took a mouthful and nearly choked.

'Oh God,' I spluttered. 'It's tough as old boots.'

'Jenny, you know this is boiling chicken, don't you?' said Lenny. 'You're supposed to simmer it gently for hours.'

My face must have been a picture as Lenny's mouth started to twitch, and then he let rip with that huge, explosive laugh.

Soon we were all roaring with laughter.

'I give up,' I smiled, ripping off my pinny. 'Who wants to go out? There's something going on down the Grange House tonight.'

Lenny was still laughing his head off as we made our way out into the buzzing streets. It was Friday night and the excitement was palpable in the air, as was the smell of weed, as young people got ready to cast off their dull 9–5 existence in the factory and party.

It was the winter of 1970, and young people were fed up. The seeds of radical change were being sown. Just a few miles away to the east, in Dagenham, women workers at the Ford factory were finally reaping the rewards of their strike, after they'd downed tools to demand equal pay with male workers. And now, two years on, all of us factory workers owed those brave ladies a debt of gratitude as the government finally brought in the Equal Pay Act.

I'd pored over photos of them on strike in newspapers, waving their placards, and marvelled at their guts, little knowing that in just a few years' time I too would be making front-page news.

But, for tonight, Lenny and I just wanted to party.

Slinging his arm around me as we bounded down the road, he ruffled my hair.

'Just as well you more tender than your meat, girl.'

We were still laughing as we pushed open the door. The party was already jumping. A wall of smoke and music blasted us as soon as we pushed our way into the hot, heaving room.

A hand grabbed me from behind.

'Jenny,' grinned an excited Gerald. 'Come dance with me.'

Soon we were writhing in time to a reggae tune.

Suddenly the crowd seemed to part as one and Lenny's furious face appeared in front of us.

'What you doing with my woman?' he thundered.

Gerald stopped dancing and held his hands up.

'Chill, brother, we just dancing.'

But this answer wasn't enough to placate Lenny and, suddenly, I saw the telltale warning signs. The same ones I witnessed with such a heavy heart that time the police stopped him. His jawline set into a rock-hard line and a vein throbbed threateningly in his temple.

'Back off, brother,' he growled. And then he grabbed my arm. 'You coming home with me,' he demanded.

Outside, the cool night air stung my flaming red cheeks.

'What the hell do you think you're playing at?' I demanded.

I was about to go on when Lenny's hand shot out and pushed me up against a wall. As my back smashed into the wall, all the breath left my body and I stood gasping for air. And then his face was just inches from mine. 'Don't show me up like that again,' he hissed.

His eyes blazed furiously as he slammed his hand on the wall behind my head. And then he was gone, bounding up the road, leaving me in a bewildered, shaking mess.

The air where he had stood seemed to crackle with the force of his anger.

What on earth . . .?

I had never seen Lenny react like that before.

We'd rowed before, sure, but he'd never laid a finger on me.

Walking home, my swirling mind began to settle and, by the time I let myself back in, I'd convinced myself it was nothing. Maybe my dancing with Gerald had been a little provocative? Besides, he hadn't actually hit me. Had he? It was probably a one-off, I reasoned.[3]

Three hours later, Lenny still wasn't home and, wearily, I decided to turn in for the night. My eyelids were growing heavy when a frantic hammering on the downstairs door woke me up.

'Jenny, wake up,' screamed a man's voice outside the window.

Blearily I pushed open the window. Lenny's friend Noel was standing outside on the street.

---

[3] Domestic violence has the highest rate of repeat victimisation of any crime. (Source: Refuge/Home Office, 2002.)

'The police got Lenny, they're roughing him up real bad.'

'Where's he at?' I yelled, already bundling on jumpers over my nightie.

Minutes later, I arrived panting at Dalston Police Station. It was 3 a.m. on a Friday night and the station was crawling with drunks and people the cops had picked up, all shouting and wailing as police forced them into cells and interview rooms.

Lenny was sat on his own in the waiting room, on a small plastic chair in the corner of the room, his head in his hands.

'What happened?' I gasped.

He looked up and I could already see angry bruises spreading over his face and arms.

'The usual,' he sighed.

I noticed the gold ring he wore on the middle finger of his right hand was totally bent out of shape.

'How did that happen?' I asked.

'I wouldn't come nicely,' he spat bitterly. 'Took four of them scum to drag me into the van by my hand.'

Suddenly he winced in pain.

'I paid the price once they got me in and shut the doors, mind you.'

I closed my eyes to block out the picture. I could only imagine the going-over Lenny would have received.

'Let's get out of here,' he said. 'No black man is safe round here.'

Back at home he said nothing as I gently bathed his cuts. No mention was made of his own rough treatment of me earlier that evening. It didn't feel right to bring it up now and, in many ways, justified what I was already feeling in my own head. Lenny's short fuse was caused by the police, no doubt. As he fell sound asleep in my arms, sleep didn't come quite so easily to me. My troubled mind was swirling with the crazy events of the evening. Lenny's anger, that push, the simmering tension and the police's increasing violence towards him. Where was it all leading?

Outside, a police siren seemed to wail a haunting response. Inside, our leaking tap dripped: *drip, drip, drip,* its noise boring into my brain. What was happening to our happy home? Inside these four walls I had always felt safe, but now? Now I just felt uneasy.

Winter gave way to spring, but despite the lighter evenings there was no thawing in Lenny's cold new persona. Ever since he'd shoved me and then got picked up by the police, I could sense a small, almost imperceptible, shift in Lenny's attitude towards me.

Outside the home he was still the same old charming Lenny. His mate Noel would never even have noticed it, but I did.

One evening, three months after he first shoved me, he came back from work with a face like thunder.

'They're making cutbacks at work,' he snapped. 'I've lost my job.'

I was devastated for him, but not surprised. Unemployment was rife in 1970. With docks and factories closing each week, there simply weren't enough jobs for all – particularly young black men.

'Goddamnit,' he snapped before I could even answer. 'Got

dog shit on my shoe. Bloody neighbour lets her dog crap on our doorstep.'

'I'm sure she's not doing it on purpose,' I replied.

'Nah,' he raged. 'It's the racists. You see that wall down the end of Stoke Newington? Someone wrote "Go home niggers" on it.'

And then he was off. Ranting and raving. I could hardly blame him. Since the first time he'd been picked up by the police, his harassment at their hands had been almost non-stop and he'd been dragged into a cell kicking and screaming another two times and then released without charge.

Each time, I'd gone to collect him with a dreadful sense of doom in my heart. Every arrest chipped away a bit of the old happy-go-lucky Lenny, slowly turning his soul to stone. The police used the 'sus laws', as they were known, to stop, search and question without a permit anyone they didn't like the look of.

The law made it illegal for a suspected person or reputed thief to frequent or loiter in a public place with intent to commit an arrestable offence.

White policemen were systematically abusing it to have a go at any black man who took their fancy.

The Lenny who gently held me in his arms, let rip with that huge, explosive laugh and cooked me incredible food just to make me happy, was gradually slipping further away from me and it was utterly heartbreaking.

To Lenny, appearances were everything. He defined his self-worth by a fastidiously put together outfit, material worth and respect from others. To be beaten and spat on for no good reason was as galling as finding dog crap on his freshly shined shoes.

And now this . . . he'd lost his job.

No job, no money, no respect. Lenny was being taken apart, piece by piece. He needed my support now more than ever. Just because times were tough, didn't mean I could bail out.

'You'll get another job,' I soothed, reaching out to touch his chest.

It felt as hard as stone. He batted my hand away and started to get changed.

'Where you going?' I asked.

'Out,' he snapped.

'Can you afford it?' I asked.

'What's it gotta do with you?' he sneered.

Hurt tears pricked my eyes. He'd never treated me with such contempt before.

'Lenny,' I gasped. 'What's up?'

'Stop your nagging, woman, and get out my way,' he muttered.

Anger boiled inside. How dare he talk to me that way?

'Well, you're not going out without me,' I raged, planting myself between him and the door.

The speed with which he moved took my breath away.

In a flash he had covered the ten feet between the bed and the door and shoved me so violently out of the way that I lay sprawled and winded on the floor. The doorframe shuddered as he slammed it shut behind him.

I lay still on the floor, trying to steady my breathing and gather my wits until I felt ready to get up. What the hell was happening here? Everything felt like it was slowly unravelling, coming apart at the seams.

Apart from rough and tumble at home with my brothers, I'd never been involved in violence of any kind. It was just baffling.[4]

As I got to my feet and ran my throbbing elbow under cold water, a small voice nagged at the back of my mind. Did I deserve that?

I slept on it, the silence in the bedsit in Lenny's absence giving me time to reflect on my situation.

Lenny was just going through a rough patch, that's all. Things would pick up. If my life so far had taught me anything, it was that you shouldn't run away at the first sign of trouble. I'd done that before and look where it had got me.

The next morning, I resolved to make the best of a bad situation.

'Morning, darlin,' I smiled brightly, setting down a cup of tea next to his side of the bed. 'I'm off to work now. Do you need anything before I go?'

I bent down to kiss his cheek and he didn't even stir. Just grunted.

I waited for him to turn around, pull me sleepily into his arms and try and make me late for work. But nothing. He didn't even open his mouth.

When I returned home that evening, Lenny was just on his way out, grabbing his wallet and keys.

---

[4] One woman in four (25 per cent) is physically abused by a partner during her lifetime. (Source: Refuge/Council of Europe, 2002.)

'You going out again?' I gasped. 'I thought after last night you and me could stay in, you know . . . catch up.'

I could feel the intimacy between us slipping away with every night apart.

Playfully, I started to tweak the buttons on his shirt. Just three months ago, that gesture alone would have been enough to have Lenny throwing me into bed while I dissolved into fits of giggles.

I undid the top one slowly and smiled suggestively.

'I miss you,' I whispered.

The punch came out of nowhere, connecting somewhere between my jaw and cheekbone.

The force of the impact nearly made me spin 360 degrees and, no sooner had I staggered to face him again, Lenny followed it up with a stinging backhander right across the other side of my face.

I landed with a thud on the floorboards and there I stayed, in a stunned, crumpled heap.

Without saying a word, he stepped over me, calmly adjusted his collar in the mirror and walked out the door.

Ten minutes later, I burst through the doors of my doctor's surgery in Stoke Newington and hysterically demanded to see my GP.

'I need to see someone,' I sobbed. 'NOW.'

Taking one look at the crop of angry purple bruises blooming across my face, the receptionist ushered me into a doctor's room.

'Now then, Jennifer,' said the doctor calmly. 'What seems to be the problem?'

'The problem?' I whimpered. I'd have thought judging by the state of my face it was obvious.

'I'm getting beaten up at home.'

I could barely speak for sobbing and, in fits and starts, the whole sorry story came gushing out, about how a shove and a push here and there had given way to this.

It wasn't the same doctor I'd seen after my breakdown three years previously, but he reminded me of him: white, middle-class and staring at me in an oddly detached way from the other side of his desk.

And then I said three words that would come to haunt me over the following years.

'I need help,' I whispered.

The silence stretched on for ever.

'So . . . C-can you, help me that is?' I stuttered.

Without saying a word, he picked up his reading glasses and started sifting through a set of Manila notes on his desk. Eventually he looked up and stared at me, hard, over the top of his glasses.

'You've had a breakdown, I see,' he snapped.

His tone was accusatory.

'Well yes, in the past,' I blurted. 'But that's not what I've come about. I'm getting beaten up at home.'

I repeated it, louder and slower this time, in case he hadn't understood. 'I'm. Getting. Beaten up. At. Home.'

He nodded, almost as if he hadn't even heard my words, and started to scrawl out a prescription.

'Valium,' he snapped, handing it to me. 'Take it twice a day without fail.'

I stared from the prescription back to him, stunned. And then I felt it, great tidal waves of anger and frustration rising up inside me. He hadn't listened to a single bloody word I'd just said.

'This is your answer?' I screeched. 'Valium?'

This doctor, in all his infinite fucking wisdom, just wanted to sedate me.

What was it with doctors and pills? Did they really believe pills were a cure-all and that dispensing them like Smarties would make a problem go away?

I was so shell-shocked I just sat and stared at him, open-mouthed.

'I'm not taking this,' I yelled. 'How the hell is that gonna help me the next time Lenny decides to hit me?' I demanded.

He sighed and ran an agitated hand through his hair.

'Please calm down. I can see you're upset.'

Too flamin' right! I'd come to him for help, not to be drugged into submission. And it was then that it struck me. This ignorant doctor was out of his depth here. He didn't have the faintest clue what to do with me. He probably thought I was just another hysterical woman provoking her poor partner into violence, and that if he calmed me down he'd calm the situation down.

Defeated, I slumped back in my chair.

'I'll also refer you to a psychiatrist,' he added.

On my way out of the surgery, I screwed the prescription into a ball and tossed it onto the growing piles of rubbish in the street. After my overdose I had made a personal vow never again to take drugs and by God I'd meant it. Of that much I was sure, but as to how I found myself in this position, I was baffled. How had a push led to a shove, led to a punch?

In the weeks that followed, the air was thick with tension. Lenny spent increasing amounts of time out of the home. He'd leave when I returned from work and not rock up until dawn broke the next morning. He became a creature of the night, going out God knows where, and with God knows who.

I could never predict what mood he'd be in when he did return, either. And if Lenny's temper had taught me anything by now, it was to not dare question him.

Suspect smell of perfume on his collar or a phone number scrawled on the back of a fag packet? Say nothing.

An iron, a kettle, a brand-new watch produced from nowhere? Ask nothing.

At times I'd get a tantalizing glimpse of the old, charming Lenny, returning with armfuls of food, rolling his sleeves up and cooking me up a feast of jerk chicken or curried goat. He still wasn't working, but I didn't dare ask where he got the money to buy food. I was just so relieved that he was happy I didn't dare risk igniting his anger again.

Other times we'd fall into bed like the old days and I'd lie in his arms, pathetically grateful for his touch.

But who was I kidding? Even curled up together in that most intimate of positions, naked and laid bare, my body was still always on red alert for trouble, my stomach a tight ball of anxiety, trying to predict when Lenny might turn angry.

And that was the trouble. Lenny could turn from charming to savage in a heartbeat. There was no telling. On the nights he did stay in, I'd feel a slow prickle of fear draw up my spine when I felt him loom up behind me.

Like the time I was doing the washing up and suddenly he was standing directly behind me, so close I imagined I could almost hear his heartbeat. Jumping, I whirled round.

'Everything all right, Lenny?' I smiled, a touch too brightly.

My trembling hands gave me away though, feverishly wringing the tea towel I was clutching.

Without saying a word, he trailed the back of his knuckles down my cheek and I stood rooted to the spot, fear exploding in my chest.

'Do you need cleansing?' he murmured.

His knuckles carried on softly stroking my cheek and his eyes never left mine for a moment.

'My sweet, sweet Jenny.'

As he talked, I realised there was something different about his eyes. Something strange. They had changed, almost as if someone had flicked a switch behind them. In fact, his whole face was different, harder somehow.

With a jolt, I realised.

He wasn't the same man I had met at all.

Now all I saw was a chilling anger radiating from his face. And something I couldn't quite put my finger on. What was he talking about cleansing for? His conversations had become increasingly bizarre of late, all rambling dialogue with some sort of hidden meaning that only made sense to Lenny.

I had witnessed this sort of behaviour somewhere else in the past, in someone else. A powerful sense of déjà vu hit me. Mam.

I buried the thought almost as soon as it surfaced, too terrified as to where that train of thought might lead.

I wanted to reach into Lenny's soul, pull back the sweet, happy Guyanese immigrant I had first met in the Grange House that night eleven months ago. I missed the boy that sang sweet reggae to me and cooked like a dream. Where was he? His body was the same, but his brain had left the building.

Finally Lenny's fingers left my face and he turned and walked to the door. I let out a slow, silent sigh of relief. I wasn't going to be hit. Not this time.

Later, in bed, I recalled the days when his touch had me longing for more, when my body melted in his hands. Now I just stiffened when he put his arms around me. The same hands that tenderly caressed me in bed could so easily be grabbing me by the arm and flinging me across the room not half an hour later.

I quickly learnt that anything could trigger a rage. A misplaced set of keys, the milk turning sour, the distant wail of a police siren outside on the street.

I thought about escaping to the safety of my childhood home, to Mam and Dad, but it felt like there was a fifty-foot brick wall between me and the M1.

I knew from Dad's regular letters that Mam was out of The Haven by now and home but, despite this, she wasn't well. The heavy medication the doctors had her on was masking her schizophrenia, but I also knew, not that Dad would ever dare say, that he was still dealing with her episodes. How could I land this on him?

Besides, I also knew what his reaction would be to the

thought of someone laying a finger on his precious only daughter. He'd be racing down the M1 with my three brothers before you could say north–south divide. They would want to kill Lenny for hurting me.

The idea of them all being here, crowded into my little bedsit, dealing with my mess was almost too much to bear. A searing shame stabbed at me. I had already put my family through so much. They belonged in the safety of Chesterfield, where men worked and women stayed at home and feathered the nest. With a sharp pang, I realised that was all I had ever hoped for with Lenny: to settle down and love and care for him.

But I wasn't in those cobbled streets. I was in the rubbish-strewn streets of Hackney in 1970. And my world was about to turn on its axis, once again.

Men and women were on strike and men could seemingly hit their wives, as long as they didn't make a fuss. It was a hard, dangerous adult world. And at twenty-four, I was old enough to deal with this. I'd made my bed. Now I had to lie in it, or somehow find a path out of this madness. However difficult, terrifying and chilling that journey would prove to be.

CHAPTER 8

The Men in White Coats

One month after my visit to the GP, in September 1970, my appointment with the psychiatrist came up.

I had absolutely no idea what to expect, but I went along with an open mind. I still loved Lenny, and I would do anything to try to get things back to the way they were before.

I walked through the doors of St Leonard's Hospital in Kingsland Road, Hackney, which had started out life as St Leonard's Shoreditch Workhouse for the poor. The irony of being treated in a former workhouse, with its roots embedded in the Victorian notion that the path to being a good citizen was through cruelty and spirit-breaking regimes, was entirely lost on me at the time.

Hundreds of destitute men, women and children lived in this shadowy institution in the 1870s, where they were offered moral and religious guidance to assist them in becoming better citizens. It was a form of brainwashing, of course. Tragically, one hundred years on, not much had changed.

I wasn't brainwashed exactly, but I was about to have my brain electrocuted. The psychiatrist wasn't remotely interested in me. He was just another faceless medical man who seemed intent on dealing with this difficult female patient as quickly as possible.

'I'm sending you for ECT treatment here at the hospital,' he advised, handing me a form and a starched white hospital gown to change into. Naively, I didn't even ask him what it was. I just stumbled up a long maze of tiled corridors until I found the door with the right number on.

I didn't have the foggiest what ECT was, but at least it wasn't pills. Nothing could be as bad as swilling back a load of mind-numbing Valium, surely?

Er, wrong, actually, as I was about to find out.

'This won't take long,' said a nurse as I changed into a gown. 'Now hop onto this couch and sign this form.'

Next to the couch was a clunky white box with cables and leads snaking out of it.

'Lie back and relax,' she ordered, as a doctor walked into the room. He didn't even look at me, just started twiddling with the knobs on the white box.

My eyes widened in dismay as the nurse popped a sort of rubber spatula in my mouth to hold my tongue down and the doctor plunged a syringe into my arm. A strange cold sensation trickled down my arm. Frantically I fought to stay conscious, but within seconds the nurse's white hat blurred into the white ceiling.

When I came round, the first thing I was aware of was my crashing headache.

'I feel like I've been kicked in the head by a mule,' I whispered, dry-mouthed, to the nurse. 'What the hell just happened?'

'You've had electroconvulsive therapy,' she replied smoothly. 'The brain is shocked using electronically induced seizures. It's very common psychiatric treatment. Now just lie there until your headache's gone.'

Gradually my headache wore off, to be replaced with something else. Burning anger. How dare they electrocute me? How was that going to stop me getting beaten up? Perhaps I'd been naïve in signing the forms and not asking any questions, but never in my wildest dreams did I imagine this.

As I staggered to my feet, I glanced in the mirror on the wall. On either side of my head I could make out red circular marks where the pads had been placed.

My head pounded as if someone was digging through my skull with a drill. I had to get out of this place. *Now*. Frantically I started to get dressed.

'You can't go yet,' flapped the nurse. 'You haven't sufficiently recovered.'

'I don't bloody care,' I said, pulling up my trousers. 'I'm leaving.'

'Well,' she huffed. 'This is most irregular. You have two more appointments. Make sure you book in on the way out.'

'I will,' I lied, as I lurched to the door.

As I staggered home feeling like a week-old corpse, my mind was reeling, but through the fug I still managed to make the second vow of my life. The first had been to never take pills again. The second was to never, ever ask a doctor for help again in dealing with Lenny's violence.

I had gone to that GP and psychiatrist to tell them I was being badly beaten up at home and this had been their answer? Pill and bed treatment and then fry my brain!

Needless to say, I never went back. My treatment at their hands had been barbaric and traumatic. Psychiatrists! I wouldn't give you a penny for a dozen of them. Their solution to my problem had been to keep me quiet so I wouldn't cause a commotion.

In their eyes *I* was the problem, not Lenny. Better for me to be subdued, compliant and quiet in society.

Although there had been some improvements in women's rights in the 1960s, the feminist movement was in its infancy but growing all the time. It was much needed. Mothers were still being forced to give up illegitimate babies, racism was rife and domestic violence was being swept under the carpet.

Gradually, a message was sinking into my psyche: *Don't make a fuss, do what's expected of you*.[5] As I let myself back into the bedsit, I was filled with a hopeless rage. I was no better off than before.

The key turned in the lock and suddenly Lenny was looming over me. One look at the tight set of his jaw instinctively told me to curl into the foetal position.

'No, Lenny,' I whimpered. 'Not now.'

I started to sob and beg. 'Please, Lenny, please, please no.'

He ignored my pleas for mercy and, as his fists rained down on me, my senses became blurred and jumbled. Lenny kept on

---

[5] Only 16 per cent of victims of partner abuse in 2008–9 had reported the abuse to the police. (Source: Refuge/BCS, 2008–2009.)

punching until I was numb to everything. When he had satisfied himself, he grunted something and then left.

My head pounded and every limb in my body throbbed. I lay very still for fear of the pain that movement would bring. As daylight faded from the room, I curled into a ball and started to cry. Desolate tears streamed down my cheeks and stained the bedclothes.

A tight fist of pain unfurled inside me, a road of misery stretched ahead, endlessly unravelling, devouring me. *What could I do? Who could I turn to? Where would this end?*

But no matter how many times I turned these questions over in my mind, there was no solution. I was in such turmoil I couldn't think straight; my brain was shot to pieces from the ECT and my body throbbing from Lenny's onslaught.

At that precise moment, I couldn't tell my left from my right, much less find an escape route. My shattered self-esteem was now so fragile I genuinely believed that this was my lot in life. Maybe I even deserved it?

Unless you are being beaten regularly, you can never truly understand the crippling fear and irrational thought processes that spin through one's mind. Mostly, though, you're in such turmoil that nothing makes sense. But as I lay there in the depths of despair, unbeknownst to me, something was growing inside me. *Something that would alter the course of my life for ever.*

It wasn't long before I was back at St Leonard's Hospital. Not for more ECT treatment, but this visit was equally shocking in its outcome. The doctor's words hit me like a truck.

'You do realise you're two months' pregnant, don't you?'

My mouth fell open.

'But how?' I gasped eventually.

After months of painful periods, a doctor had told me my fallopian tubes could be blocked as a result of ovarian cysts I'd had at sixteen, and he wanted to flush a green dye through my tubes to take a closer look.

It was during this routine scan that he'd found a tiny heartbeat. I'd always been convinced that I would never be able to conceive, the very fact that I had never fallen pregnant during my year as a runaway, despite having unprotected sex, and again with my first husband Reg, had convinced me it wouldn't happen for me.

I walked home with tears of joy flowing down my cheeks. Nothing else mattered. Paperboys cried out the latest news: 'Read all about it, rock legend Jimi Hendrix found dead in London.' People were weeping in the streets, but it didn't even touch me. *I was going to be a mum!*

Of course my situation was far from ideal, but the fact that in the midst of this chaos a tiny life was blossoming inside me brought me immeasurable joy.

I clutched at the hope that perhaps this might change Lenny. That it would shock him into being the kind of a man he used to be. We had created a baby. Our baby. If this couldn't bond us again, then what would?

Of course I was being naïve. But, back then, I had the smallest glimmer of hope that this tiny seed of life could change everything.

'I'm pregnant,' I blurted out as soon as I got home.

Lenny looked up in surprise.

'Really?' he said.

And then, as the news sunk in, a slow smile spread over his face. 'Hey, that's great. I'm going to be a dad!'

I nearly sank to the floor in relief. With Lenny you never quite knew what way things were going to go, but he seemed genuinely happy at the news. And, for a while, it felt like our baby could achieve the impossible and get us back on track.

Lenny calmed down and stopped raising his fists to me. From the moment the doctor told me I was expecting, something inside me clicked. I stopped smoking, stopped going out altogether. I still went to work, but at the end of the day I couldn't wait to get home.

I cleaned the bedsit like crazy and wrote letters home to Mam and Dad gushing over my amazing news.

'We're so thrilled for you, love,' Mam wrote back. 'My little girl's having a baby.'

Lenny laughed when he caught me sticking my tiny bump out in the mirror and proudly rubbing it.

'You're only a few months gone,' he chided.

But I didn't care. This baby meant everything to me. My primal instinct to nurture and protect kicked in and I rested as much as I could and ate as much food as I could afford, which wasn't much admittedly.

Lenny still wasn't working, so by the time we'd paid the bills there was very little left over.

As my belly swelled, I knitted little booties and cardies, dusted the skirting boards and spent hours imagining what our baby's face would look like.

During my pregnancy the world around me was changing at a bewildering pace. *Apollo 14* landed on the moon, world heavyweight champion Joe Frazier defeated Muhammad Ali and the decimal currency was launched in Britain, but none of those events even pricked my consciousness. I was cocooned in my own bubble of happiness, all the while tentatively hoping and praying Lenny truly was a changed man.

The Divorce Reform Act also came into effect, allowing couples to divorce after a separation of two years, meaning Reg and I could divorce.

But as my bump started to fill out, I noticed Lenny started going out incessantly. Barely a night passed when he wasn't out at some party or shebeen, as if the bedsit was no longer big enough to accommodate me, him and my growing bump.

Deep down, I knew it was dawning on him that he had extra responsibilities coming his way and that with no regular job, he had no financial security. I was paying the bills with my wages, but pretty soon I wouldn't be able to work at all. Then what?

A cold finger of suspicion stabbed my heart. Who was he seeing, night after night? One night, when I was five months gone, I grew bolder. Somehow knowing I was going to be a parent gave me a renewed confidence in myself.

'I don't want you to go out again tonight, Lenny,' I demanded. 'We should be saving money. Besides, look' – I gestured to the window – 'it's snowing.'

He snorted. 'Forget it, I'm going out, where are my keys?'

Sighing, I shook my head.

'I don't know, Lenny.'

The warning signals flashed alarmingly before me as he started to gather steam.

'You've hidden them to stop me going out,' he ranted.

Tutting, I turned my back on him and sat down on a bean bag on the floor. *Big mistake*. His kick landed squarely in the centre of my back, knocking the air clean out of my body. Instinctively I grabbed my bump and gasped for breath. Hot shards of pain sliced through my abdomen and from somewhere deep inside I felt the baby jolt.

How dare he endanger our baby?[6] Anger coursed through me and I leapt to my feet, grabbed my green coat and threw it round my shoulders. I chased him out into the snow-covered streets. I knew it was a dangerous, impetuous thing to do, but I'd had enough. Months of bottled-up abuse and neglect pumped through my veins as I scurried after him, slipping and sliding on the icy pavement.

It was everything: the neglect, the beatings, the crippling poverty, the endangering of *our baby,* and now this, his bitter betrayal, all crystallized together in a single bolt of pain and fury.

'Lenny!' I hollered through the muffled air.

'STOP.'

He whirled round and looked stunned to see me.

Soft snowflakes fell and settled in his eyelashes. Angrily he wiped them away and I saw his disbelief flash to brittle rage at my defiance.

'I want to know where you're going every night!' I yelled. 'You're seeing someone, aren't you?'

---

[6] Between four and nine women in every one hundred are abused during their pregnancies and/or after the birth. (Source: Women's Aid/Taft, 2002.)

His cold breath billowed out like a dragon's as he surveyed me coolly.

'Go home, Jenny,' he muttered, turning and stalking off down the street.

But I wasn't going to be fobbed off any longer, and I was right behind him.

'You're messing around,' I yelled. Then, louder, 'I want to know where you're going.'

Suddenly he whirled round.

'I said, GO HOME,' he bellowed.

His fist smashed into my face with a sickening crunch. My head snapped back and blood showered from my nose. Staggering, I reached out to a wall to steady myself but, quick as a flash, Lenny was there again. He grabbed my wrist and twisted it until I slowly sank to my knees.

Once I was on the floor, he didn't stop there. He systematically beat, punched and kicked me until I had no voice left to protest. My muffled groans filled the thick white air as I tried in vain to protect my bump.

In the chaos I was dimly aware of startled onlookers gasping in shock at the horrific scene unfolding in front of them. Then I heard their footsteps quicken as they hurried past.

If one of the many police on the streets of Hackney did witness a pregnant woman getting beaten up in the snow, they certainly didn't come to my aid. Finally Lenny stopped. His voice, when it came, was low and threatening.

'Now. Go. Home.'

I lay twisted in the blanket of snow, my crimson blood seeping onto the cold white pavement, staining my beloved green velvet coat. But I didn't care about that. All I cared about was my baby.

Limping home, a sense of doom coloured everything and the sky felt heavy, like an omen. Inside I started to shake uncontrollably as the shock hit me like a juggernaut. How my baby survived Lenny's attack, I don't know. But she did.

From that moment on, I trod on eggshells around Lenny, just counting down the days until I gave birth.

Every fibre of my being was focused on getting through the pregnancy, giving the gift of life to the little baby inside me.

Hoping, praying, holding on . . .

There can hardly be a less dignified position for a woman to find herself in than naked from the waist down with both legs in stirrups. The contractions were coming thick and fast now. The pethidine I was on wasn't even touching the sides and as I felt another one gather momentum inside me I shut my eyes and gripped the bedsheets for dear life.

A calming voice soothed me from the side of the hospital bed.

'Come on, love,' urged Mam, my hand gripped in her warm palm. 'You can do it. You're nearly there.'

Just hearing Mam's soft Derbyshire voice made the pain dull and, looking over at her beautiful face, I had to pinch myself for the fiftieth time that she was even here at all in my hour of need.

My precious Mam.

From the minute I'd looked out the window to see her stout, stockinged leg emerge from the taxi, I'd been gobsmacked. She'd said she was coming, but she'd still arrived totally unannounced, and on the very day my labour began.

How she did it, travelled all the way to London as a sick woman, on her own, and how she knew that was the day I would give birth, I have no idea. A mother's intuition, I guess. I just thank God she was there as I gave birth, a shining beacon of love all wrapped in a warm overcoat and sensible shoes.

I'd barely seen her since The Haven, but the drugs she was on had obviously given her the strength to travel 150 miles on her own.

'Mam,' I'd cried when I'd let her in. 'You should have let me know you were coming.'

Thank God Lenny was out – they'd not met him – and I saw her eyes flicker round the tiny bedsit before coming to rest on me.

'You're so thin, Jenny love,' she'd gasped, pulling a container of home-made soup from her bag. 'Has tha' not bin eating?'

How could I tell her there was barely enough money to put food in the fridge, or that I was so terrified of Lenny I was too scared to eat.

Having Mam by my side meant the world. She'd remained utterly unflappable, even when my waters broke and the ambulance arrived. And here she was now, still by my side at the Mothers' Hospital in Clapton Pond.

After two more contractions, and twelve hours of unrelenting pain, I heard it – my baby's first cry. The most precious sound in the world. At 5.58 a.m. on 2 June 1971, I became a mum for the first time. When my little girl was gently placed in my arms, my pain just melted away.

In fact, everyone in the room seemed to vanish as I locked eyes with the little girl I had fought so hard to keep.

Francesca was just a scrap of a thing, four pounds, fifteen ounces. She was so tiny but, oh, she was the prettiest little thing with enormous brown eyes and a mop of dark hair. Gazing at her minute features, I found myself marvelling that I had created something so perfect.

'Well, hello,' I whispered, planting a delicate kiss on her soft, musky head. 'You look just like a little dolly.'

I heard Mam sniff back a sob behind me.

'She's beautiful, Jenny love, just like her mummy. I'll leave you two in peace.'

Sadly we didn't get much time together, as Francesca was so small she was whisked off to an incubator. But before she was taken away, I kissed her again and, just like that, my whole heart was consumed with the most fierce love.

When she was returned to me, two days later, and I got to breastfeed her for the first time, I was locked in a blissful bubble. The love you have for a child is like no other on earth. The centre of my universe had shifted. Everything was now about the tiny creature cradled in my arms.

As she suckled, I gazed over every part of her soft, warm body, drinking in her tiny features. And I knew then, with certainty, that I would move heaven and earth to protect this little girl.

Such was the force of my fixation on Francesca that I barely registered Mam leaving or the tap on the shoulder from a midwife.

'Francesca's father's here,' she smiled.

Lenny!

'Here you are,' he said, bounding into the room. I smiled back rigidly.

When he took her from me, I wanted to rip her back. But I couldn't and I watched in silent horror as he cradled his daughter for the first time. As he rocked her in his arms, he was clearly buoyed up.

'We've been given a housing association flat in Cadogan Terrace in Hackney,' he beamed. 'It's got one bedroom, a toilet, a living room, a kitchen and a backyard. We're moving up in the world.'

As I listened to him chatter and sing to his baby girl, I prayed this could be the fresh start we both needed. More space and a better living environment had to help.

'And work?' I ventured nervously.

'Don't you worry about that,' he said, giving me back Francesca. 'You concentrate on looking after my little girl. I'm off to move our stuff to the new place.'

A week later, we were discharged from hospital and I took our little girl back to our new home in a taxi. The midwives had fussed over me as I left, insisting I was too skinny and that my milk would dry up quickly if I didn't get more food, so I decided to rely on formula rather than continuing to breast-feed. They never said as much, but I suspect they knew I was in an abusive relationship.

But how could they help me? They couldn't wave a magic wand and produce a fifty-pound note or a safe place to stay.

The urge to protect is the most powerful instinct in mankind and as the taxi bumped its way across Hackney to our new home, I held Francesca tight in my arms; no such thing as baby car seats in those days.

'Welcome home!' Lenny grinned, as he threw open the door

to our new home. He ran around like a little kid, throwing open doors, proudly showing me the kitchen. Then, taking my hand, he led me into the living room.

'Look,' he beamed. 'A lounge with no oven in it.'

'Unimagined luxury,' I laughed.

The decor nearly made my eyes go out on stalks, mind you. The walls were patterned in a shiny, bobbly wallpaper covered in garish green palm trees and a thick, brown shagpile carpet covered the floors.

As I put Francesca down in her cot and sat down to rest, I watched Lenny walk about the place, tidying up. He obviously loved this flat.

Our new-found bliss lasted precisely a day. The next morning I opened the fridge. It was empty.

'Lenny,' I ventured. 'I need some money for formula for the baby and some milk and bread for us.'

He glared at me before throwing down a few bob.

'Money's tight, Jenny,' he warned. 'I'm brassic.'

'So get a job,' I wanted to scream, but knew that it was more than my life's worth to say that. So we limped on. Scraping together money from the odd bit of work Lenny could get here and there, and a little bit of Social and Family Allowance.

By now I had my suspicions that Lenny was stealing, but we were in survival mode and I just didn't care any more.

Fortunately, I then discovered that formula milk was free from the clinic I took Francesca to, but for me the only meal of the day was usually a few pieces of toast in the morning and whatever Lenny brought back with him if he came back in the evenings.

The sparkle of having a new flat quickly wore off. What good was it having a fridge for the first time if you had no food to put in it? The poverty was crippling.

Family Allowance covered the basics, like nappies and a bit of food, but the rent had to be covered by Lenny's non-existent wages. He had worked out how to get the lock off the gas/electricity meter and just ran the same shilling through over and over. But, apart from that, there was still food to buy and bills to pay. With money we didn't have.

Day after day, I sat in, staring at that damn palm tree wallpaper, trying my hardest to care for my baby, despite the crippling hunger in my belly. Most days my head swam with exhaustion, worrying how long I could eke out the Family Allowance. Our home was an intense melting pot of pressure with Lenny firmly at its centre. So much for our new start.

When Francesca was six weeks old, Mam sent the train fare so we could visit. Stumbling into their warm kitchen, I was nearly overcome with relief when Mam put her arms around me, and Dad took Francesca. After a good meal in my tummy, I began to think more clearly.

Dad bathed Francesca in the sink while Mam and I sat by the fire with a cup of tea. I loved watching my dad, a tough old miner, turn to putty with his granddaughter in his arms as he gently splashed warm soapy water on her and made clucky noises just to get a smile.

'She's beautiful, love,' marvelled Mam.

And then, scrutinising me more carefully . . .

'You sure *you're* all right though? You've no meat on your bones.'

'Aye,' laughed Dad from the sink. 'I've seen whippets with more on 'em.'

My heart started to beat a little faster.

This would be the time. *Now*. Now I could confess everything, about the poverty, the beatings and abuse. I need never go back again. I hesitated . . . Then I remembered Mam's illness.

No. No. No.

Lenny would be straight up here, causing scenes. Mam's mental health couldn't take it. How could I be the one to drag her down again? Plus, my self-esteem was so low, if I left Lenny who would want me now?

'I'm fine, Mam, don't you worry,' I said. But her green eyes seemed to be searching my face for clues that I was lying.

Just then Dad started to laugh, and I turned round, grateful for the interruption.

'Eye up,' he chuckled. 'I've been washing and washing her, but I can't seem to get her clean.'

We all fell about. He didn't mean it in a nasty way, far from it. He adored his granddaughter. But black babies weren't something you saw often in a 1970s pit village.

By the time I took the train home, I felt rested and stronger. Better able to take whatever the future held. But even I could never have guessed at what was hurtling my way.

CHAPTER 9

Cursed

Francesca was just four months old when Lenny arrived home one evening. I had just put her down to sleep when the door banged open and she woke with a start.

'Lenny,' I fumed, walking into the lounge. 'I just got . . .'

But my voice trailed off when I saw the state of him. He was clearly terrified; his eyes were rolling round in his head and he was panicking so much he could barely breathe. In his trembling hand he was clutching a small glass bottle of what looked like dirty water. Thick sediment swirled in the bottom of it.

I watched in utter dismay as he uncorked it and took a large swig.

'Whatever's wrong?' I gasped. 'And what the hell's that?'

'I've been having an affair,' he gibbered.

I knew it.

But what he said next made his adultery pale in comparison.

'With an African girl,' he went on. 'When her mum found

out, she didn't like it. She put a curse on me, so I had to go to the *obeah* man to lift it.'

'Oh, Lenny,' I groaned. 'You didn't.'

In the African and West Indian community an *obeah* man is a witch-doctor who can combat black magic and voodoo with spells and potions. It's a load of rubbish to me, of course, but to most in the community the fear of 'obeah' or black magic is serious business.

'You don't understand,' he trembled. 'I had to see the *obeah* man. She's cursed me, bad things will happen.'

Bad things were already happening. Seeing the fear in his eyes, I felt a deep dread. I knew it was rot. These *obeah* men have certain members of the black community by the short and curlies; some are so terrified they will pay any amount of money for a potion to lift a curse.

More than likely what Lenny was clutching in his trembling hand was a bottle of dirty water, but I knew trying to get him to believe that was impossible. Wringing his hands, he stood up and started to pace the room.

'I need to be cleansed, I have to be cleansed,' he muttered over and over.

What was he talking about cleansing for? Cleansing what? None of it made sense. Suddenly I felt very tired.

'We'll talk about this in the morning, Lenny,' I sighed. But, as I drifted off to sleep, I knew this was the beginning of the end for Lenny's already fragile mental state.

I knew all too well the devastating consequences of mental illness. I had witnessed it for years with Mam, and seen first-hand how it ate away at someone's personality until there was nothing left. How it tore apart everyone close to that person. I knew precisely how the reverberations of mental illness echoed down through the years. Now, tragically, it would seem mental illness was featuring in my life again.

Despair swamped my brain. Was that why I had been so attracted to Lenny? After my experiences with Mam, had I been compulsively drawn to him?

I didn't know. All I knew was the so-called 'curse' set in motion a strange and chilling sequence of events that would see my life spiral even further out of control.

The next morning, Lenny got up early and left. There was no sign of his dirty water potion, but when he returned later, he was clutching a Bible. He didn't look like he'd eaten, or even washed. He just looked possessed.

'I've joined a church,' he blurted. 'And you need to as well. We all have to be cleansed of the curse.'

We?

'Lenny, this is madness, can't you see?' I protested. Suddenly he was on me like a wild animal, hitting, beating and kicking.

'Lenny, no!' I cried, as I crashed to the floor. 'Francesca!'

Francesca was lying in her cot, watching through the bars, her huge brown eyes snapped open in alarm.

As he kicked me harder and harder, her little face crumpled and she started to scream and reach out for me. Whatever pain I felt was diminished by the mental torture of not being able to go to my baby.

'Let me go,' I screamed, fighting back with a savage fury, but he had me pinned to the floor, his hands squeezed round my neck.

I couldn't move. I felt as if the life was slowly being drained from my body.

'Nooo,' I managed to choke. 'Not in front of Francesca.'

'Francesca,' he murmured, releasing his grip.

Had the mention of her name brought him to his senses?

'Of course, Francesca!' he cried, his eyes flashing with a wild and eerie determination. 'We all need to be cleansed.'

And suddenly he was on his feet, dragging me by my hair over to her cot.

'What are you doing?' I gasped.

I watched, dumbfounded, as he raced to the kitchen and returned to the bedroom with two candles and a Bible. Then I watched in horrified silence, trembling, as he turned off the lights, lit the candles and carefully balanced them on the end of her cot. Then he turned to a well-thumbed page in the Bible.

'Psalm 127,' he said in a suddenly calm voice. 'Read it to her.'

The look on his face was so chilling, so possessed, I started to cry.

'No, Lenny,' I sobbed. 'Please no.'

'DO IT!' he thundered, his face switching between calm and frenzied anger in a heartbeat.

I started to read, my voice barely above a whisper.

Unless the Lord builds the house, the builders labour in vain.
Unless the Lord watches over the city, the guards stand watch
in vain.

My voice broke off. This was madness. Total madness.

'Don't make me angry, Jenny,' he warned. 'Read.'

Closing my eyes to block out Francesca's bewildered face, I carried on:

> In vain you rise early and stay up late, toiling for food to eat, for he grants sleep to those he loves.
>
> Children are a heritage from the Lord, offspring a reward from him. Like arrows in the hands of a warrior, are children born in one's youth.

The air was thick with tension and the threat of violence. Lenny stood over me as I choked out the words, his deranged face bathed in the flickering candlelight, his glazed eyes as cold and fathomless as the bottom of the ocean.

I broke down, unable to go on and he continued, his voice loud and sure:

> Blessed is the man whose quiver is full of them. They will not be put to shame when they contend with their opponents in court.

When he'd finished, Lenny snapped the Bible shut and gripped my chin in his hands.

'We will cleanse your soul, Jenny,' he said slowly through clenched teeth.

A cold finger of terror drew up my spine. I knew in that moment that it wasn't Lenny's fists I need fear, but his mind.

After that, he spiralled dangerously out of control. When he was home, he was reading the Bible compulsively or chanting Psalm

127 over and over. Or else we would have the whole candle-lighting ceremony and Psalm-reading over Francesca's cot.

My punishment if I refused? He would thrash me with the Bible. It was the first time I had ever experienced religion as a weapon.

By the time Francesca was six months old, Lenny's mental state had plunged to new depths. I came back from the baby clinic one afternoon to find him writing on the living room wall.

'Tougher legislation,' he'd scrawled in Biro.

What the hell?

This wasn't just a fragile mental state any longer, this was full-blown psychosis. When he spotted me, he ordered me to read the Psalm to Francesca again. Something inside me snapped.

'No,' I yelled. 'I won't do it.'

From out of nowhere I saw a silver flash of steel and gasped as the tip of the blade sliced into my knuckles.

Lenny had a knife!

'Do it,' he ordered, thrusting the blade in my face.

Lenny had never used a knife on me before. I did as he said, feeling my soul shrink with every word I muttered.

A knife! Now I knew with certainty. It wasn't *if*, but *when* he would kill me.[7] His mind was escalating out of control at such a rapid pace it was only a matter of time before he went too far.

---

[7] A study of 200 women's experiences of domestic violence, commissioned by Women's Aid, found that 60 per cent of the women had left because they feared that they or their children would be killed by the perpetrator. (Source: Women's Aid/Humphreys and Thiara, 2002.)

Afterwards he put down the knife and beat me.

Blocking out Francesca's frightened cries, I rolled into a ball and tried to shield myself from his blows. I felt a sudden, sharp sensation on my back as he plunged his teeth into me.

Catatonic with fear, I lay still, almost like a dead animal, praying for him to finish. The violence was on a scale I could scarcely imagine. Lenny bit, kicked and punched me and when I lay trembling on the floor, unable to take any more, he sat back and lit a cigarette.

Suddenly an unearthly howl rang out as the smell of burning flesh filled the air. I was shocked to realise it was me.

I felt foggy and confused and then I realised Lenny had stubbed his cigarette out on my back.

The burning flesh I'd smelt was mine.

I prepared for death as his violence exploded again. Surely no one could survive this.

In the midst of the swirling chaos and screams, Francesca's terrified cries rang out.

'Please, Lenny, let me go to her,' I begged.

But he ignored me, and instead dragged me to the bathroom where he started to run the bath. When it was half full, he threw me fully clothed into the water.

I screamed when I worked out what he was going to do next.

'No, Lenny,' I begged.

But my words faded to nothing as he plunged my face under the cold water and held me under. Frantically, I fought back with all my strength, but Lenny's was superior. I started to feel dizzy when his hand yanked me back up again. I was gasping for air, water pouring all over the floor.

'You have to suck the water through your nostrils, Jenny,' he urged maniacally. 'It will cleanse you.'

'No, Lenny, no,' I spluttered as he dunked me back under.

Over and over I went under, holding my breath until he brought me dripping and gasping for breath back up to the surface again.

Each time his manic face hovered over mine, chanting: *Suck it up, suck it up. It will cleanse you.*

Eventually he dragged me out and I fell to the floor in a heap, my head swimming.

By the time he walked out of the flat, I was a broken woman. I crawled, sopping wet, across the carpet, took my baby in my arms and, too beaten to cry, I sat and rocked her gently, both of us whimpering.

My body was a patchwork quilt of scars, burns, bruises and bite marks and as I staggered to my feet I saw the outline of two purple and black bruises circling my haunted eyes.

I bathed my cuts and bruises and sat bewildered and more scared than I have ever felt in my life. Every joint and muscle in my body throbbed and it hurt to move.

It's impossible to describe the fear of impending death. At that moment in time I didn't even feel human. I certainly didn't resemble anything human.

Maybe you're thinking, why didn't she run, just get the hell out of there with her daughter?

But even if Lenny hadn't locked the door, I wouldn't have run. I was too weak, too damaged and too terrified. Fear is all-consuming. It strips all logical thought processes from your brain and suffocates you. Had I been alone, I think I would have fled, but I had a baby to consider.

If Lenny found me trying to escape with her, he would have killed me on the spot. Of that I had no doubt. Besides, even if I did run, where would I go? The medical profession had done nothing to help me. The racist police? Don't make me laugh. I could almost hear them now: *You shacked up with a black man, you've made your bed* . . .

I had no money, no friends, nowhere to turn. And far more damaging than the cuts and burns was the aching guilt. What was this doing to my baby girl?

Six months old and she had already witnessed unimaginable violence.[8]

In time, if I survived this, my cuts and bruises would heal, but what of the damage to Francesca's young brain? I should be protecting her the way I'd vowed to in hospital right after her birth. Every fibre of my being was attuned to her, to reaching out to her and soothing her cries.

The pain of not being able to go to her had destroyed me, had cut far deeper than Lenny's knife ever could. Looking at her now, finally settling in my arms, I wanted to weep, knowing what she'd seen and the damage it might have done.

Lenny was destroying us.

A few days later, there was a knock at the door. Lenny was out.

Gingerly, I opened it a fraction. It was Noel, Lenny's old mate.

---

[8] In households where domestic violence occurs, in 90 per cent of incidents children were in the same or the next room. (Source: Refuge/ Hughes, 1992.)

'Jesus, Jenny, what's going on?' Noel gasped, taking in my bruises and the scrawled writing on the wall. 'What's with Lenny and this church? He's gone all weird.'

'I don't know,' I mumbled. 'You'd better go.'

I slammed the door, terrified in case Lenny came home and saw me talking to Noel.

I sank to my knees and wept.

Slowly but surely, my world was closing in.

There was no escape. I was a prisoner in Lenny's madness. I scurried from the flat to the shops and back again, talking to no one, hardly even daring to lock eyes with anyone.

The violence was now on a scale scarcely imagined before. Sometimes days would go by with nothing, other days he would beat me relentlessly, hour after hour, day after day.

Weak with hunger, I couldn't make sense of anything. Day drifted into night and back again. I began to lose track of what day and week it was. My own sanity was slipping from me. All I could do was keep feeding my little girl and do my best to shield her from the worst of Lenny's cruelty.

There was no rhyme or reason to his beatings and it was the uncertainty, the not knowing whether today was the day all hell would let loose, that was driving me slowly insane. But underpinning everything was this crazy new religion, this terrifying urge to cleanse me and Francesca, the endless reading of Psalm 127.

The mental torture was worse than anything.

When Lenny went out, I never knew whether he would be gone two minutes or two days, or what state he'd be in when he returned. Sometimes he'd lock me in, other times not. I came to dread his key in the lock and his chilling demands.

'Wear your hair tied back and no make-up,' he ordered one evening. 'I don't want you talking to no one.'

I didn't dare question him. I did as I was told.

Every time he walked out and I heard the key turn, signalling once again that I was Lenny's prisoner, I was transported straight back to my time on the streets when that Irish guy had locked me in.

Except this was worse. Because my captor was a man I loved. Yes, loved. That's the hardest thing for anyone who has not been a victim of domestic violence to understand. How can you love a man that beats you?

But I didn't fall in love with a man that deliberately hurt me. I fell in love with kind, sweet, funny Lenny. And a part of me was clinging to the hope that that handsome young man still existed.

It's also incredibly hard to admit to anyone, most of all yourself, that your relationship is such a dismal failure. That's why beaten women become so isolated. To admit it feels like not only a betrayal of your partner, but also accepting that your life is a mess.[9]

The only person I spoke to was my next-door neighbour, Rose, and even then we never discussed the violence. Rose was a lovely Jamaican woman with a couple of kids and a husband who worked as a tailor.

I was on the way back from the shops when she'd invited me in for a cup of tea. I'd hesitated.

---

[9] On average, a woman is assaulted thirty-five times before her first call to the police. (Source: Refuge/Jaffe, 1982.)

Cursed

'Go on,' she'd urged. 'Just a quick one.'

So I had. Her kindness and companionship were as soothing as balm. I never once mentioned Lenny's beatings, but she wasn't daft. I wore permanent black eyes and the walls were as thin as paper. She must have heard my screams for mercy night after night.

She didn't bring it up either. Just offered me tea, and told me to come again when I'd leapt up like a scalded cat and announced I had to go.

When Lenny was out, I guessed he was either at church or out thieving, depending on what mood he was in when he woke up. But one chilly December morning, soon after Lenny had tried to 'cleanse' me in the bath, I discovered the lengths he would go to achieve his sick goal.

'Come on,' he snapped. 'You're coming to church with me.'

'I have Francesca to look after,' I protested.

'We'll get Rose to look after her,' he replied. 'I know you're friends with her.'

Rose obliged, and soon I found myself being led by the hand to his church. It was what I call a hallelujah 'jump-up' church. I felt uneasy as we paused at the door.

'Welcome, brother Lennox,' nodded the priest.

Suddenly Lenny whirled round to me, eyes blazing.

'You're not coming in here,' he spat at me. 'You're the devil.'

To my utter astonishment, he started to beat me round the head in front of the entire congregation in the doorway of the church. Over and over, he slapped and punched me until I curled up defensively against the doorway.

Not one person came to my aid. They all studied their Bibles or looked the other way. As I stared up at the altar, with the figure of Christ gazing down at me, I despaired.

'You're the devil,' Lenny hissed again, shoving me out the door.

As I fled home in tears, I began to wonder: was I in fact invisible?

The violence I was being subjected to was as plain as the black eyes on my face. The local shopkeeper knew it, the police must have known it, my neighbour knew it, my doctor certainly knew it, and now the local priest had witnessed it. Yet no one did a single thing to try and help me. They all just turned a blind eye.

In 1971 domestic violence was viewed as a personal matter between husband and wife, to be settled behind closed doors. Most of the time I think the general perception was that the woman must somehow have provoked the poor man. It certainly wasn't viewed as a criminal act. I'd have had more help had I been belted in the street by a perfect stranger.

The common police reaction was to view it merely as a 'domestic dispute' and that you should just kiss and make up. And as for leaving your husband or partner? Forget it. The sanctity of marriage was still held in high esteem. Marriage was viewed as the cornerstone of society. Better to stay put and suffer than break up such a revered institution. Besides, where would you go if you did dare to leave?

A woman who left her partner and her home was deemed by Social Services to have deliberately made herself homeless, and therefore couldn't be automatically rehomed. Not only that, she also risked having her children taken into care by Social Services if she did. Even if she did have the money to buy a new house, in 1971 women were still refused mortgages unless they had a male guarantor.

The women's movement was just getting going; the previous year had seen the hosting of the first Women's Liberation Conference, but its groundbreaking work was still a long way off making its mark. Women were treated like second-class citizens, and if you were beaten you never dared to break the unspoken code of silence.

As far as I could see, there were simply no laws in place to protect women being subjected to extreme and life-threatening violence and no safe place for them to run to.

If I did manage to convince the police to take it seriously, what would happen? They would arrest Lenny and then what? He would either be bound over to keep the peace or bailed pending a court case. Either way, he would be back in the home within days and, my God, if I did that to Lenny I would be made to pay. I was utterly isolated. My only option was to run away and beg on the streets.[10]

As I collected Francesca from Rose's house, I knew with a heartbreaking certainty that there was no way I could subject her to the misery of being homeless. I had survived it once by the skin of my teeth. I knew that, with a baby in tow, I wouldn't

---

[10] In a study by Shelter, 40 per cent of all homeless women stated that domestic violence was a contributor to their homelessness. Domestic violence was found to be 'the single most quoted reason for becoming homeless'. (Source: Woman's Aid/Cramer and Carter, 2002.)

have the same luck twice. And with nowhere for me to turn, Lenny's violence continued unabated.

Soon after the beating in church, he ordered me to read the dreaded Psalm. When I refused, he thrashed me over the head with a wooden stool. When the blood started to pump out of the gash on my head, he sighed in irritation and took Francesca to Rose's house before dragging me down the road to Hackney Hospital to get it stitched.

As punishment, he kicked me all the way down the street until we got to the hospital door before shoving me in with blood pouring down my face.

Every single passer-by looked the other way as he booted me up the street like an animal, blood-spattered and whimpering. This was Hackney in 1971, not Dickensian London. But it may as well have been the Dark Ages. As he kicked me, I didn't even feel like a second-class citizen. The blank stares of bystanders told me I was worth nothing.

People's total unwillingness to step in and help, shattered my faith in human kindness and crushed what spirit I did have left. I may as well have curled up in the gutter and died. I no longer felt human. My senses and self-worth had been stripped down to the bone and my mental and physical strength was in tatters.

A positive pregnancy test in February 1972 when Francesca was eight months old was no cause for celebration this time, and a deep dread settled in my heart. We could scarcely cope financially with one child, what would the added pressure of two mouths to feed do to Lenny?

Despite the horrific circumstances, I drew strength from the little life growing inside me and fell in love with my baby from the moment I felt the first flutter inside. Strangely, while I was pregnant Lenny barely touched me. The mental torture continued though. I was still locked in and had to wear my hair tied back at all times.

As my bump grew, I opened letter after letter from Mam and Dad, each one imploring me to get in touch, to come and visit, that they were missing me. Their kind words pierced my heart and tears fell and splashed onto the page, the words becoming a jumbled mess. I longed to visit them, but how could I let them see me like this? A gaunt, haunted young woman with black eyes, burn and bite marks and a baby bump.

How?

I could no longer cover or hide Lenny's abuse and questions would be asked. Questions I could no longer give answers to. With a hollow heart I crumpled their letters up and threw them in the bin.

From afar, their love and tenderness could do nothing for me. I was like an animal in survival mode. How that little life grew in my frail, underweight body, I will never know.

And when Rebecca was born on 2 October 1972 at the Mothers' Hospital, she was as tiny as Francesca had been. As before, love flooded my heart and that incredible sensation that comes with cradling a fresh new life in your arms.

'I love you so much, my sweet girl,' I sobbed.

The tears wouldn't stop. The nurses thought my tears were that of a hormonal new mum. In truth, they were the tears of sheer guilt. Guilt that I was taking home a little girl who I already loved with a fierce passion back to the most miserable of homes, the most miserable of starts. What hope did she have?

My little girl was just five pounds and so undernourished that she had to be kept in hospital to be tube-fed milk for two weeks.

But, unlike Francesca's birth, with Rebecca there was no promise of a fresh start. Just fear and uncertainty for what the future held. As I scurried back and forth from home to the hospital with expressed milk for my baby, I looked like a terrified mouse. I saw the pity in the nurses' eyes. They knew I was being abused but, like everyone else, their hands were bound, rendered powerless by the law to act.

I dreaded bringing Rebecca home, but at two weeks old she had put on enough weight to come back. In my heart of hearts I knew what would happen. Lenny's ceasefire wouldn't last. Sure enough, the beatings resumed just weeks after I'd brought Rebecca home.

'You're the devil,' Lenny hissed one night, producing a knife from his pocket and holding it to my jugular. Frozen with fear, I stood rooted to the spot, my heart thundering in my chest.

He traced the blade slowly and chillingly down my neck before nicking my knuckles with the point as a final warning shot. It didn't puncture the skin, but I knew that next time it would.

From that moment on, I sank into a pit of fear and despair. My life was in mortal danger. I wanted to grab my babies and run, run, run like the wind, but where? Who the hell would take me and my illegitimate family in? In society's eyes, as an unmarried mother with two black babies and a set of black eyes, I was nothing.

The garish palm-tree-covered walls seemed to shrink an inch with every passing day. The permanent cold lump of fear in my throat was suffocating.

A sadistic voice whispered in my ear: *You'll never escape.*

No, the only way I'd be free from Lenny was when he'd finally killed me. But whenever I looked at my beautiful babies in their cot, I felt a swell of strength, a part of the old Jenny who wouldn't let that be her fate.

Francesca and Rebecca were my whole world and, as long as I was their mother, I had to keep figuring a way out. I couldn't let them see me being carried out in a body bag. I just couldn't.

Sick images came to me in snapshots. My lifeless corpse covered with a sheet, the streets buzzing with the news of my death, the look on Mam and Dad's destroyed faces. Francesca and Rebecca taken into care and me just another grim statistic.

No. No. NO. There had to be another way out.

But time was running out. The net was closing in.

Lenny's fast-moving and dangerous mind was unpredictable, as I found out when, on the twenty-sixth day of Rebecca's life, he made a shocking announcement.

'We're getting married,' he growled on the morning of 28 October 1972. 'It has to be done,' he said darkly.

In a stupor I trailed after him, pushing baby Rebecca and Francesca, now sixteen months old, in their pram, disbelief at what was about to occur ricocheting round my shattered brain.

Panic set in with every footstep.

Once married it would be even harder to get away. I would be Lenny's possession for ever.

We climbed the steps to Hackney Town Hall and the clock struck one. A church bell chimed ominously.

Rebecca slept and Francesca frowned as I bumped the pram

up the steps and in through the doorway. A registrar was waiting for us in the foyer.

'Hello, Mr Smith, my name is Terence Griffiths and I will be assisted by Deputy Superintendent Registrar Ivor Husbands.'

'Any nerves?' Lenny grinned at me.

I smiled weakly. Dressed in a dark-green suit with the faint outline of a bruise on my jawline, I couldn't have looked less like a blushing bride if I'd tried.

'Where are your witnesses?' the registrar asked.

Lenny looked blank.

'You have to have two witnesses to get married.'

A glimmer of hope surfaced.

Lenny bounded out of the door. A minute later, he came back in with two puzzled-looking African men.

'Good, good,' said the registrar. 'We can begin then.'

As we parked the buggy at the back of the room, I was almost in a dream-like state as Lenny and I took our places in front of the registrar.

It was a wedding, but the sombre mood made it feel more like a wake. Empty green leather chairs lined the room, Francesca cried a little from her pram at the back, and the bored witnesses looked slightly uncomfortable. Lenny, meanwhile, stared straight ahead.

It was unspeakably awful and I went through the motions in a trance. Even as I mouthed my vows it felt as if someone else were saying the words and I was looking down on the whole charade from another place.

And then I found myself saying the most meaningless words of all: 'I Jennifer do take thee, Lennox Ignatius Smith, to be my lawful wedded husband, to have and to hold from this day forward, for better for worse, for richer for poorer, in sickness and in health, to love, cherish, and to obey, till death us do part.'

Never did a vow feel more like an omen.

Five minutes later, we were declared husband and wife. A scream caught in my throat. My life was now officially over.

We were married, which in the eyes of the law meant I was now more trapped than ever before. Most young married couples celebrate the start of married life with a honeymoon. For Lenny and I, it was a return to Cadogan Terrace, where Lenny upped his campaign of terror.

Now that I was his wife, barely a day passed when he didn't beat, knife, burn, kick, punch or bite me. Anything could provoke violence. A misinterpreted look, or words as simple as: 'Have you got—?'

I couldn't think straight, couldn't function, couldn't look after my babies in the way I knew I should. My body and mind were in ceaseless turmoil.

Every time I heard his key in the door, one thought went through my mind: *Is today the day I will die?*

A week after the wedding on 5 November, we got the girls christened at a Church of England church in Hackney Wick. At the back of my mind I did it to form links with the church in the vainest of hopes that perhaps a different faith to Lenny's could help me.

When I had suggested it, to my amazement, he agreed, but I don't really think he understood the differences between religions.

I wondered whether an alliance with a new church could

provide a vital escape route. I was clutching at straws, but I was fast running out of options. Hope and luck was all I had now.

A kindly but elderly clergyman baptized the girls. As he splashed holy water on their foreheads, I wasn't thinking about their religious rite of passage, I was scrutinising the man's face, questions burning into my brain.

Could he be the one to rescue me from this madness?

Ten days later, my faith in the church was put to the ultimate test. I can't remember what sparked the beating, but there was a new edge to Lenny's violence. His fists rained down on me, pummelling my face. My lip split like a dropped watermelon and blood spurted down my chin. As his boot connected with my shin, I fell and crashed into the table, sending cutlery flying. I rolled into a ball and lay panting under the table.

Something inside my head clicked. Think, Jenny, think.

Then I remembered: the church.

It was a risk, but I could tell by the way Lenny was clenching his teeth that this beating would be worse than the rest. I could read Lenny like a book by now and I had decided I wasn't hanging around to see what would be served up to me next.

Rolling out, I leapt to my feet and raced to the door. Lenny made a grab for me, but I dodged him at the last minute. Breathlessly, I made it to the door. It was unlocked.

I yanked it open and raced out onto the road and ran for dear life, my heart jumping round my chest like a tennis ball. Once at the church I crashed through the door and landed at the clergyman's feet.

My words fell over themselves.

'Please help me, please, he's going to kill me. I need your help. You've got to help me, I beg you.'

I was crying hysterically, blood streaming down my face and dripping onto the church floor.

'Hush now, child, calm down,' he said, gently pulling me to my feet.

He stared at me long and hard. I will never, ever forget what he said next. In the dark gloom of the church he drew a steady line in the shape of a cross over my head. His words, when they came, were low and said with no flicker of emotion.

'Go home, my child, and make your peace.'

I stared at him in disbelief before turning and walking out in defeated silence. The only door I had believed was open to me was now firmly shut. I was a dead woman walking.

Lenny was waiting for me in the dark when I returned. His eyes raged with an inky-black fury.

'Psalm 127,' he growled. 'Read it.'

I closed my eyes, stepped forward and accepted my punishment.

CHAPTER 10

The Refuge to the Rescue

The world turns on tiny things. All our lives are dictated by mysterious forces too great to explain. Call it fate, if you will, all I know is that in May 1973, when Rebecca was seven months old, I went to the corner shop to get some milk and something compelled me to pick up a copy of the *Daily Mirror*.

Flicking through, an advert jumped out the page at me. It was tiny, no bigger than the size of a playing card, but the words made me stop in my tracks.

'*Victim of domestic violence? Need help?*'

My heart started pumping. I could scarcely believe what I was reading. There was a phone number to call too. I bought the paper, stuffed it under my jumper and raced home.

By now I was so, so, so tired I could have laid down and died. My head was so scrambled it felt like someone had removed my brain and replaced it with porridge. I was so beaten and broken down that logical thought processes were now almost completely impossible.

But one thought now stuck and repeated itself, over and over in my mind like a mantra.

I have to get out. I have to get my babies to a safe place.

With one eye on the door, I carefully tore the advert out of the paper and frantically scanned the room. There, in the corner of the lounge, was a frayed edge of carpet. Hastily I pulled it up, stuffed the advert under the carpet and smoothed it back down – just as Lenny walked in.

'What you doing?' he snapped, eyeing me suspiciously.

'Nothing,' I said, my heart thundering as I rose to my feet. 'Just clearing up.'

If he found that hidden advert he would kill me. No questions asked.

He glared at me before stalking from the room.

I knew just what I had to do next. It was a few days before I got the chance to go back to the corner shop.

Lenny left one morning and the door banged unlocked behind him. I knew I had to act fast. Lenny could return any minute.

Leaving the girls in their cot and rescuing the advert from its hiding place, I ran to the shop. Every corner I turned, I braced myself, half expecting to run smack bang into Lenny, but I made it to the shop. The bell on the door jangled as I opened it and I jumped instinctively.

The young girl behind the counter stared at me curiously.

'Please help me,' I burbled. 'Can I use your phone?'

She stared at my stricken face and compassion shone in her

eyes. I'd been in there enough times with black eyes for her to know exactly what was going on.

She looked around and then, lowering her voice, she smiled reassuringly.

'Yes,' she whispered. 'Follow me.'

She led me out to the back of the shop and showed me where the phone was. I could have kissed her there and then, but there was no time. My hands were shaking so much it took me three attempts just to pick up the phone. Even when I dialled the number and it started to ring, the blood in my veins was pulsing so fast it was all I could hear. The blood roared and whooshed through my ears as I tapped the phone impatiently.

Please pick up.

'Chiswick Women's Aid,' said a softly spoken woman.

I could scarcely speak and my words came out in short, sharp gasps.

'I'm a battered wife, can you help me?' I panted.

'Can you make your way here?' asked the woman. 'We're at 2 Belmont Terrace in Chiswick.'

'I'll try,' I said. And then the tears started coursing down my cheeks.

Someone was listening.

'That's 2 Belmont Terrace,' she repeated slowly. 'Just try and get here.'

'I've got no money but I'll try,' I wept gratefully, replacing the phone in the cradle.

'Thank you so much,' I said to the shop assistant.

She smiled and looked at me with such an expression of pity.

'Good luck, love,' she replied.

On my way home I chanted the address over and over so it burnt into my memory. It was all I could think of. I didn't have a clue where Chiswick was, it could have been on the other side of the moon for all I knew, but nothing else on earth mattered as much as getting there. It was my last chance and my life depended on it.

That night, Lenny used my head like a punchbag, battering me so hard I knew my face would be all shades of the rainbow. Francesca's pitiful cries as he beat me hardened my heart and yet tore at my soul. If it wasn't for my babies, I would have curled up and accepted death.

But now I had a chance. One shot at escape. I knew taking it would put my life in even more jeopardy, but for them I had to take it.

The next day, my eyes a flaming kaleidoscope of yellow and purple, I waited until Lenny went out before hammering on Rose's door. She took one look at me and ushered me inside.

'I've got to get out, Rose,' I whispered.

'I'm telling ya, darling, you'd better,' she said in her broad Jamaican accent.

'Can you loan me just enough money to get a taxi to the station?' I asked.

I would have begged if necessary.

'I will,' she said.

'Thank you,' I replied, closing my eyes in relief.

Together we made a plan.

'When Lenny next leaves the house, I'll bang on the wall. Look out the window and once he's round the corner, call the taxi.'

'OK,' she said. 'I'll do that.'

'But wait until he's well out of sight before you call the taxi,' I cried, compulsively wringing the hem of my top. 'You hear me?' I sobbed. 'If he sees that taxi pull up, he'll come right back and then . . .' I broke off, exhausted sobs wracking my body.

'I hear you, Jenny,' she said soothingly.

That night I didn't sleep a wink. Dawn crept over the horizon and Lenny woke up as usual. I tried to act casually, but inside I was a mess. For hours he just hung around, not doing much. It was sheer agony. I had psyched myself up and it had to be today. It just had to be.

I watched, barely breathing, as finally he drained his mug of tea and slowly pulled his jacket on. Calmly I took his cup and stood, like a coiled spring at the kitchen sink, waiting for the bang of the door behind him.

The door thudded shut.

I leapt into action and raced to it. It was unlocked. Thank God. Every nerve-ending in my body was on fire. There was not a moment to waste.

Glancing out of the window, I saw his back disappear round the corner and I froze stock-still in the middle of the lounge. I was paralysed with terror. I couldn't move a muscle. I started to whimper. I had never been more terrified in my entire life.

Could I run? At that moment I honestly didn't know. Fear knocks the guts out of you. You think you know yourself, think you have strength, but you just don't know until you're in that situation. What last shred of strength I had seemed to have deserted me.

I had run fourteen years ago, when the call of the road had

beckoned, but now the stakes were far higher. Back then I was running from my mother's illness, now I was running for my life. Then I heard it. Francesca's little voice behind me.

'Mama,' she cried. I whirled round and she threw her sticky little hands out to me from her cot, her big brown eyes gazing straight at mine.

'Mama,' she burbled again.

She and Rebecca were so heartbreakingly beautiful, pure and innocent. How could I expose them to any more violence? They had already seen too much.

Something stirred inside me. An instinct to protect my children so powerful it took my breath away. Now. Now. Now. I had to do this.

All our lives depended on me finding my backbone. Her cries galvanized me into action. Pure adrenaline pumped through me. I felt like my blood was on fire. I hammered on the interconnecting wall between mine and Rose's flat and then, grabbing an old carrier bag, I raced round the flat throwing in bottles and formula.

Scooping my babies into my arms, I glanced round the flat and nearly imploded with fear. Come on, taxi, please. Come on. If Lenny came home now and found me about to run, he would kill me on the spot.[11]

Beep. Beep.

I jumped out of my skin. It was the taxi beeping its horn

---

[11] The period during which a woman is planning or making her exit is often the most dangerous time for her and her children. (Source: Woman's Aid.)

outside. There was no time for backwards glances or a last look around. Those precious extra seconds could make all the difference between life and death.

How I made it down those stairs I'll never know, and when the fresh air hit me on the pavement the blood in my veins turned to ice.

'Bethnal Green Tube Station,' I yelled at the taxi driver as I flung myself, Francesca and Rebecca in the back. Checking out my wild eyes, ringed with black bruises, the taxi driver looked stunned.

'Now, you've got to leave NOW,' I screamed, feeling hysteria rising in my chest.

Any second I waited for the thud of a hand to smack down against the car window, for the door to be wrenched open. And then, after an eternity, the taxi slid away from the kerb.

At midday on a seemingly ordinary weekday, a woman falls out of a taxi outside Bethnal Green Tube Station clutching two frightened children and a carrier bag.

She is trembling so much she can barely purchase the ticket to get her from east to west London. By the time she makes it onto the Tube, she sits rocking back and forth in her seat, clutching her babies tight in her arms as the Tube screeches and rattles its way across London town.

Commuters stare curiously from over the top of their papers, taking in her black eyes and crying children and then, pretending not to have seen, going back to their daily paper.

That woman was me, and by the time I made it to Chiswick Park forty-five minutes later I was gibbering as I lurched out of the Tube. I thought Rose's generosity and bravery were outstanding, but it seems two acts of kindness were to save my life that day. A policeman standing outside the Tube smiled at me.

'Can I help you, love?' he asked.

'Do you know where Belmont Terrace is?' I cried. 'My babies need feeding.'

His face softened. 'I do,' he smiled, gently taking Francesca from me. 'Come on, I'll take you there.'

Mute with gratitude and exhaustion, I followed him until he stopped outside a small, innocuous terraced home and knocked on the door for me. It swung open and suddenly a woman's face was smiling back. Light and warmth spilled out from the doorway and seemed to frame her like a halo.

Gently she reached out and guided me in.

'Come on in, love,' she soothed. 'You're safe now.'

Overcome with relief and exhaustion, I literally fell in through the doorway and broke down.

Through my tears I noticed there were women *everywhere*. One took my babies, one took my carrier bag, and then another was guiding me up a small wooden stairway. Inside what looked like a small office, a large woman dressed in a kaftan-style dress rose from behind the desk and, without saying a word, folded me into her arms.

I was so overcome, I barely registered the fact that there was another man and a woman inside the small room. Something about this woman with the flowing robes, short blonde hair and soft, calm smile inspired total trust. The relief was utterly overwhelming and I broke down in her arms. For the first time in years, I felt protected.

'It's OK. You're safe now,' she soothed me. 'You're safe.'

That woman was called Erin Pizzey and though I didn't know it at the time, as she gently rocked me in her arms, she was to have an enormous impact on my life and shape me into the woman I was to become. But at that precise moment in time, as I sat shivering in a strange house, with no possessions, no future and no clue where I was, I was nothing. I felt barely human. It had taken every last shred of courage and nerve to get me here and now that I knew I was safe, I couldn't string two words together. I was shivering violently and my teeth were chattering.

Erin ushered me to a seat and gently placed a blanket round my shoulders. My body was so rock hard with tension I barely felt her hand on my shoulders.

'It's the shock,' she explained.

Someone pressed a steaming mug of hot, sweet tea into my hand and I gulped it down gratefully.

'I'm Erin and this is Anne Ashby,' she smiled, nodding to the other woman in the room. 'She's my right-hand woman.'

The affection between them was clear to see.

'The most vital moment is the moment you stepped through this door,' she went on.

Her voice was calm and gentle, but there was a quiet edge of determination that ran through it. This was a woman with a steely inner core. I sensed her strength and power immediately.

'You are amongst people who understand,' she said, gazing straight into my eyes. 'People who will be with you, stay with you, care for you, help you to feel safe until you work out what you need to do next. You and your children are safe now. I repeat, you are safe.'

I smiled and then started to cry again, but this time the tears were of sheer and unrelenting relief.

With every tear shed, I started to feel more human. No one pressured me, no one asked unnecessary questions or tried to get me to do anything beyond drink hot tea. And despite the noise, hustle, bustle and the shrieks of small children, which rang up through the floorboards, there was such a feeling of calm and positivity radiating from every joist and corner of this shabby little terraced house.

Finally I started to 'come to' in my surroundings.

'This is a newspaper reporter from the *Sunday People*,' smiled Erin, nodding to the man the other side of her. 'He's here interviewing me about the refuge.

'Chiswick Women's Aid is an open community and we never turn anyone away. The women who live here, as well as visitors, be that doctors, students or reporters, are the lifeblood of that community. Our doors are always open and we encourage anything that spreads our vital message. Would you mind telling him what's happened to you? You don't have to,' she added.

I thought about it. I'd never really told anyone what had happened to me. What did I have to lose? I'd already made the hardest step.

'OK,' I said falteringly. 'Well, where do I start?'

'From the beginning?' smiled the reporter encouragingly, as he picked up his camera and started to take photographs of my black eyes.

I took a deep breath and plunged in.

'My name is Jenny,' I said. 'My husband, Lenny, has beaten me for the last three years. I have finally left him.'

And with that one simple sentence everything hurtled into sharp focus. I felt like I'd emerged blinking from a never-ending nightmare.

I'd done it. I'd actually left him!

It was Oscar Wilde who said: 'We are all in the gutter but some of us are looking at the stars.' I had been down in the gutter for years, but now, finally, because of the refuge, I could start searching for stars instead of staring at darkness. I began to see that even though I was at rock bottom, I could claw my way out of the hole.

I had no possessions, no money, not even a proper bed for me or my girls, but I had found something infinitely more precious than six feet of floor space to sleep in at number 2 Belmont Terrace.

Safety.

Every day and in every way people take for granted that most basic of human rights – the need to feel safe. When you live every day in a near-paralytic state of fear and in danger of your life, to suddenly understand that at long last you are safe takes a while to sink in.

Years of grinding pain and fear don't magic away overnight. For two weeks, nothing much registered. Not the women, not the house, not my surroundings. Nothing. I was as close to a zombie as it's possible to be. It was like watching old Mrs Lee's TV set back in Hoole Street. Everything was grey, fuzzy and blurry round the edges.

Life seemed to come into sharp focus and then blur out again. I couldn't keep control over my thoughts. I was given a spot in a room overflowing with other battered women, all sleeping on mattresses. Just a single mattress with a sheet on the bare floorboards; a pillow too if you were lucky, nose to tail with other women and children.

Lengths of cheap brown hessian material hung at the windows as makeshift curtains and someone had painted the shabby room bright orange in an attempt to cheer the place up, but it was as basic as they come.

The mattresses even snaked out of the bedrooms and up the narrow hallways. It looked like a refugee camp, which in some ways I suppose it was. We were all hiding and running from a regime of terror.

I slept, I ate the most basic of food, I fed my children and I tried to melt in. I didn't so much as poke my nose outside the door. I just wanted to shut the outside world and my memories away.

Despite my aloofness, everyone showed me such kindness and compassion, cooking for me, helping to find clothing from a box of jumble, sorting out Francesca and Rebecca for me, but I felt like I was moving about in a dream. I think it was my body's way of coping with the shock.

After a few days, Anne, Erin's right-hand woman, came and sat down next to me in the communal lounge.

'How are you, Jenny?' she asked, touching my hand gently.

'Fine,' I replied, smiling. 'I've just put Rebecca down for a sleep.'

'She's gorgeous, Jenny,' she smiled. 'Both your girls are.'

Something about this softly spoken woman in her mid-thirties with an unassuming smile and a mop of unruly dark red curls invited trust. She was so warm and friendly and gave off such a maternal air that it made you feel you could confide anything in her.

She wasn't a larger-than-life character like Erin, but in her own way I could sense she was a quiet force to be reckoned with.

I later found out that she was a qualified nurse and midwife who had met Erin in 1971 in a park. The two women talked and clicked and Erin persuaded Anne to join her and come and help out at the small local women's community group she had formed in Belmont Terrace.

Apparently Erin had originally seen the derelict property and she'd persuaded Hounslow Council to loan it to her as a place where women could come and share with a playgroup and a community room.

Women came, drank coffee and chatted. Then a woman had come in and confided that her husband had beaten her and no one would help her.

'Stay,' Erin had replied. So she had.

Word spread and, before long, the terraced four-bedroom house with only an outdoor lav was inundated with battered women seeking refuge from their violent partners. Women were turning up with black eyes, broken ribs and burn marks.

Erin Pizzey founded it and called it Chiswick Women's Aid. A women's shelter, a refuge, a sanctuary, a safe haven, call it what you will – it was the first place of its kind ever in the world.

Erin had stumbled on a hitherto unknown crisis brewing in homes the length and breadth of the land.

Before Chiswick there had simply been nowhere for battered women to go, apart from the streets. Put simply, Chiswick gave these women a chance. It gave them a safe place to recover and plan their next move.

And now, two years on, in May 1973, thanks to the publicity Chiswick Women's Aid was attracting in the news, I reckoned there must have been thirty-five women and children squashed into this house, sleeping on every bit of available floor space going.

With so many women and kids all crammed into four rooms and only an outside lav with no bathroom, the acrid smell of unwashed bodies was intense. Nappies and dirty washing piled up in every corner and kids were running everywhere. It was organised chaos.

'We haven't been ignoring you, Jenny,' said Anne, smiling, as she sat down next to me clearly exhausted. 'When a woman first comes here it's vital she learns to trust us. Sit back, watch and observe, Jenny, then you can find your feet.'

Just then a gaggle of children raced past in a whirlwind of noise, tripping over Anne's legs and landing in a tangled heap of limbs. A woman on the communal payphone nearby was having a heated argument with someone, and the radio blared Slade's 'Cum on Feel the Noize' from the nearby steam-filled kitchen.

Anne sat, composed, in the middle of the fug of cigarette smoke that hung over the living room, like she was sitting in the eye of a storm.

'Anne, can I have a word?' interrupted a woman in a pair of tight denim flares, a tank top and a mullet hair-do clutching a small, crying child in one arm. 'I need some help with a form.'

'Of course,' Anne answered, completely unruffled. 'Let me just finish talking to Jenny first.'

'Anne,' hollered a voice from the hallway. 'Fella from the council's here.'

'Be right there,' she called back.

Despite the interruptions and bedlam exploding around her, the soft smile never once left Anne's face. She was totally unflappable. I wouldn't have been surprised to find the words 'Keep calm and carry on' imprinted on her chest. She radiated gentle love and capability from her very core.

'It might seem like chaos here, Jenny,' she laughed. 'But that's because we never turn away a single woman who needs our help. Erin was very clear on our open-door policy right from the start. How can we turn away a beaten woman and her children and say, "No, sorry, no room."? Can you imagine how you would have felt had we said that to you two weeks ago?'

I shuddered to think where I would have found myself if the door to 2 Belmont Terrace had been closed in my face. Dead most likely!

'Every woman in this place has been through so much, just like you; and not one of them deserved what you got,' she added. 'Most are like you. They've asked for vital help from doctors, priests or Social Services and been denied it and so where do you turn? It's no wonder the women just keep coming. They come here in their droves. We are getting over one hundred calls a day and every day sees a new arrival often with no clothes, not a penny in their purse and so desperate. All they . . . *all you* need, Jenny, is safety, time to think, time to reorganise your lives, and that's what Chiswick Women's Aid want to offer.'

I could see Erin and Anne were passionate about this cause, and thank God too, because it was this very same steely determination that was to save my life in just a few months' time.

I found that the refuge was governed by certain rules, but with a strong heart beating at its core.

'The only rules are these,' she went on. 'When you are ready to be included and you have adjusted to your surroundings, there is a cleaning rota which the women take in turns to do. There is strictly no drink, no violence, and you are not allowed to bring boyfriends or husbands into the house. All the women have the right to vote you out, just as they also have the right to vote the staff out. This is your house, treat it with respect.'

Her face softened.

'If you need to talk about anything, Jenny, anything at all, come and find me or Erin. We live nearby and we go home at night but, apart from that, my family joke that I live here. I'm on call in the night too.'

'Twenty-four hours, eh?' I asked.

'Twenty-four hours,' she repeated.

What a wonderful woman. I was literally speechless at her and Erin's kindness. It had been a long, long time since anyone had shown me any compassion and their thoughtfulness broke down my barriers.

Anne got up to go but, as an afterthought, squeezed my hand in hers.

'It may not seem like it now, Jenny, but you will recover. We are a community of women. You are totally supported.'

Her words stirred something deep inside me and suddenly, in a flash, I felt a powerful sense of nostalgia so strong it took my breath away. The last time I had been in a group of nurturing women had been the remand home I'd been sent to after I'd run away from home.

Northenden Road Girls School had been a powerful force for good in my life. Elegant Mrs Mary McIntyre Brown had given me so much and taught me I had so much to give. Lenny had knocked that belief out of me with his fists.

The psychiatrist who had given me the ECT treatment, the doctor who just seemed hell-bent on pumping me with sedatives and the police and church who ignored my pleas for help had only compounded my sense of isolation and total failure.

Perhaps Anne and Erin were right. Maybe I needed to open my eyes to my surroundings? It may have been noisy, chaotic and bursting at the seams with women and children, but they were all in exactly the same boat as me. Our bruises may have been in different places, but we all carried the same mental scars inside.

And, despite the less than ideal living conditions, everyone seemed cheerful and the atmosphere was calm and positive. Incredible when you consider some of the homes women had run from.

And when you looked at the overcrowded living conditions, the women must have fled something horrific to be prepared to live this way.

There was no privacy, no peace, no quiet corner to escape to, not even a proper bed. All life had to be played out publicly. But it was free from cruelty and violence.

As I glanced round the room, I saw the telltale signs of abuse. Black eyes, bruises, angry children and the defensive, belligerent scowl on some women's faces which gave way to a heartbreaking flash of vulnerability and fear.

Some women squabbled over the rota, others were rough and cackled like old fishwives telling filthy jokes, others sat quietly in the corner like me, smoking and letting it all wash over them. But they were all *exactly* like me in one respect. They had all been trapped in a cycle of violence and subjected to a horrific brutality they had not done anything to deserve.

It was a powerful realization. Society had turned its back on us. Easier to ignore the problem, perhaps even imagine we had asked for it or stuck with it because in a sick way we liked it. I wondered how many other women in this house had run for help and had their brains fried or been pumped full of drugs by a lazy, ignorant doctor.

Thanks to Erin and Anne's pep talk, I emerged from my dreamlike state and my reawakening was powerful. *I wasn't alone any more. I was part of a community again.*

And, as I knew from growing up in a tight-knit community and living in one at the girls' school, only good things could come from the power of a group.

This community might not swap recipes or gossip over the garden fence, like the women of my childhood, or hunt for runaway girls and trade beauty tips like at the remand home, but it sure as hell could swing into action when a man had left you beaten and broken.

Stubbing my cigarette out, I wandered into the tiny kitchen where the noise level rose a few decibels.

Hordes of children sat while a woman served them up beans on toast and another prepared little dishes of jelly and poured cups of orange squash. A huge pot seemed to be constantly bubbling on the stove, sterilizing countless baby bottles. Every surface was covered with boxes of cereal and cutlery was barely washed and dried before someone else was reaching for it.

In the midst of this, the radio crackled out tinny disco hits and two women stood folding sheets, shrieking with laughter and joking with another woman washing clothes in the sink. Another went round wiping kids' grubby faces whilst a wiry woman in flares, a halter-neck and a big perm ducked down and caught a stream of snot from a little boy's nose in her hankie.

'Gotcha, yer little bleeder,' she grinned affectionately at him.

It was impossible to tell if it was her child. In fact, I had no idea whose child was whose.

There, in the midst of it, sat Francesca, happily tucking into her beans and giggling with a child next to her.

Such a hot, heaving house of women and snotty kids may have sounded like hell to some. But suddenly I realised. It wasn't just a safe house. *It was my home.* I lived here now! I had no idea how long for, but Erin had made it perfectly clear: I could stay for as long as I needed. And seeing Francesca now, coming up to two years old, safe, protected and well fed for the first time in her little life gave me a jolt of happiness.

'Hi,' I said shyly to the woman pouring squash. 'I'm Jenny. Can I do anything to help?'

'Hello, darling,' she said back in a thick south London accent. 'You're new 'ere, ain't yer? How's yourself? I'm Paula.'

'That your little girl over there? She's gorgeous. 'Ow old is she, love?'

'My God, she's two in a couple of weeks,' I gasped.

'Don't worry,' she grinned. 'We'll throw her a party. We always have parties with cake and jelly when the kiddies have a birthday.'

'That'd be great,' I gushed. 'She's never had a party before.'

And suddenly there it was again. A tidal wave of guilt so strong I virtually had to hold on to the kitchen counter for support. My own daughter had never had something as normal as a piece of cake before. There were so many things she'd never had: *trips to the park, new shoes, playmates* . . . Her life had been nothing more than watching her mummy being beaten and terrorized.

Sensing my despair, Paula put her arm round me.

'Come on, love. She's happy now. I'll introduce her to my lot. Got four of 'em I have, for my sins.'

Four? I gulped. I thought my life had been hard dealing with Lenny's violence and two kids. How the hell would I have coped with four? It didn't bear thinking about.

Once lunch was served and cleared up and the kids sent out into the tiny garden to play, I helped Paula wash up and she confided some of her story to me.

'My old man used to beat me something rotten,' she sighed. 'It was years before I could get away . . . Well, I was always pregnant, weren't I?'

Her voice trailed off and I didn't push her. I sensed there was an unspoken respect between the women of this house not to probe too deeply. No one wanted to discuss the horrors that had driven them to all live under one roof. They just wanted to concentrate on building a future away from fear.

'Your old man?' she asked.

I shrugged.

'It's complicated,' I replied, instinctively crossing my arms and rubbing the part of my back where Lenny had sunk his teeth into me.

Under my top I could feel the raised bumpy scar tissue where his teeth had torn through my skin.

She smiled. 'It always is, love. That's why we're here, ain't it? You're here now though, and that's what counts.'

Anne saw us talking and smiled. 'Great to see you making friends, Jenny,' she whispered as she walked past.

'Can you put me on the rota now, please?' I asked.

And with that one simple act I went from being an onlooker to a fully fledged new member of this warm community.

Four weeks after my move to Belmont Terrace, around June 1973, Erin had some news.

'As you know, the conditions here are getting pretty over-crowded and intolerable,' she said.

Everyone groaned and laughed.

With the arrival of summer, the smell of unwashed bodies all sleeping top to toe on mattresses had made the air pretty pungent, to say the least.

'We can't carry on living like this and nor should you have to,' added Anne.

'Too bloody right,' yelled Paula. 'What's the council doing about it?'

Seemed as if Hounslow Council couldn't do anything. As we were living in a refuge and not technically residents of Hounslow borough, we weren't their responsibility, so Erin had taken matters into her own hands as usual.

She'd managed to secure funding for the refuge from the Department of Health and Social Security.

She explained how, thanks to a man named Neville Vincent, a businessman with experience of property, and the help of the board of directors of Bovis, a construction firm, they had secured us a new, far bigger, house to live in.

'It's got three indoor toilets too,' she smiled.

A huge cheer went up round the room. I don't think there was a single one of us in that room not in awe of Erin. She was a remarkable woman and utterly fearless.

Anyone prepared to take on what seemed like, at face value, such a hopeless cause and champion our right to a safe place to live was a saint in my eyes.

She was a pioneer daring to tackle an issue that had long been swept under the carpet.

'It's just round the corner,' she said, eyes gleaming. 'Who wants to come and have a look?'

I'd have followed her to the ends of the earth if she'd asked.

The Big House

The Big House in Chiswick was a large Victorian semi-detached home set back a little from the road. Big bay windows looked out onto a leafy street. It was a perfect sanctuary.

But once you stepped inside, it was totally derelict. The walls were peeling, paint and plaster was falling off the ceiling in chunks, the exposed floorboards needed patching up and there was no hot water. It needed more than a lick of paint. It needed rewiring, plastering, painting and a whole lot else besides. But it did have one vital ingredient. Space and lots of it! The rooms were huge and airy and it spread over four floors, including the basement.

Erin saw the potential instantly and she and Anne were bursting with enthusiasm.

'There's space for an office and community rooms,' Erin announced, dashing from room to room. 'We're going to convert the basement into a playgroup for the children. And just look at the outside,' she said, throwing open the back doors.

There was a near stampede as the kids ran whooping round the large hundred-foot garden. I laughed out loud as I watched Francesca charge after her new playmates, pudgy little legs pumping ten to the dozen, a determined grin plastered over her face. She'd never had much space to run round in. Judging by the kids' ecstatic reaction, nor had most of them. The space, fresh air and freedom instantly went to their heads, as it did to us all as we explored our new home.

There were four large bedrooms on the first floor with a further two dormer rooms in the attic and reception rooms downstairs on the ground floor to be used as community rooms. Erin had earmarked the smallest room as her office to make maximum use of space.

I bumped into her on the first floor.

'Luxury, isn't it, Jenny?' she said.

'I'll say,' I laughed.

Erin hired a lovely workman called Harry who came in daily, with his small team, to carry out the much-needed renovations. There was no time to wait until the house was finished. We simply moved in and they worked around us, often clinging precariously to the side of the ladder as we served up the kids' breakfasts.

Harry was an absolute darlin' of a man, like a favourite granddad. He was as wide as he was round and always wore a bright, jolly smile. His constant whistling and cheery patter as he worked made the house start to feel like a home. And if he was intimidated by such a large group of women, he didn't show it.

'I don't know how you women do it,' he chirped as he painted. 'Now, make us a cup of tea, Jenny, me tongue's hanging out.'

'Anything for you, Harry,' I laughed back. 'Now make sure you look at my bedroom next. Not sure I can stand staring at that crumbly old ceiling much longer.'

He laughed and as I turned to leave he called me back and pressed a crumpled pound note into my hand.

'Treat your girls to something,' he winked.

He was a diamond to his core. It wasn't just me he slipped money to either; I lost count of the times I'd seen him hand out notes to other women. It was just a small act of kindness, but it made a real difference to my state of mind.

Humming to myself, I bounded up the stairs two at a time, but when I got to the doorway I froze. Several women were standing round looking a little shell-shocked.

'It just come down, Jenny,' murmured another mum.

A huge chunk of ceiling plasterboard had fallen onto my mattress.

'That'd have killed you outright,' she gasped.

'Thank you, God,' I said, looking up heavenwards through the great exposed hole in the ceiling.

'Here, Harry,' I shouted. 'That ceiling wants fixing now.'

'Cor blimey,' he chuckled, scratching his head as he joined us in the bedroom. 'So it does.'

There was no point getting cross about it, we were living in extraordinary times and it was just part and parcel of life. There was no time for Health and Safety inspections and form filling. It was like living in one giant experiment and not a single one of us could afford to be precious.

No matter that the roof over my head was crumbling, at least it was there, just about. The house was fulfilling a pressing need, as we were rapidly finding out. We'd only been there a few weeks, but it had filled up with battered women and their children in a heartbeat. In all my years I had never seen anything like it.

I shifted up my mattress and made room for the countless women arriving daily. I hadn't been there long when Tracey arrived. She was a small, wiry, battle-scarred woman from London with five kids in tow. She had a smart gob, but I liked her immediately. Perhaps we were kindred spirits. Once I'd shown her the ropes and helped her settle her five bewildered kids, we shared stories over a cup of tea and a fag.

'He used to come home from the pub and give me a good hiding,' she said. 'Final straw was when he held a bloody shotgun to my head. Bleedin' coward he was, deep down. I threatened to leave, but he wouldn't listen.'

She sighed and drew on her cigarette, her hands trembling ever so slightly. 'Too busy with his fists, I suppose.'

'You should have poured boiling oil in his ears when he was asleep,' quipped a woman sitting nearby.

Tracey's frown vanished as her face creased into a wide smile. Soon we were both cackling away like a couple of old fishwives. Tracey had a sense of humour just like mine, and the camaraderie between us crackled into life.

It felt good to laugh again. When you've been stripped of

everything else: money, dignity, freedom and safety, having a sense of humour buried deep down in your soul is something a man can't ever take from you.

It wasn't just mouthy, funny Tracey who gently brought me back to life. So many women in that place started my healing process. Each of us had our own unique character and story that contributed to the complex make-up of the house. The stories of relentless abuse wove a familiar tapestry, the tales of fear so strong I half wondered if they weren't recounting my own.

There was a lovely black lady and a mum of six kids by the name of Jerry. Jerry never stopped smiling and was so laid-back it was a wonder she never fell over. Her beautiful wide smile and huge brown eyes were a familiar sight around the house, as was the Afro wig she'd pop on each morning. Lovely, gentle Jerry never spoke of the violence which drove her to the house, but given that she had fled with six kids in tow it must have been bad. At night one of her older kids used to bang his head repeatedly on the pillow. It was heart-wrenching to watch, and his anguished compulsion conveyed that family's suffering more powerfully than a thousand words ever could.

Then there was Ivy. Poor old Ivy had a shocking drink problem. Alcohol was banned from the house, so she'd head out most nights and come back pissed as a pudding. She drank blackcurrant and rum until she could barely stand, and when she staggered home each night she always had a red-stained mouth and her bloodshot eyes looked like two red and blue marbles. No one judged her. We simply helped her look after her two lads and put her to bed. Ivy had endured years of beatings and no one was going to fix her overnight, so we didn't try. We were simply there for her when she needed us.

Drinking wasn't the only side effect of years of relentless violence and control. One woman used to head out daily up the high street with her kids all tucked up in a big old-fashioned pram. When she returned, she'd lift up the pram mattress and it would be stuffed with stolen tins of food. Poor woman. She'd been forced to do it for so many years in order to feed her kids it was now second nature. Shoplifting had been a survival technique and it would take years to wipe out the ingrained instinct to feed her kids at any cost.

I knew from my desperate year on the street when I stole milk off doorsteps, what lengths you'd go to just to survive, so I was never going to judge her. And what was wonderful was that no one else in the home did either. The women represented a solid wall of solidarity and battle-weary humour.

Thrown into the mix was no-nonsense Bridgett.

Bridgett was an Irish lady in her forties who, now she was free from her husband's violent rages, was determined to find the fun in life.

Her husband came to the refuge many times to beg her to return. He was a familiar sight. We all saw him sitting out there on the doorstep but, to her credit, she stayed strong and refused to see him.

'It's this place,' she explained. 'It gives me the strength to say no. I've got my courage back.'

I'd not been there long when Bridgett had a date. Socialising was encouraged by the house, as long as you had someone to watch your kids and with all those women in the house that was never a problem; you had built-in babysitters.

Tracey and I had agreed to look out for Bridgett's four daughters and we even gave her a makeover. Bridgett was a bit rough round the edges, but she had a heart as soft as marshmallow. Before her date she appeared in a pair of jeans and an old slummy T-shirt.

'Let's make you look a bit feminine,' announced Tracey.

'Come on, Jenny, gis a hand.'

Together we rifled through the donated jumble clothes until we came across a lovely sky-blue Crimplene maxi-dress and some wooden wedges.

In the bathroom we zipped her up in the dress and Tracey did her make-up.

'There you go, love, you look lovely,' beamed Tracey.

'Cheers, girls,' she grinned back.

And with that she gripped her fag between her teeth and suddenly hoisted one leg up into the sink to wash her feet, revealing her nether regions.

'Blimey, girl,' cackled Tracey. 'Best not do that on your date.'

'I don't have time for a bath,' she laughed in her thick Irish accent.

We came from all over England. Brenda was from Bolton in Lancashire. She was a great laugh and as down to earth as they come. A fellow northerner, we got on well. She had run from seven years of violence and, like me, seen an advert for the refuge in a newspaper.

'My husband used to give me a real good hiding. I thought

he was going to kill me,' she used to say. 'Once we heard a commotion out in the street. It was a man beating his wife up. My husband said, "Int that disgusting, a man beating his wife." I says to him, "But that's what you do to me."

"Ay," he replied. "But that's different. You're my wife."'

I laughed along in wry despair. Sometimes laughter was the best defence we had. Because sometimes the scenes left you breathless – women with bruises the colour of aubergines spreading over their face and arms. And they were just the ones you could see. Bite marks, broken ribs, burns from cigarettes, smashed teeth . . . the list of appalling injuries went on and on. Men were clearly abusing women with any weapon they had to hand. One poor soul even came in with scalded legs where her fella had poured boiling hot water all over her.

If you get the impression, reading this, that it was just working-class women like me who streamed through the doors, you'd be wrong. Domestic violence cuts across all classes.

She only stayed a couple of weeks, but Iris was very posh, the wife of a lawyer who used to taunt her that she would never leave. He was outwardly highly regarded and clever too, which made his abuse mental as well as physical.

'Who would believe me over him?' she told us. 'He's a respected lawyer, for God's sake.'

His abuse had taken its toll on her in every way possible. We noticed that when she started coming back to the house she had frozen chicken fillets stuffed down her trousers.

She was never chastised by anyone for her secret shoplifting. She was simply surviving. Her story taught me that violence doesn't discriminate and a well-to-do doctor's or lawyer's wife is just as likely to be abused as a cleaner's or charlady's wife. Each and every woman who crowded into the house was so different from the last. The only common denominator was violence.

The phone never seemed to stop ringing or the doorbell going. Every time you opened the door there stood a new woman, her face frozen in fear and, more often than not, clutching small children in her arms.

Sometimes she'd even be dressed in slippers and a nightie, other times she might just about have had time to throw a few possessions in a bin bag.

I did the same thing that had been done for me: took them to Erin and went and put the kettle on. The house was only licensed to hold thirty-six, but before long that number had swelled to forty, then fifty, then more, and still they kept coming.

Erin's mantra remained the same. 'We have an open-door policy. I will never turn a single woman away.'

True to her word, she didn't.

In and amongst the tidal wave of women that seem to wash up weekly, Harry and his team kept on hammering and painting, and Erin and Anne worked harder than ever. They were busy round the clock, interviewing new staff, workers to run the playgroup, doing newspaper interviews, liaising with council and local Social Security offices so women could claim the Social, filling out forms, organizing jumble sales and coffee mornings to generate much-needed funds, and overseeing the renovation of the home and giving talks.

The house hummed with Erin's seemingly tireless reserves of

energy. She was a one-woman whirlwind and we all marvelled at her extraordinary stamina. And yet, despite the paperwork the charity must have generated, she and Anne still found time to talk and comfort new women, sit and chat with us in the communal lounge or cuddle a bewildered child.

Students came to help, reporters kept turning up, and a psychologist interviewed us for a study into battered women. There was no time for Erin to deliberate over the protocol of anything; all the urgent demands being placed on the house meant that rules were made up as she went along. Besides, Chiswick was the first of its kind in the *world*. There was nothing to compare it to!

Erin and Anne were a tireless source of energy and each day they and all the women who lived in the home seemed to breathe new life into it. The Big House even seemed to take on a personality of its own.

Chiswick was arousing interest from around the country and the phone rang off the hook with reporters wanting to talk. Erin encouraged the interest and recounted the story each time with passion. Her enthusiasm was infectious, and Tracey, me, and the rest of the women found ourselves swept up and clinging to her coat-tails for the ride.

But with more women came the need for organization, and Erin hired more staff. Anne's husband, John Ashby, helped out and other men came in the form of Michael, Jeff and Graeme, three lovable, gentle, long-haired hippies in their twenties whose job it was to run the playgroup under the guidance of Jeanne, the playgroup leader.

Erin was adamant the children needed positive and nurturing

male influences in their lives. At first, some of the children were clearly terrified to encounter men, but the lads showed nothing but kindness and were incredible role models. To children whose whole lives had been ruled with a rod of iron by a violent male, to then see a man displaying affection, patience and gentleness, must have been an eye-opener.

Every day I still felt the creeping fear of what witnessing their father's violence must have done to my girls' innocent young minds. I saw it in Francesca, who clung to me as if her life depended on it. Hardly surprising when you consider the fear she'd felt all her life.

I saw it in the older children at the home too. When they fought, it wasn't a half-hearted play-fight. They fought with genuine aggression and they fought to hurt. It wasn't just fights either. Some of the kids wet their beds or suffered horrific nightmares. Others had terrible fights, then big, showy, emotional make-ups, just like they'd witnessed their parents do. It broke my heart seeing the children's despair and behaviour.[12]

But they, like Francesca, were never punished. The playgroup workers just held them gently until they had calmed down. No one judged the children's behaviour. How could we? Instead, we treated them like our own. If a child was crying, you put your arms around them. If a nose needed wiping, you

---

[12] At least 750,000 children a year witness domestic violence. (Source: Women's Aid/Department of Health, 2002.) One in seven children and young people under the age of eighteen will have lived with domestic violence at some point in their childhood. (Source: Refuge/Radford et al, 2011.)

wiped it, or a nappy changing, you changed it. You didn't wait to be asked. You'd just do it. It was a general unspoken agreement that life at such close quarters would be a lot more pleasant if we all just helped one another.

Cooking wasn't arranged by rota as with that many women it would have been too much to organise, so women were responsible for feeding themselves and their own kids. But as friendships blossomed, communal meals started, with tasty Caribbean favourites getting served up alongside spag bol or shepherd's pie.

The playgroup workers often ducked in to share a cup of tea and sample the women's cooking. Not that we minded their presence in the house one little bit. We were so grateful to them. The lads were daft as brushes and just like big kids themselves and all the children reacted so well to them.

But the one I adored was the 'house mother', JoJo.

Or, as the women came to know her, JoJo '*Pop a little pill, darling*' for her eagerness to get most of the mums on the contraceptive pill, which had been in use for twelve years by 1973.

JoJo was the linchpin of the house and, like her title suggested, the mother figure of Chiswick Women's Aid. Her talents were seemingly endless and her day spent in a whirlwind of activity. She was in her early forties and quite posh in my eyes, with smooth, dark, shiny hair but, despite her glamour, she was never aloof. She wouldn't have lasted two minutes had she been. She was warm, inclusive and brought everyone together. Her voice could be heard all over the house.

'Come on, darling, let's get up, shall we? Calm down, darling, let's get you a cup of tea, shall we? No rows, darling.

What shall we cook for lunch, darling? Who's on the cleaning rota, darling?'

Our 'house mother' was as inexhaustible as Erin and Anne; putting an arm round women when rows broke out, soothing, fussing, calming, cajoling, pouring oil on troubled water and generally keeping the house happy and positive. I, like every woman in the house, fell a little bit in love with darling JoJo.

Thanks to Erin, Anne, JoJo, Harry and the playgroup workers, life at the Big House soon fell into a comfortable routine.

Tracey and I were always first up. We'd wash and feed our kids. Then, gradually, other mums would start drifting down and do the same, before the whole lot were taken to the playgroup. Then the fun would start.

Out would come the mop and bucket and a constant stream of jokes and mickey-taking would flow, as we scrubbed the place from top to bottom.

Finding my voice again was a revelation.

'Come on, ladies, let's get this place spick and span,' I'd chivvy, as I piled mattresses against the wall and started mopping the floors. 'We don't want no diseases here.'

Tracey was every bit as vocal, and she'd turn up the radio to blast out reggae when it came on and bop and mop at the same time. Around this time a new Jamaican artist called Bob Marley started to get airplay for his album *Catch a Fire*, and I for one was smitten.

'Ooh, I love a bit of Bob,' said Tracey as she powered over the floor surfaces wriggling her skinny hips in time to the bouncy reggae beat. 'Hands up if you would.'

A sea of women's hands shot up and we all fell about laughing.

'Hands up if you got it last night,' I added.

A few hands shot up and the laughter nearly lifted the ceiling.

People might have winced at our raucous chat but, you have to remember, we were young women in our twenties, and now that we had found freedom we were determined to look for the fun that had been sorely missing from our lives.

In walked Bridgett.

'Here she is,' I laughed, 'the great white hope. How did your date go, old Ma Clampett?'

'Be away wit' yer, Jenny,' she laughed, affectionately swiping my arm.

Then Jerry walked in and I saw Tracey wink at me. Quick as a flash, Tracey whipped off Jerry's wig and threw it across the kitchen to me.

''Ere, Jenny, catch.'

The wig sailed over the kitchen and landed in my hands. Sucking her teeth and shaking her head, Jerry started to giggle.

'Come on, man,' she laughed in her beautiful, lilting Jamaican accent. 'Give it back.'

The wig flew in a perfect arc back over the kitchen to Tracey and soon Jerry was laughing helplessly.

Jerry had a wonderful sense of humour and Tracey and I only teased her because we knew she could take it.

'Blimey, you've got a gob on yer, Jenny,' chuckled Harry as he walked in the kitchen. 'Bleedin' madhouse it is here.'

It was too but, gradually, through the madness, the chaos, the fun, banter and jokes, I was finding myself, *my real self*, again for the first time in years.

Of course there were some women who didn't join in, preferring to stay in their rooms but, as I quickly learnt, that was OK too.

In any community you have different characters and some women were so traumatized they weren't really socialized and didn't know how to behave. They never picked up a cloth or a broom. They were happy to lie-in until midday and leave their kids unparented. So it was up to the stronger women to lead by example, and show them how to behave in the house.

Crucially, there was never any blame culture. All us women had been slagged off for too long, and no one needed any more of it.

Picking up a mop and mucking in was second nature to me, perhaps because I'd been brought up to be tidy and house proud by Mam. Even though she was far away physically, Mam was never far from my thoughts, and not long after we moved to Chiswick, she came hurtling back into my life. I'd been simply too beaten and ashamed to contact her, but somehow she found me.

After we'd cleaned each morning, all the women would sit down in the community room and have a coffee with Erin and Anne at about 10 a.m., while Erin would open all the morning's post. A house meeting, Erin called it. It was a chance to air any issues we had, discuss news, and for Erin to tell us developments with the movement. Those meetings were perhaps part of the reason we adored her.

They were amazing, and to be made to feel a part of her

movement and her openness in discussion gave us all a sense that we were part of history in the making. Not only that, but she gave us free rein to help run the refuge as we saw fit and make decisions that affected day-to-day life – like which visitors and researchers we allowed in and which journalists we wanted to speak to. It was *us* women answering the phones and *us* women who were encouraged to decide the rules as we went along. She gave us back the control that had been missing from our lives.

Being trusted with the decision-making was incredibly empowering and her belief in us boosted our self-esteem no end. Erin didn't lock herself away in an office. She was right there by our sides, sharing every letter and laugh. The more publicity she did, the more letters of encouragement and support flooded in. She was incredibly charismatic and when she walked into a room it seemed to light up.

'Keep up the good work, ladies,' she read out loud from one letter. A ten-pound note slipped out at the same time. 'I wish there had been somewhere like Chiswick when I was being beaten,' she read poignantly from another.

It wasn't just letters. It was bags of jumble, food, clothes, gifts and money, all piling up in the middle of the floor. Then Erin was reading out another letter.

'*I'm looking for my daughter, Jenny, and I wondered if she is living there,*' read Erin. '*Her husband has been up here in Chesterfield looking for her, is she there?*'

My head snapped to attention and suddenly every pair of eyes in the room was on me.

My mam was looking for me.

And then, chillingly, the full enormity of what she had said hit me. Lenny had been to my home.

'Oh God, no,' I choked. The tears were upon me in an instant.

Mixed feelings swamped me. I missed Mam so much it was like a physical pain in my chest, and I couldn't bear the thought of Lenny up there in Chesterfield, pestering her in her fragile state of mind.

Erin said nothing, just folded me into her arms. Later, she and I talked privately in her tiny office, which by now had been nicknamed the cubbyhole.

'I haven't seen my mam in nearly two years, since I took Francesca up there when she was a baby. It's like I'm cocooned in here from the outside world,' I sobbed.

'I know,' she soothed. 'But you need this time, Jenny. You need time to recover. Use the community to help you and re-energize you,' she urged.

She was right, of course. And, later that day, I went out with Tracey and Jerry and tried to forget Mam's letter. As we ran simple errands like food shopping, picking up the Social or going to the launderette, emotionally we were leaning on each other. That mental and physical crutch gave you a bravery you just would never have had on your own.

But then, living in the community, you were never truly alone. Lending mutual support, even with the most mundane of tasks was vital and dealing with the pain of Mam's letter was eased with my new friends by my side.

We spent so much time together I even sensed us starting to look alike. As we pottered about Chiswick, a small army of women with matching perms or mullets, denim flares and tight denim waistcoats or cheesecloth tops, giggling, smoking and gossiping, we looked like every other 1970s housewife.

Except we weren't average housewives. We were women running from our pasts, bonded by our unique and shared experiences.

The local neighbourhood treated us with kindness and respect. They all knew where we were from and whenever they saw us out and about they only ever smiled or waved. That same tree-lined street that is now filled with anonymous coffee chains and expensive delicatessens was a little scruffy round the edges back then. Independent hardware stores jostled for space with family-run butchers and bakers.

Tracey and I always used to visit a little butcher's shop where the owner always slipped us a couple of extra rashers of bacon just because he was a thoroughly nice man.

During the shopping trip I resolved not to write back to Mam. Not out of callousness, but because I genuinely believed I was protecting her. If she didn't know where I was, she couldn't tell Lenny. I needed to be in the bubble of the refuge, I desperately needed the support of the community, to be warm and safe. I wasn't ready to deal with the outside world.

Sadly, the outside world found me. Shortly after Mam's letter, JoJo cornered me.

'Jenny, darling,' she said softly. 'Lenny's called and he wants to meet you. He's asked to see the kids in the local park.'

My heart plummeted and soared at the same time.

'I . . . I,' I stuttered.

'You don't need to explain,' she smiled. 'Do what you think is right, we'll support you whatever.'

I took a deep breath and made a decision.

'I have to let him see his kids,' I said.

'Do you want someone to come with you?' she asked.

'It's OK,' I replied. 'It's broad daylight and the park. I'll be OK.'

That would have been inconceivable six months ago when I fled our home, but I felt stronger now. But my heart still raced ahead of me when I walked into the park and saw him standing with his back to me by the swings.

'Lenny?' I called out softly.

He turned and a part of me wanted to run. But my feet stayed glued to the tarmac and I gripped Rebecca a bit closer to me.

Francesca ran to me and hugged my leg.

'It's OK, love,' I said. 'You go and play.'

Reluctantly she let go and clambered onto a swing. I watched in a dream-like state as Lenny started to push her, and her face broke out into a delighted smile.

'Higher,' she ordered.

'OK,' he laughed.

'How did you find me?' I asked.

'Rose's husband told me,' he replied.

'I'm so sorry, Jenny,' he said. 'What else can I say? It's been tough, you know, but I should never have done them things.'

'No you shouldn't,' I snapped.

I scanned every inch of his face, looking for the angry, troubled man I ran from. But I didn't see him. He looked genuinely remorseful and, as he pushed his daughter on the swing, I felt a pang of regret. This was what my children needed. A father!

'Please come home, Jenny,' he begged. 'I need you.'

I stared long and hard into his brown eyes, as if somehow they would allow me access to his soul. They no longer blazed with anger, just remorse. I started to cry and gently he took my hand in his.

'I'm so sorry,' he whispered.

I looked from him back to our daughters. Was this old Lenny back? Or was I deliberately not searching too hard for the signs? Was I so blinded by the desire for a normal life that I was conveniently rewriting history in my head? I don't know, and what I said next will have many shaking their heads in despair.

'OK,' I agreed. 'Let's try and make it work.'

Madness, I know, but deep down I harboured the impossible dream. Perhaps me and the girls had a shot at a normal family life?

Back at the house, no one tried to talk me out of it. Women returning to their partners wasn't an unusual occurrence, it happened all the time, so my reunion with Lenny wasn't viewed as abnormal. Most of the women craved a normal family life just like me. And, just like me, some of the women still even loved their partners.

'We're always here for you,' said Erin, as I stripped down my mattress and the small cot Rebecca had been sleeping in.

'Take care, Jenny,' said Anne, giving me a cuddle.

Stepping back into the flat was a surreal experience and every footstep I took felt like someone else was controlling my body.

I put down my carrier bag and stared round the room that just six months ago had been my prison cell.

The flat was a total mess and Lenny frantically started gathering up cups and flinging open the windows.

'Sorry about the state of the place,' he said.

He seemed so pathetically pleased to see me.

The girls clung to me as I sat down awkwardly on the settee.

As he cleaned, I found myself studying him – every twitch, every grimace. Was it the prelude to violence? Was he still mentally ill? But there was no mention of church and I couldn't see his dreaded Bible anywhere. Perhaps my leaving had given him the shock he needed?

'I've arranged a babysitter for tonight and I've booked us in for a meal at an Angus Steakhouse up west.'

I was flabbergasted. I didn't recognise this Lenny at all.

'Great,' I muttered, trying to show enthusiasm.

But that night, instead of feeling relaxed as we tucked into our steaks and onion rings, I had never felt more ill at ease. I felt like an actress playing out a role. It was all a hideous, sick charade. Eager couples and families tucked into their meals, eyes shining with excitement at being 'up west'. I should have been happy like them. This was the Lenny I longed to see after all, happy, calm and clearly keen to impress me.

But I wasn't. A feeling of sick dread crept over me, gathering pace until I felt like my head was about to explode. Suddenly he leant over the table and I froze.

'Give me a kiss,' he smiled.

I smiled, but my cheeks were rigid and as he kissed me why did I feel the urge to scream?

Back at home, I put the kids into a local playgroup and tried to go about my normal life.

Or as normal as it was possible to be, but the threat of violence hung over me like a storm-filled sky before the rains start. Even the clouds were the same colour as angry purple bruises.

I felt permanently on edge and I missed Chiswick. I missed Erin's contagious energy, Tracey's filthy gob, Anne's quiet calm and JoJo's cheery efficiency. I missed Harry's banter. I missed the laughter and camaraderie of the house meetings. I even missed my patch of floor. But, mostly, I just missed the home.

I'd been back in Hackney three weeks when Lenny came in. Something about the way the door banged set my teeth on edge. After years of studying him to try and second-guess his moods, I was so attuned to him that even the closing of a door could arouse suspicion.

My suspicions were right. The row was over something so trivial I can't even remember, but the way he suddenly reached and grabbed me by the throat brought everything flooding back. His eyes blazed and his jaw was set into a rock-hard line. The real Lenny was back.

His face was pressed just two inches from mine and as he spoke, flecks of spit landed on my face.

'You. Ever. Leave. Me. Again,' he seethed. 'And I will take the kids. You hear me.'

You stupid, stupid fool, Jenny.

Of course he couldn't change. Deep down, I think I even knew that all along. But he had never mentioned taking the kids before. Over my dead body. When it came to my girls, I would fight like a lioness.

The minute he left the flat, I flipped out. Racing round the room, I flung a few possessions in a bag then rang the girls' playgroup.

'Don't you dare let anyone take my kids except me,' I yelled. 'I'm coming to get them now.'

I ran up the road like a woman possessed. When I got there, Francesca and Rebecca were in Reception with the playgroup leader.

'Thank God,' I cried.

'It's all right, girls,' I wept. 'We're going back to our old home now. Everything's going to be OK.'

Back at Chiswick, no one uttered a single word of recrimination when I walked in. Erin and Anne beckoned me into the office.

'I've been a bloody fool,' I sobbed.

'No you haven't,' they insisted.

That's the real meaning of compassion. Not Erin, nor Anne, nor JoJo, nor any of the other women judged me for my mistake, not once.

'Good to have you back,' winked Tracey, when I walked into the communal lounge. 'I missed you.'

In my absence a number of things had happened. There were now more women than ever in the house. There were too many even to count, but I guessed there must have been close to seventy women and kids, or even more. Space was now at an absolute minimum and women were living cheek by jowl.

There were so many women and children crammed in the

rooms that women were changing behind pinned-up sheets to protect what little modesty could be found. The kitchens were overflowing, so you had to keep your tins and packets of pasta in a bin-liner by your bed.

Somehow, though, Erin had managed to get her hands on some iron bunk beds. Sitting down on mine, I realised the mattress was as lumpy as bag of marbles but, no matter, it beat sleeping on the floor.

'Eh up, Tracey,' I joked. 'I'm going up in the world.'

'Heaving here now, isn't it?' she replied, looking around at the overcrowded room. You literally couldn't see a spare inch of floor space for the bags, clothes, nappies and small children.

'I'm telling yer,' I said, shaking my head in dismay at the sight.

I shouldn't have been surprised. I knew better than anyone how violent men could be. I guess I just didn't know how many were out there.[13]

'Erin told us there are homes like these, modelled on Chiswick, popping up all over the country,' said Tracey. 'And, guess what? We're going to be famous. There's a film crew coming in to film us for a documentary about battered wives.'

Erin told us more about it at the next house meeting.

'I've always said that Chiswick is an open community with an open door. Our address and phone number are public, and we need to make public the vital work that we do here. You

---

[13] Domestic violence accounts for between 16 per cent and 25 per cent of all recorded violent crime. (Source: Women's Aid/Home Office, 2004; Dodd et al., 2004; BCS, 1998; Dobash and Dobash, 1980.)

women are the lifeblood of that community; you are the fore-runners to the next generation of battered women. That said, no one has to appear if they don't want to.'

'I'm game,' I said.

'Me and all,' replied Tracey.

As we waited for the film crew and arrangements were made, a feeling of excitement grew in the house.

Because of Erin's inclusivity, no one was ever made to feel like an outsider, a miracle when you consider how many new women were turning up each day.

We all felt a part of something, a part of this movement, or, as Erin said, an inspiration to the next generation of battered women.

I started to have long chats with Erin in her office – just she and I. Talking about violence and why some men felt the need to display violence and why women tolerated it.

Erin told me about the book she was writing, how she documented how many women came and went, and how she was also compiling a dossier on the services that refused to help battered wives.

'Why do I love it here so much?' I asked. 'Despite the fact that we're living on top of each other?'

'It's the power of the group,' she replied simply.

'There's strength in numbers. After years of feeling lonely and isolated and cut off from families, for women to suddenly find themselves in a house full of nurturing, caring women, that's what's important. And women discover something else, they actually quite like other women and that they can draw tremendous support from them.'

I nodded. From just six months or so, I already knew the women of the house would do anything for one another. But never in my wildest dreams could I have imagined how the house would swing into action when put to the ultimate test.

The fight for life.

My new-found peace was about to be shattered.

Racing my way was a riot of noise, panic, pandemonium and unadulterated terror.

Lenny was coming to get me . . .

CHAPTER 12

Danger in the Safe House

Whistling to myself as the kettle bubbled to the boil, I felt good for the first time in a long time. Life was looking up. I had no regrets about leaving Lenny, I'd settled back in well in the house, had good friends and even the girls seemed content.

Francesca didn't cling to me quite as much as she did in the early days. She and Rebecca were downstairs now, in the basement playgroup.

It was the end of 1973, and it had certainly been a traumatic year. It had been approximately seven months since I'd first arrived, but the changes had heralded brave new beginnings.

I should never have gone back to Lenny. I realised that, but hindsight is a wonderful thing.

I wandered into the communal lounge with my tea and made myself comfy in a battered old armchair. I was just about to light a cigarette when something about the way a woman was chatting on the communal payphone made me stop.

She had stopped talking and was staring straight at me, ashen-faced. Her knuckles turned white as she gripped the phone. Trembling a little, I set down my mug and sat up. Wordlessly, she slammed the phone down.

'Jenny,' she blurted. 'It's your Lenny. He says he's coming to kill you. Says you're the devil.'

Sitting bolt upright, I froze.

What the hell?

'He's on a payphone at the end of the road. You've got to hide,' she urged. 'NOW.'

Pandemonium broke out as the whole house switched into panic mode. You could smell the fear in the air. A violent man was threatening to come into a refuge full of battered women. It was the very worst thing imaginable to each and every one of these women.

Flapping about, I jumped to my feet and realised I couldn't move. The fear had literally rooted me to the spot. Women's terrified faces were milling everywhere. Mouths moved up and down, but nothing made sense. And, suddenly, there was Anne, pushing her way through the sea of terrified women.

Her voice was calm but insistent as she gripped my arm and started to lead me from the room.

'Lenny is outside the house now, we have to get you upstairs,' she said firmly.

'My girls,' I whimpered.

'They are OK,' she insisted. 'They are being looked after in the basement. It's *you* he's after, Jenny. There's no time to lose.'

My legs were shaking so violently she had to half-drag, half-pull me up the stairs to the first floor. When we reached the first-floor landing, we heard the smashing of glass from the basement, followed by a terrific thud.

'He's in the house,' screamed a distant voice.

'Quick, Jenny,' urged Anne. 'Into the attic.'

Then I heard it. Lenny's voice.

'Where is she?' he thundered from the bowels of the house. 'She's the devil. I've come to kill her.'

He was here. Actually here, inside my sanctuary. I could have collapsed and died on the spot from fear.

Instead, I frantically scrambled up the stairs into the attic.

Breathlessly, I paused at the doorway to the attic room. Anne's husband, John, had joined her on the first-floor landing, along with another woman. In her hand Anne was gripping a spirit level, a grim look of defiance plastered over her usually placid features. They stood shoulder to shoulder, a human barricade, barring the stairs to the attic room.

My heart was roaring in my ears as I slammed the door. Frantically I scanned the room for a weapon, anything to protect myself from Lenny. Because when he made it up here, and I had no doubt he would, I had to be prepared to fight to the death. There was no doubt in my mind – he had come here to kill me. But there was nothing I could use in self-defence – just clothes, sheets and carrier bags.

There was an almighty crash down below, followed by more wild screams. He was getting closer.

Barricading myself in was the only option. Slipping on clothes, I frantically raced across the room and gripped the edge of an iron bunk bed. I pushed with all my might until I had it wedged up against the door.

I don't know where I got the strength from, but I managed to push another against the door too, until there were two bunks wedged tightly against it.

They were strong. But I knew when Lenny was in a rage he was possessed with the strength of fifty men.

There was nothing to do but sit and pray. I sat with my back against the wall, my feet jammed up against the end of the bunk beds, pushing them as hard as I could against the door.

I closed my eyes as the fear took hold of my body.

Fear is riveting. Every drop of blood in my body diverted from my organs and raced to my skin, anticipating a knife wound or a blow. My veins pumped with wild adrenaline in readiness to run.

But there was nowhere to run. I was trapped in this tiny room with my husband on the rampage one floor below.

'Please, please, please,' I chanted over and over. 'I don't want to die.'

Lenny's wild screams grew louder and closer.

'She's the devil,' he raged. 'She must die.'

He was possessed. Terrified screams and shouts echoed round the house. It sounded like a riot. I could hear women shouting and tussling and I imagined my friends fighting Lenny off. But I also knew they would be no match for Lenny. For he was out of control, a human wrecking ball, hell-bent on hunting me down.

I squeezed my eyes even more tightly closed and prepared myself for death. The sound of crashing and blood-curdling screams grew even closer.

'Where is she?' he roared.

His voice sounded like he was directly outside.

He was outside! Oh God. Oh God. Oh God.

The only thought that spun round my terrified mind was of my daughters. My head slumped into my hands and I started to whimper and shake violently. My girls were just babies. This wasn't my time to die. Not here, not now. Not when I'd already survived so much. Huddled into a ball, my body froze and began to shut down.

I don't know how long I stayed that way until suddenly, through the gloom, I realised the shouts were growing more distant, fading through the house.

I don't know how long I sat there, frozen to the spot. It could have been minutes, it could have been hours. Finally, there was a gentle knock on the door.

'Jenny, love,' called out Anne. 'It's me. It's OK. He's gone. You can open the door.'

Stumbling to my feet, I very nearly crashed to the floor again. My legs felt like water. Try as I might, I couldn't get the bunk beds away from the door. The same strength that had imbued me not twenty minutes before had all but deserted me now.

The door thudded and reverberated as people tried to push it down. By the time Anne's face peered round the crack, I was a total mess. Frantically she threw open the door and gathered me into her arms.

'I thought I was going to die,' I sobbed, gripping on to her for dear life. 'I thought he was going to kill me.'

'I know, but you're OK now,' she soothed. 'You're safe, he's gone. The police have got him. The girls are perfectly fine too.'

I was shaking so violently, but held tight in her arms I could hear her heart thudding against mine.

'Are you OK? What happened?' I gasped.

She was half-laughing, half-crying and still trembling from her exertion.

'It's all right,' she gulped. 'When he got to the first floor, we fought him back.'

'But how?' I asked, flabbergasted.

'I hit him with a spirit level,' she shrugged.

I stared stunned at the formidable and stoic lady holding me up. A former midwife, a campaigner for battered wives, and now my lifesaver. At that moment in time, and still to this day, I have never felt such gratitude towards another human being.

I always knew you could hang your hat off Anne Ashby. Now I knew you could rely on her as if your life depended on it.

'He managed to kick poor John in the balls though,' she added.

As she and a slightly sore John guided me downstairs, I stared in disbelief at Lenny's trail of destruction. You could see exactly where he'd been by the broken glass, upturned furniture and shaken women.

We all sat around in the communal room drinking tea in a state of disbelief at what had just happened and the whole story unfolded. Lenny had broken in through the basement playgroup by smashing the windows and then hurling himself in, in front of dozens of bewildered kids. Then he ran from room to room, hunting me out.

Erin, meanwhile, collected as many children as she could

find elsewhere, herded them back into the basement playgroup along with the rest, and planted herself in front of the door armed only with an empty bottle of orange squash for self-defence.

Lenny tore through the human barricade of women until he reached the first-floor landing. But he was no match for Anne, who hit him with a spirit level and drove him back down to the ground floor. He tried to get back downstairs into the basement playgroup, but instead encountered formidable Erin and her squash bottle.

He was restrained and bundled out of the house by John and Anne, but even that didn't stop him. He managed to get back in *again* through the basement window.

Finally, the police arrived, but it had taken them a full twenty minutes just to get him in the van.

'You should have seen it, Jenny,' gasped Tracey. 'He fought like a madman, the van was rocking all over the place.'

I shook my head in dismay and we all sat in stunned silence.

'Any shit that's thrown at me sticks, doesn't it?' I said eventually.

Tracey cracked up, then Anne started to laugh.

As a euphoric feeling of relief swept over me, I stared hard at her and realised I owed her and Erin more than just a sanctuary, a safe place to sort myself out. *I owed them my life.* They had promised me I would be safe in the home. They hadn't broken that promise.

It later transpired that, in the entire history of Chiswick Women's Aid, Lenny was the only man who succeeded in breaking into the Big House and I very much doubt that any who witnessed his psychotic rage or fought him off will ever forget it. I certainly won't.

Plenty of blokes had hung around outside, shouting abuse or pleading forgiveness like Bridgett's husband, but none had ever actually made it in until that fateful episode.

From his police cell Lenny went to court and from there was sent to a Category B men's prison, Wormwood Scrubs in west London, known locally as 'The Scrubs'. There he did some of his time in the medical ward.

I received a letter from the governor informing me that Lenny had been diagnosed with a personality disorder and transferred to the psychiatric ward of Hackney Hospital, where he was receiving medication.

As strange as this sounds, I felt desperately sorry for Lenny. I knew from witnessing Mam's struggle, that no one chooses to have a mental illness or a sick mind. And I was in no doubt that the trigger for Lenny's loosening grip on reality and, in turn, his violence was his mental illness, exacerbated by racist treatment. I'm not making excuses for the violence; I'm just trying to make sense of it.

That's what I was doing the day I got on the Tube to Hackney to visit Lenny in hospital. Tracey came with me and held my hand as I timidly pushed open the door. But, instantly, I knew I had nothing to fear. The Lenny who had broken in, blazing with rage and accusing me of being the devil, had vanished.

In his place was a shrunken, defeated, broken man, lying in a hospital bed, sedated out of his mind.

A prison guard stood watch. But Lenny wasn't going anywhere. He was meek and mild as a lamb. The contrast was startling.

'How are you, Jenny?' he asked.

'I'm fine,' I replied quietly. 'How are they treating you in here?'

'OK,' he nodded.

There was a long pause as he scrambled to try and form a sentence.

'I think I'll be better off back in Guyana,' he mumbled eventually.

I nodded my agreement.

It was pitiful. He didn't ask after the girls, no mention was made of him breaking into the refuge, or his violence. It reminded me of visiting Mam in The Haven. There was the same air of hopeless despair and confusion etched on people's faces.

On the way out, Tracey turned to me.

'That was bloody grim.'

'Ay,' I replied. 'But mental illness is something you can't fight. If I didn't have sympathy for him, I wouldn't be human.'

She patted my arm. 'Come on, let's get back to Chiswick.'

After Lenny was released from hospital, it was agreed that it would be for the best to get Lenny to return to Guyana.

It was one of the most emotional experiences of my life. Anne Ashby, her husband John, me and Tracey, picked him up from hospital and drove him to Heathrow. Me, Tracey and Lenny sat in the back, with Tracey in the middle. Anne sat in the passenger seat and John drove.

Lenny was still so heavily medicated he didn't have the energy to hurt a fly, so there was no fear there, just sadness. He talked a little.

'I think I'll be better off back with my mum,' he murmured, as the grey streets flashed past.

But he was in an almost trance-like state, and we drove through the suburbs to the airport mostly in silence.

Once there, we helped him check in and then waited for the medical escort the hospital said would accompany him. No one turned up. That hit home more than anything.

That was the problem. In this country Lenny had no one. No family, no friends, no roots. He was a confused, angry, sick man with no support.

'Take care, Lenny,' I said as he reached the departure barrier. He shot me a sad little smile, then he was gone.

As I waved goodbye and watched him disappear through the departure gates, I felt nothing but intense sadness for him and what his future might hold.

He would get family support in Guyana, sure, but the right medical treatment? I doubted it very much.

Tracey and Anne linked arms with me and walked me back to the car. There were no words. It was indescribably sad.

Back at Chiswick, I rang the airline to check he had definitely boarded the plane. He had.

I never saw him again. And the girls would never see their father again. It was over. Soon after, I had a letter from his mother: 'Lenny is in no fit state to look after his affairs,' it said, 'so it's best you get on with your life. Please kiss the kids for me.'

With Lenny gone, I began to experience a freedom that I could only previously have imagined. This was helped by the fact that myself, Tracey and two other women in the Big House were given a new home all to ourselves.

On 24 March 1974, approximately ten months after I joined Chiswick, I moved to a place in Marlborough Road, a four-storey house in a quiet side street just around the corner from the Big House.

Erin had managed to get a short-term lease from the Notting Hill Housing Trust and, in return, for a rent of one pound a week, us four women and our eleven kids would have, joy of joys, a bedroom to ourselves and our own kitchenette. No more overcrowding and jostling with dozens of other women and kids just to get a cup of tea or queuing for the bathroom.

Second-stage housing, Erin called it. She explained that it was still a community house and close enough to Chiswick for us to feel supported, but it was also a gradual return to normality.

Absolutely bloody marvellous, I called it. I had the support of my best mate and the other women but, crucially, me and my girls now had space and freedom away from the overcrowding to allow our confidence to grow.

Had I been forced to leave and go it alone, isolated and lonely, I'm not sure I would have coped at that stage, and I often wonder what my fate would have been if that had been the case.

But that was the genius of Erin and Chiswick Women's Aid. They put the needs of the women first and really cared and thought about our safety, not petty bureaucracy or the fear of reprisals over overcrowding.

The house on Marlborough Road wasn't the smartest of places and it was pretty shabby round the edges, but what did I care? By moving me there, Erin was showing to me that she thought I had it in me to move on. It was a subtle message. I was growing in strength and confidence daily. And just knowing that Lenny was finally out of my life for ever, I could concentrate on healing.

Tracey was just as delighted as me. I was just moving some boxes of stuff round the corner when I heard her foghorn voice ring out down the street.

''Ere, Jenny,' she hollered.

I looked up to find her perched precariously on the window ledge two floors up. Her legs dangled casually over the edge and a fag was clamped between her teeth.

'Come on up,' she grinned wickedly. 'Let's have high tea.'

I cackled and shook my head. 'You're a mad cow you are.'

'I know, but you love me, doncha?' she yelled from the window ledge.

I did too, just as I loved all the women in our unconventional home.

As I unpacked, I took stock of my life. I was nearly twenty-eight by then and, like Tracey, finally ready to start taking risks in my life and moving on. I'd been imprisoned, shot at, drugged, electrocuted, beaten, stabbed, kicked, burnt, bitten, nearly drowned and narrowly avoided a ceiling falling in on my head. Not to mention my ex trying to kill me because he was convinced I was the devil. But I wasn't dead yet. Seems it would take more than that to finish Jenny Smith off.

When I'd finished unpacking, I joined Tracey on the window ledge for a fag and a cuppa. Falling off held no fear for us. I reckon we thought we were invincible!

'You know what,' I said, drawing on my fag and smiling as I puffed smoke rings into the air. 'I may be a battered wife, but I reckon the batter's fallen off.'

Most days we returned to the Big House so our kids could play at playgroup and we could join in the house meetings and keep in touch with what was going on. We were so bonded to Erin, Anne and JoJo that it was inconceivable not to see them all the time.

Shortly after our move, the documentary *Scream Quietly or the Neighbours Will Hear* was aired on Thames Television. We all crowded into the communal lounge to watch it. It was very simply but effectively shot in black and white, with no voice-over or special techniques. The director, Michael Whyte, had filmed us going about our business, the kids playing in the garden, us making our dinner and day-to-day life in the house. He interviewed some women about their stories and Erin too. He also took starkly shot photos of each of us women and occasionally they would flash up on the screen, accompanied by groans and laughter from all of us.

'Oh God,' I shrieked, when my photo flashed up on screen. 'I don't look like that, do I?'

We joked, but our laughter hid our fears. You could see the raw pain etched deep into every woman's face.

Tears pricked my eyes when the documentary cut to a scene of our sleeping arrangements. The camera slowly panned round the overcrowded bedrooms, showing the crush of mattresses, all of us sleeping in tight rows with our children huddled next to us.

That's when it really hit me. We had all been prepared to live this way because the alternative was too frightening to even contemplate. My heart broke a little as I gazed at us sleeping on the floor next to our babies with next to nothing. It was sad beyond belief.

And yet the sadness was mixed with great pride. Particularly when Erin flashed up on screen, railing about the inefficiency of Social Services, government, police and local authorities in dealing with battered women.

She highlighted for the first time ever how ridiculous it was that a battered woman who leaves her home couldn't be rehoused by Social Services because she had deliberately made herself homeless and could then risk having her kids taken into care. How the police could arrest an abusive husband, then release him straight back home and to his terrified wife, who would doubtless be forced to drop all charges.

She also talked of the forgotten victims of domestic violence – our children. Of their bewilderment and fear, and how they grow up not understanding the limits of violence.

As the camera cut to a scene of a smiling Francesca being pushed through the garden in a little wooden cart, surrounded by dozens of other kids, my heart broke all over again.

This was the reality of her childhood. She should have been safe and nurtured in a secure home environment, not watching her daddy break in threatening to kill Mummy and forced to sleep on a mattress on the floor.

I comforted myself with the fact that at long last we were being given a voice and that the powers-that-be who ran this country would at last wake up to what was going on behind closed doors and in our little community.

But, most importantly of all, it showed that in 1974 Britain had a big and growing problem on its hands, a problem that for too long had been ignored.

It took a feisty woman in a kaftan and a small army of battered wives to show them.

We were all enormously proud to have played a part in the making of the documentary. We were the early pioneers and we were determined to support the place that had saved all our lives.

Erin's book of the same name had been published just before the film. The book and the documentary caused shockwaves throughout the nation and started to change the way people perceived domestic violence, which made it historically very important.

This wasn't a personal matter to be dealt with behind closed doors between husband and wife any more. This was an issue that simply wasn't going away. Not if Erin had anything to do with it. We knew this because from that moment on Chiswick Women's Aid started to receive sack-loads of mail and donations daily from all over Britain, and people flooded to the house to volunteer their time to help in any way they could.

At the point of filming, the house held eighteen women and forty-six children, nearly double the number when I had first joined the refuge at Belmont Terrace, but those numbers were growing daily, reaching epidemic proportions.

The house was overflowing with children, women and noise. Later on, they even had to put bunk beds in the sheds in the back garden for some of the older children to sleep in. Every morning that Tracey and I returned to the Big House, there seemed to be a new woman and her children there.

'I can't close the door on them,' Erin shrugged. 'How can I?'

She remained undaunted by Hounslow Council's repeated orders to reduce the number of women and children living in the house. The council said it was a Health and Safety issue with so many people crowded in, which I suppose in a way it was. But I understood her defiance to not turn anyone away and she refused to be bullied or intimidated by council officials. She and Anne knew all too well that, legally, they were only allowed thirty-six women and children in total, but by this stage there must have been closer to seventy, with women sleeping everywhere from the kitchen floor to the overflowing bedrooms.

But, unlike the other refuges now opening up and down the country, Chiswick remained the only one with an open-door policy. I sensed that for as long as Erin had breath in her body, it would remain that way too.

I may have been living round the corner, but I wanted to do my bit, however small, even if it was sorting the donations, showing visitors around, or answering the phone and telling a desperate woman how to get to us.

Every time I did so, my mind cast back to the moment I had rung from the corner shop with the same plea for help.

'Just get here,' I urged. 'Whatever you can do to get here, just do it.'

I hoped my response offered the same hope it did to me when I had needed it. And, slowly, I gathered that my part, however small, was valuable. I was now the older generation of women who had something worthwhile to offer to the newcomers. The terrified woman who had first arrived was slowly vanishing and, through the healing love and support of other residents, I felt I was becoming the woman I was destined to be.

This community was like being embraced in a womb that had nurtured me back to life. Suddenly I found the words of my old headmistress at the remand school echoing through my brain.

You have so much to give, Jenny.

Finally, I knew what.

CHAPTER 13

Finding My Voice

My brain felt clear for the first time in years, as if the dust had shaken off and I was seeing again for the first time.

I set about my work with gusto, cleaning, supporting newcomers and inviting some of them from the Big House round to mine for tea. It was my duty now to dish out tea, biscuits and a shoulder to cry on. No one directly told me to do this, but the way Erin had set the refuge up to run like one big, albeit slightly shambolic, family, encouraged us to take personal responsibility for everyone's welfare. Not just our own.

That's how I met Sally. I introduced her two girls to mine and cooked them all fish fingers and then, when they were happily playing, I fixed her a cup of tea.

'It's nice to escape the madness for a while,' she smiled gratefully as she sipped her tea. 'Not that I'm not grateful to the home, you understand,' she added nervously.

I could see she was a timid thing, racked with insecurities.

Hardly surprising when she told me a little of what her husband had subjected her to.

Sally's husband had terrorized her for years, abusing her mentally and physically in front of their two daughters.

'I just couldn't get the bottle up to leave him. I blame myself for that,' she whispered.

She stared at her girls playing and her eyes glazed over with sadness.

'I dread to think the effect this'll have on them, I just couldn't . . .'

Her voice trailed off as she started to sob.

'I was so weak,' she wept. 'So bloody weak.'

Leaping to my feet, I gripped her shoulders.

'Listen here,' I said. 'You're stronger than most women in this country. You left a violent man and that takes guts. Trust me, I know. I've been on the end of flying fists for years too. This is the start of your new life, right here, right now.'

She sniffed, blew her nose and smiled weakly.

'Perhaps you're right. I've been invited out on a date, you know,' she went on. 'A bloke I met up the shops, but I won't go.'

'Why ever not?' I gasped.

'Me, on a date,' she snorted. 'Can you imagine? My husband would go spare.'

'Your husband used to beat you to within an inch of your life,' I said, staring her right in the eye.

'You've escaped all that now. This is your time. You've got to stand up for yourself, Sally, otherwise who else will?'

She stopped and set her teacup down.

'Perhaps you're right, Jenny,' she said.

'You know it,' I laughed. 'Now you're going on that date, like it or not.'

Laughing, she held her hands up in surrender.

'OK, OK,' she said, smiling. 'But I've got nothing to wear.'

'I'll loan you something,' I replied.

'And my hair's a state,' she added.

'Leave that to me and Tracey. We're old hands at make-overs.'

Together we all set about transforming Sally from drab, battered housewife to sexy single woman.

By the time we'd zipped her up into a long purple maxi-dress, persuaded her to wear some wedges, brushed her hair and gave her a thick coating of mascara, she didn't even look like the same woman.

'Now go on and have some fun, I'll look after your girls for you.'

Her eyes shone with gratitude. 'Thanks, Jenny,' she smiled. 'I'll never forget this.'

I watched her out the window as she walked off down the road in search of a new life.

Erin was right. This was about much more than politics. This was about women supporting other women, about community and empowerment.

But for every Sally there was a woman whose story filled me with despair. Not all women could be repaired so quickly. And some couldn't be repaired at all, as I found when I met dear sweet Peggy.

Peggy was eighty and new at the Big House. She had been

very badly beaten and was quickly admitted to Charing Cross Hospital in Hammersmith, West London.

Erin asked if Tracey and I could go and visit and cheer her up. We were only too happy. But even two gobby women like us were totally silenced when we met Peggy.

She was a tiny, frail little thing who seemed dwarfed in a hospital bed. Her lined face was beaten black and blue. I tried to hide my shock at the sight of her, and smiled brightly as I gave her a bunch of grapes and some chocolate.

'Everyone at the Big House sends their love, Peggy, and hope to see you back there really soon,' I said, taking her hand in mine.

'Bless you, dear,' she smiled weakly. 'I don't like to trouble anyone.'

When she was discharged, she came to stay with us at Marlborough Road as it was that bit quieter and Tracey and I did our best to look after her. Her story, as it came out bit by bit, was utterly harrowing.

It transpired that her abuser wasn't her husband but her son. *Her own son.* I felt my heart shatter when I heard that. How could someone beat such a lovely old lady, their own mother, and treat her with such contempt?

I never did find out much more about her than that or how she came to arrive at Chiswick, as Peggy was fiercely loyal to her son and felt she would be being disloyal if she spoke out about him.

I sensed her self-esteem could never be repaired, she was simply too old and the years of mental abuse had taken its toll on her mind.

And sadly her body . . .

'I'm so sorry, Jenny, love,' she admitted one morning, not long after she arrived. 'I've messed myself.'

She started to cry and I gathered her in my arms and hugged her tight. Her frail body felt as if it might snap in two.

'Don't worry, Peggy, we'll get you cleaned up in no time.'

I tried to remain cheery and upbeat in front of Peggy, even when her physical condition worsened and she spent hours crying. But, privately, I raged at a world which allowed a man to beat his own mother until she was so scared she couldn't even control her own bodily functions.

Tragically, Peggy didn't stay with us long. It quickly became obvious her medical needs were too great and she was readmitted to hospital.

'I've failed her,' I wept to Anne. 'We should have been able to look after her.'

Anne shook her head.

'I'm sorry, Jenny, but Peggy is an old lady. She needs serious medical care.'

Peggy died in hospital. She was in her eighties. A victim of her sadistic son. Her death tore my heart clean in two and I vowed to keep fighting and supporting Chiswick Women's Aid with every breath in my body until people like Peggy, Sally, Jerry and Bridgett and all the other battered wives of Britain could live free from fear.

Erin was imbued with fresh fighting spirit too.

As she upped her campaign of publicity capitalizing on the wave of public support generated by the book and film, so too did Hounslow Council. They had offered to take over the financial concerns and management of the refuge, an offer which Erin turned down flat, quite rightly fearing for the future of the women once Hounslow got its claws into it.

So, instead, Hounslow started to send letters, threatening court action if she didn't reduce numbers and comply with their regulations. By early 1975, she had received a court summons ordering her to attend court on grounds of overcrowding.

By that stage there must have been nearly ninety women and children at Chiswick, but those numbers fluctuated. She ripped the summons in two and simply gave it back to them. Chiswick was in jeopardy, but Erin stood firm.

'Do you want this place to close?' she asked the assembled women at the morning meeting after she had received the summons.

A chorus of defiant 'no's drowned her out.

'What do you fink?' hollered the loudest voice, probably mine or Tracey's.

'Then they won't close us down,' she insisted.

A roar of approval rang out.

'And I won't stop the open-door policy,' she insisted. 'What matters is public opinion.'

Every woman in Chiswick backed her 110 per cent. With that in mind, we took our cause to the streets to campaign.

Wielding our home-made banners and placards saying 'Battered Women Need A Refuge', we started carrying out peaceful protests with our children. We went wherever we thought we could be seen or heard, without ever being rowdy or rude.

We even stood with our placards at the end of 10 Downing

Street dressed in kaftans, tank tops and bell-bottom jeans, small children peeking out from behind our knees. What a sight we made! It made a colourful change from the stuffily dressed politicians who usually trod the famous cobbled street.

At that time there were no gates at the end of the street, so we got quite close to number ten, watched over by two disbelieving police officers. I had to pinch myself. Me, a miner's daughter from a pit village, standing at the door to the Prime Minister's house, a part of this powerful movement! I'd come a long way from the frightened girl who had first run away to London aged thirteen.

Everywhere we went, you could either sense the support or the utter disbelief that women were daring to try to get their voice heard on such a sensitive subject. But these were no ordinary times. It was 1975 and Harold Wilson was in power, but it was also the year the Conservatives had chosen their first women leader: Margaret Thatcher.

The punk movement had begun and unemployment had climbed to one million. People were sick of strikes, power cuts and three-day working weeks. Unrest and unease were brewing in the air, and Chiswick Women's Aid was to be a part of the sweeping changes to come.

By now Erin was becoming a famous face in her own right, appearing regularly on TV and in the newspapers. She had burst into the public consciousness by daring to tackle and speak publicly about a taboo subject. She challenged us to do the same.

'You are representatives of the world's first refuge, tell people your story,' she urged.

I'd have jumped off a cliff if she or Anne had asked me, but more than anything I wanted to help protect the home from threat of closure. *Our home.*

The first time I gave a public speech, I was so nervous I don't think I even registered where it was or who I was speaking to. But sitting in the front row of the packed hall were Erin and Anne, smiling encouragingly.

'You can do it,' Erin mouthed.

My heart was hammering as I opened my mouth and surveyed the sea of professional, suited men and women. Defiance kicked in and I jutted out my proud chin, like I'd seen my dad do on so many occasions when we were growing up.

I wasn't just a battered wife. I was a battered wife who had survived. And now I had something to say.

'My name is Jenny and for three years I was beaten,' I began.

My mouth was dry and I felt sure I was babbling, but I fixed on Erin and Anne. By the time I got to the end, I was actually enjoying myself. People were listening. To me!

'Chiswick has an open-door policy for a reason,' I concluded. 'When you open a door and there's a woman there in the state that you know what it's like to be in, are you going to close the door because it's too crowded? Are you hell! You're going to put another mattress down and welcome her and her children in. You're going to give her a cup of tea, talk to her and tell her about the house. You give her a hug, make her feel welcome and safe. Just as Erin did to me when I first arrived.'

I felt my pride soar as the audience erupted into applause.

After that we all worked tirelessly and I gave many talks and interviews around the country, from radio station interviews in

Portsmouth to talks to doctors, lawyers, psychiatrists and family groups.

From swanky offices to draughty halls, I, along with many other women, became a mouthpiece for Chiswick. Doors were no longer closed to me like they had been back when I was with Lenny.

'Just point me in the right direction and I'll use this,' I said, pointing to my gob.

By now Francesca was enrolled in a local school and Rebecca was at playgroup, so I had the freedom, time and inclination to help. But, more than anything, I believed in our message and with every footstep I took, I felt my self-esteem and belief in the cause grow. Plus, with the backing of Erin and Anne, I had oodles and oodles of confidence. My spirit soared and, for the first time ever, I felt a strong sense of my own purpose in the world. For years I didn't have a voice. Now you couldn't shut me up.

'Chiswick Women's Aid gave me a place of safety,' I told anyone who would listen. 'No man has a right to beat a woman, and we will never stop fighting to protect the rights of women.'

I even went to a support group for violent men in Primrose Hill in North London. They wanted a battered wife to go along to talk so the men could see the consequences of their actions and for them to get to the bottom of why they used aggression.

From the minute I walked into the room, I shuddered at the waves of anger and hostility present. My legs started to shake as I sat myself down in a chair and gazed round at the nine angry men staring at me.

'Jenny,' smiled the counsellor chairing the group.

'Could you share your story, please?'

Shakily I managed to tell my story and, afterwards, the counsellor asked if I would like to ask a question. I directed it to a man opposite me with his arms crossed defensively.

'Why did you feel you couldn't contain your violence and at what point do you let go?' I ventured.

I watched his fists tighten as his eyes narrowed.

'She just knows what buttons to press,' he said in a low voice. 'She goads me into it.'

Then he fixed his gaze on me with a look of hatred so strong it took my breath away.

'She asks for it.'

I have never felt so intimidated. There were men in the room I sensed who genuinely wanted to change and were reaching out for help. But he was just an out and out nasty, violent bully.

I never went back.

It may seem strange, a battered woman going to talk to a room full of abusive men. I daresay it wouldn't happen now, but back in 1975 there were no set rules in place. It was all one big experiment and I was willing to try anything that might work.

I turned out to watch Erin and Anne give talks too. I remember Tracey and I going to watch Anne give a talk to a group of high-powered businessmen.

She was calm, measured and articulate. Her soft voice resonated with the crowd and she held them in the palm of her hand as she put forward Chiswick's case.

But, afterwards, in the toilet, she yanked up her maxi-dress, revealing a pair of old tights covered in holes and ladders.

'It's a good job they couldn't see my tights,' she laughed.

I looked at Tracey and we had one thought. Giggling, we ripped them off her. Our howls of laughter must have been heard echoing outside in the corridor.

'You buggers,' laughed Anne.

The campaigning against Hounslow's threat of closure was working and by 1975 Erin had many supporters, including The Who and comedian Spike Milligan, who often gave money to the refuge.

Erin inspired devotion in her followers. With her strong beliefs and ability to argue her case, she had her critics too, but I put her on a pedestal.

But it wasn't all work, work, work. With freedom and safety, came the desire to have fun. And lots of it.

Most women, when they break up from a man, have a new haircut. But Chiswick women weren't most women and our circumstances weren't like others. I bought a cheap Toni home-perm kit and, before long, most of the women were walking round Chiswick looking like they had microphones stuck on their heads.

By day we helped Erin campaign, but by night, boy, did we want to let off steam. With our permed hair, maxi-dresses and wedge heels we thought we were it.

Most days we woke to mountains of jumble on the doorstep. One morning I was over the moon to find a stunning cream Ossie Clark dress with a bronze print. Most women would have given their back teeth for a dress from the iconic 1960s fashion designer, but I found it first in the jumble. I teamed it with a pair of bronze platforms and I really felt the business.

'Ooh lovely, Jenny,' cooed Jerry when she spotted me in it. 'Did it come in?'

That phrase could be heard echoing somewhere in the house at least once a day.

'If I ever get round to writing a book, I'm going to call it "Did it come in?",' joked Anne.

Free from fear for the first time in years, many of the women, myself and Tracey included, just wanted to have fun. You could see the sparkle return to women's eyes and pretty soon we were like kids in a sweet shop.

We had live-in babysitters; we knew our kids were safe so, naturally, like most women in our twenties, we wanted to party. Erin and Anne encouraged us to go out and lead a normal life. Why should we cower away inside? People might have expected us to be browbeaten and terrified, but a lot of the time we were young women given a second chance at life.

Jerry had started dating a nightclub manager of a well-known reggae club in Shepherd's Bush, not far from Chiswick, and heading down there with a big gaggle of women became a Saturday night ritual.

From the moment the doors on the bus outside the refuge slammed shut, we were like any other crowd of boisterous young women determined to have a laugh and forget our responsibilities for a few precious hours.

Our perms were so stiff from chemicals they could have withstood a force-ten gale and our heavily kohled eyes would sparkle with mischief at the promise of the fun times ahead. The stench of Charlie perfume hung in the air as we made silly jokes and waved at young fellas driving alongside the bus.

Everyone was so friendly in those days, chatting, laughing and sharing a fag and a joke. We didn't have much, just enough for a couple of drinks and the taxi fare home, but we didn't need much either. Taxis and drinks were so cheap in them days everyone could afford the odd night out, not like now where you virtually need a mortgage for a Saturday night out in London.

From the moment we spilled out of the bus onto Askew Road, the doors to the nightclub were thrown open and we were treated like royalty by Earl the manager.

'Welcome, ladies. I'm glad of the custom,' he beamed.

It was dark and throbbing with reggae. Downstairs in the basement was a dance floor always packed with revellers and upstairs served delicious Jamaican food and cold beer on tap. It was heaving, and half of Chiswick seemed to end up there, bumping and grinding against each other in our skin-tight flares. Black and white alike let their hair down and partied with wild abandon.

But no one partied quite like the Chiswick girls, laughing like drains and taking over the dance floor.

We were an uproarious tribe of women, bonded by the pain of our pasts but, for a few short hours, determined to live for the moment. We may have come from different backgrounds, but we all had one thing in common. A bloody wicked sense of humour, and on those nights we laughed until we cried.

We may once have been downtrodden, violated, controlled, beaten, bitten, burnt, punched, kicked and told daily how useless we were, but at a deeper level it had instilled in us resilience, and with resilience comes humour. It was wonderful to see that flowing out of the women.

Lots of girls copped off with guys and, sure, there were one-night stands, flings and relationships formed, as with any other group of young women our age. Our lovely house mother, JoJo, was on hand to make sure everyone got the contraceptive pill. But, mainly, we just needed to let our hair down.

Tracey and I were too daft to get into anything serious and heavy with another fella. We were more interested in pushing each other about in shopping trolleys, playing daft pranks on each other or dancing to reggae at Askew Road.

It was at this nightclub that Tracey and I met a guy called Alvin 'Seeco' Patterson, a percussionist with Bob Marley & the Wailers. He was a lovely, gentle man who invited us down to the Island Recording Studios to watch the band rehearse.

We were huge fans and, at that time, Bob Marley was so famous he had a god-like status. Needless to say, we didn't need asking twice.

A few days later, we hovered nervously outside until Seeco spotted us and beckoned us in. Bob Marley was the loveliest man you can ever imagine and watching them play together was a real privilege.

The air in the studio was thick with cannabis and everyone was smoking thick cone joints.

Bob sat in a corner strumming on his guitar and bobbing his head.

'I can't believe we're in the same room as Bob Marley,' hissed Tracey under her breath.

'Tell me about it,' I muttered.

Suddenly Bob looked up at me and grinned.

'Play us something, Bob,' I blurted out before I could stop myself.

'OK,' he replied, and started to pick out a tune on his guitar.

I gasped as his beautiful voice, one of the most recognisable in history, started to drift melodically around the studio.

'*Yankee doodle went to town, a-riding on a pony, stuck a feather up his arse and called it macaroni.*'

There was a stunned silence before we all fell about laughing. He was only messing around and I fell in love with him for his sense of humour alone after that.

It made me realise something else too. For every nasty, violent man in the world, there was also a Bob. Meeting lovely fellas like him taught me that, fortunately, men could also be funny, talented and lovely to be around. Watching these incredible, gentle musicians was such an honour and we returned to the Big House full of it.

In the summer of 1975, when I had been at Chiswick for two years, Erin had a proposition for me.

'How do you fancy coming on a road trip round Europe with me and some of the other women?' she said. 'I've been asked to make speeches and speak to groups opening refuges in Europe.'

Leave Britain? I'd never even crossed the Channel before.

Was the Pope Catholic?

'Count me in,' I grinned.

Tracey kindly agreed to look after the girls and me, Erin and two of the other women who were also coming, plus some of the play staff, got packing. We were to be gone a couple of weeks and, rather than stay in hotels, Erin hired three camper vans for us to stay in. Me and two mums were in one, the male playgroup workers in another and Erin and her kids in the third.

I kissed Francesca and Rebecca goodbye, hugged Tracey and set off from Marlborough Road with a heart full of butterflies.

Everyone came out to wave us off.

'Chiswick Women's Aid on tour,' I yelled out the window, as we slid away from the kerb to much beeping, tooting and cheering.

We travelled from Harwich to the Hook of Holland. As I stood on the blustery ferry deck and watched the misty cliffs of England disappear behind us, I felt as if I was doing more than just travelling abroad. My little adventure was the start of a whole new life, a brand-new me.

I pushed down a wave of sadness as an image of Mam and Dad's face popped up into my mind. They would be so excited to hear about this trip, to know how well I was doing. And yet, for some reason, I still didn't feel strong enough to get in touch. That area of my life was simply too raw and too painful to revisit just yet.

By the time we got to Holland and began our drive to Amsterdam, there were plenty of distractions to keep my mind off Mam and my girls. We had designed posters publicizing the refuge and why battered women needed a safe house, and had plastered them to the windows of our vans. As we rattled through the sleepy Dutch countryside in our rickety vans, we certainly caused a stir and at the first campsite we came to we even drew a crowd. Though perhaps not for the reasons we had hoped. It seemed the person who had translated our posters into Dutch had mistakenly written the words 'battered women' as 'prostitutes'.

I screamed with laughter when an embarrassed young Dutch woman explained the error.

'We've travelled right across the Channel demanding refuge and better rights for prostitutes,' I hooted.

Erin quickly changed the words and we vowed to make a better impression for the rest of our trip. On our first night I was determined to make myself useful and cooked the group a meal of beef with aubergines, tomatoes and rice over a tiny portable gas cooker.

As darkness fell and we huddled round the flickering camp-fire and tucked into the stew off old enamel plates, the prostitute debacle was quickly forgotten. It was idyllic. Erin told ghost stories as the warm evening air rustled through the trees and wood smoke curled into the darkness.

I lay on my back and stared up at the stars. The peace and quiet of nature was so calming. After years of turmoil and over-crowding, this was the first time I was fully immersed in tran-quillity. A warm glow of contentment spread through my belly as the fresh night air lulled us all to sleep.

Our trip couldn't have been more basic. We used condensed milk in our tea, slept in the van on paper-thin mattresses and scrubbed our clothes by hand in the campsite sinks. But in emotional terms I had never felt so rich. I was on the adventure of a lifetime.

We visited a refuge that had opened in Amsterdam. I couldn't understand half of what the women said, but there was no mistaking the look of pain, relief and suffering in their eyes. It made me understand that my experiences were shared by women the world over.

The problem might have been highlighted in Chiswick, but its roots spread across oceans. But with every mile we covered, I felt my confidence and belief in myself grow stronger still. The beaten and defeated Jenny wouldn't have recognised this woman! And every night we spent under the stars, I felt more happy and fulfilled than I had in a lifetime.

Erin had arranged a schedule of talks, speeches, meetings and visits in order to publicize Chiswick and we drew enormous support. Everywhere we went, people were so interested in us and hearing about the refuge.

'Where do you sleep, what do you do with your children, who decides the rules?' Questions were fired at us from every angle and we answered them all as honestly as we could.

The world's first refuge was a fascinating subject that caught people's imaginations in a way we could never have imagined. I did my bit by giving talks or being interviewed whenever I was asked.

As we travelled through Holland, Germany, Belgium and, finally, France, I was stunned at the sights: policemen with guns in Germany, barges and markets in Amsterdam, magical forests, ancient towns and castles and, finally, the splendour of Paris.

As we climbed up to the top of the Eiffel Tower and I looked down over the jumble of medieval rooftops that seemed to slide down into the Seine, I was awe-inspired.

'Chiswick really has been the very worst and the very best of times,' I thought to myself.

But somewhere, deep inside, I sensed it had to come to an end. I couldn't stay cossetted in the refuge for ever. This trip had shown me that there was a big wide world out there waiting to be explored.

Perched on top of the Eiffel Tower, I pondered the important question. Did I have the guts to leave?

The answer, which I didn't yet know, was that in reality I wouldn't have a choice. As I travelled and dreamed in Paris, 220 miles away in Hounslow, the men in suits had plans up their sleeves.

Plans that would throw all our lives into peril . . .

CHAPTER 14

Eviction

In our absence, things had been heating up and just three months after our return from the continent, a number of letters were winging their way to Chiswick. The first was a love letter to me and was delivered to me one morning at Marlborough Road in a small white envelope with a German postmark on it.

Ripping it open, I stared, bewildered, at the words.

'*Ich bewundere dich für deinen Mut,*' I read out loud over the breakfast table to Tracey, who was in having a cuppa with me.

'What the hell does that mean?'

Grinning, Tracey snatched it off me and, putting on a silly voice, carried on reading.

'*Sie sind sehr schön,*' she said.

Her eyes lit up with mischief.

'It's only a bleedin' love letter ain't it,' she grinned triumphantly.

'Don't talk daft,' I scoffed, ripping it back off her.

'It is too,' she crowed. 'Look at the hearts.'

Sure enough, the writer had signed his name, Hans, with a flourish and surrounded it with hearts and kisses.

'Jenny's got a love letter, Jenny's got a love letter,' Tracey teased.

'Give over,' I chuckled, but deep down I was quite chuffed.

'You must have made an impression when you were doing them talks in Germany,' she giggled.

'I don't remember meeting any Hans,' I said, wracking my memory. 'I wonder who he is.'

'Dunno,' laughed Tracey. 'But I bet he wants you on your *Hans* and knees. Bumpsy daisy and all,' she screeched.

'Shurrup,' I cackled.

We were laughing that hard we barely heard one of the other mums at Marlborough Road come in.

'Come on, girls,' she said. 'We've got to get round the Big House. Erin wants us all there for the morning meeting.'

Coffees were drained and fags hurriedly stubbed out as we made our way there. Walking into the house, we were hit by a solid wall of noise. The place was literally bursting at the seams with women and a crocodile of children were being led down the stairs to the basement playgroup by the playgroup workers.

'Got your hands full there, Michael,' I teased as the lovable, long-haired hippy rushed past me after the stream of babbling youngsters.

'Don't I know it, Jenny,' he shouted over the noise.

Inside, mattresses were piled up against the wall as usual, as every available floor surface on all levels was obviously being used as some poor woman's bed.

New faces mingled in with other long-termers and I was dismayed at how many women needed to fit in a house designed to hold just thirty-six.

Veterans and newcomers alike pitched in and finished off the morning clean while others fixed coffees and plates of biscuits. Despite the frantic air and bumping of bodies as people jostled past each other, there was a fantastic energy in the house, almost as if the more people that joined, the more the house seemed to come to life.

Snippets of conversation drifted my way.

'Will you come with me to my solicitor's meeting, later?' said one woman to another as they passed me on their way to the communal lounge. 'I daren't go on my own.'

'Course, love,' smiled her new friend.

Another group of women were already huddled together. 'Don't forget I'm babysitting for you tonight,' one said.

'As if I'd forget that,' her friend replied. 'I'll do tomorrow night for you.'

I ducked down, grinning, as a teabag came sailing over my head as two women mucked about in the hallway. It was chaos, all right, but it was fun, controlled chaos. I could see new friend-ships and support groups bursting into life in front of my eyes. Just like the one I had with Tracey and Jerry and all the other long-termers and I knew just how powerful and sustaining those friendships would come to be to these women.

But I also knew how all the social workers and suits at Hounslow Council would view these scenes.

One social worker had even been quoted in the *Guardian* as saying: 'It's like moving from one sort of hell to another.' But he or she, like so many others who seemed hell-bent on closing us down, were missing the point entirely. Unless they had lived in a violent relationship, they could never hope to understand what Chiswick, in all its glorious mayhem, was doing for us. It was *exactly* this busy, lively atmosphere that was healing us. It wasn't hell. It was heaven.

Who had time to dwell on the past or feel a moment's isolation or loneliness in a place like this?

Sometimes *not* being able to hear yourself think is a good thing.

Chiswick was still the only refuge in the country to have an open-door policy. Many of the similar refuges set up by groups and local authorities housed three or four families, maximum, and then rang around to try and rehouse any women that turned up.

But seeing as their phone numbers and locations were secret, apart from to police and Social Services, it seemed that Chiswick Women's Aid, the mothership, was still taking in women in crisis from the length and breadth of the country. Ours was the only phone number and address to be made public and the only, or so it seemed to me, to be run with any imagination or initiative. And the need was clearly there, as the huge amounts of women now pressed into the community room testified to.

'Hello, darling,' said JoJo, her voice sounding even more breathless than usual as she sat down next to me in the lounge.

'How many are here now?' I whispered.

'I reckon about 120 women and children,' she replied, shaking her head in astonishment. 'Some of the women here had been turned away by six refuges before they came to us.'

JoJo was as inexhaustible as Erin and Anne, a good thing too judging by the number of women now living here.

When the documentary had been filmed in the year I arrived, 1973, there were sixty-six women and children. Nearly three years on, that number had doubled. I could tell by my regular visits that the house had more structure now. There were better cooking facilities so women didn't need to leave bags of pasta in bin-bags by their beds like I'd had to, and there was even a proper cooking rota overseen by JoJo. Thanks to Erin's campaigning, the refuge now had a £2,000 a month grant from the Department of Health and Social Security and a £10,000 a year Urban Aid grant from Hounslow Council, not to mention the donations that flooded in every time she or anyone did interviews with the press.

Erin walked in and I felt a prickle of excitement ripple round the room. To all of us, myself included, Erin inspired great devotion. She was the only one prepared to put herself out and take on the suits to protect us.

At a time when society seemed so uncaring, her approach was worth its weight in gold. She inspired huge feeling, either for or against her. Her critics accused her of being bloody-minded for her refusal to comply with regulations. Support from the local neighbourhood had worn thin and apparently there were complaints from residents over the noise and overcrowding.

Other refuges criticized Chiswick for being the only refuge to have DHSS money and an Urban Aid grant. Social workers had run Chiswick Women's Refuge down in the newspapers, accusing the refuge of starting with the right intentions, then allowing its political imperative to take over. Anonymously, of course.

One women's aid centre run nearby had even said in a news-paper: 'Chiswick has too many women. There are other dangers too. The husbands know where to find their wives. We've seen frightened women who daren't stay there because of the men prowling outside.'

And underlining it all was Hounslow's determination to close us down, and repeated threats to take her to court.

'Hounslow Council is bearing the brunt of a national problem, being asked to sort out the rehousing problems of women from all over the country. Our ratepayers just won't stand for it,' a spokesman was quoted in the local paper as saying.

'If Erin Pizzey wants to go to jail, that is her prerogative. We'll keep a sharp eye on the situation.'

But love her or loathe her, you could never accuse Erin of backing down or sitting on the fence.

The more Erin was backed into a corner, the stronger she came out fighting. And now it seemed she was prepared to go to war for us.

'Morning, everyone,' she smiled. 'As you know, I have been repeatedly ordered by Hounslow Council to reduce numbers, but as I have always said, if a woman in crisis knocks on our door, then we can't turn her away.'

A murmur of support echoed round the room.

'Now Hounslow have withdrawn part of our Urban Aid grant unless we comply with regulations on overcrowding,' Erin went on. 'As a consequence, last week our electricity was nearly cut off, but we won a seven-day reprieve. Without the Urban Aid grant, how can we pay our bills? This just makes it more of a fire hazard.'

She sighed and drew in a deep breath, as if summoning up every ounce of her courage.

'Our lawyer has warned us it's going to get very serious if we continue to defy their orders but, if it comes to it, I will go to jail rather than comply with regulations, so now I face a custodial sentence.'

It appeared Hounslow had no intention of backing down from their determination to get Erin in front of magistrates for contempt. The knives were out for Erin and the refuge. The place that pledged to take any woman in crisis was now in crisis itself.

A stunned silence fell over the room as the news that Erin could end up behind bars for helping us filtered into our brains, and then a lone voice rang out.

'We're right behind you, Erin.'

Soon more and more voices entered into the fray.

'You backed us, now we'll back you,' cheered another.

Soon every woman in the room was fired up.

Erin received a tidal wave of support from every woman living in the hostel and seemed cheered by the warmth towards her, but I could see the strain that her constant fighting was having on her.

Her face was pale and her eyes puffy. But her rallying call was heard, and several of the women went straight off to make banners to hang out the windows of the Big House.

The strain was also showing on Anne, who now virtually lived at the refuge alongside Erin.

'You all right, Anne?' I asked once the morning meeting had dispersed.

I had never forgotten the high price she was prepared to pay for defending me from Lenny and I was forever in her debt.

'Fine, Jenny,' she smiled, wearily pushing back a lock of her red curly hair from her face. 'You know me. We fight on.'

'But how do you find the strength to keep going?' I asked.

If it were me and I had a nice, cosy home and a husband to return to, would I have the incentive to fight? I'm not so sure.

'We had a woman in last week, Jenny,' she went on in her soft voice. 'Her husband had pulled her trousers down and poured boiling water between her legs. He'd beaten her too, so she had six broken ribs and bruises and cuts all over. Her children were suffering too. We took her straight to hospital, but she's back with us now. How could I turn her away, Jenny? How?'

There was no answer to that and, suddenly and with enormous clarity, I saw the reason why she and Erin fought on. That woman was upstairs now, recovering. Had she gone to another refuge, she would have been forced to suffer the indignity of going to refuge after refuge, shunted around until she found someone prepared to take her on.

From that moment we took our campaigning to another level. I can't profess to know the politics of it or even where we went. I left that side of things to Erin. All I know is that if she asked us to appear outside a certain place with our placards, she could count on my support and I would be there, proudly standing right behind her. The human face of why she was fighting so hard.

My scars and bruises may have healed, but the damage done inside would take longer to fix. I owed it to Erin to make sure the world knew just how vital her work was.

Our placards expressed our sentiments: 'Us women need Erin Pizzey!', 'While Erin's free, so are we! Leave her alone!' and 'Women are battered each year. Who is going to help us support Erin Pizzey?'.

Back at the Big House, we hung giant painted sheets out the window. Our points were made crystal clear to every passing motorist or journalist who stopped to take pictures.

'Hands off Erin Pizzey' and 'Erin, we love you' they boldly proclaimed. Motorists tooted their horns in support and headlines were splashed across every national paper. Our battle was leading the news agenda. 'Fight for the wives in fear' proclaimed the *Daily Mirror*, the very paper I'd first read about the refuge in.

But, six months later, in April 1976, I had problems closer to home. Four months earlier, I'd registered on the council's housing list as I'd been living in the borough for two years, only for them to write back saying that no active consideration could be given to my request for another year, until December 1976. It was no surprise, really, but it didn't matter in any case, as I always had a roof over my head at Marlborough Road.

Or so I thought.

It was me who ripped open the letter, but Tracey and the two other women living at Marlborough Road had all received identical letters and were soon gathered in my bedroom.

'Notice to Quit' read the heading.

I read on, my heart thundering in my chest.

It seemed that Notting Hill Housing Trust, who owned the property and first leased it to Erin, now wanted it back for redevelopment.

'Well, we'll write to Hounslow Council,' blazed Tracey.

'They'll have to rehouse us.'

A feeling of doom settled in my tummy.

'They won't do that,' I replied flatly. 'They've already said I need to be on the housing list for another year.'

'Then what?' gasped Tracey.

'They'll send us back to where we came from,' I whispered.

The faces of each and every woman in the room paled. It wasn't as dangerous for me, as Lenny no longer lived in Hackney, but sending Tracey and the others back to the boroughs where their husbands still lived was like handing them a death sentence.

'I ain't going back there,' gasped Tracey. 'I can't, I just can't.'

Another of the women in the room was eight months pregnant. She clutched at her tummy and looked like she might pass out.

'They can't make us leave. They can't. If I go back home he'll find me.'

'Let's go to the Big House,' I suggested.

At the Big House, Anne got straight on the phone to Hounslow and also to the office of MP Barney Hayhoe, our local MP. But the news, when it came back a few days later, was just as we feared.

'Hounslow Council say that since Mrs Smith came to Chiswick Women's Aid from Hackney, under the London Boroughs Agreement, it has been confirmed by the London

Borough of Hackney that they will accept responsibility for Mrs Smith's rehabilitation.'

The letter was signed by the MP Barney Hayhoe's private secretary, dated 2 April 1976, and sent from the House of Commons. And, just like that, all my hopes of a new life came crashing back down around my ears.

I was to be sent back to Hackney, with all its ghosts and memories. I thought of lying in the street, heavily pregnant with Francesca, while Lenny beat me and of the time he kicked me down the road to Hackney Hospital while I was bleeding from a head wound.

I remembered, with a stabbing pain of betrayal in my chest, the Hackney priest who sent me back to my home to 'make my peace' and into the worst beating I'd ever received.

But, worst of all, I thought of the time I'd received electric shock treatment at the hospital when I'd run to them for help.

Hackney and my terrible old life had seemed a million miles away, but now I was to be sent packing back there. Away from the community and warmth of my friends, and back to an isolated bedsit and an uncertain future.

'What we going to do, Jen?' sighed Tracey, sitting down heavily on my bed back at Marlborough Road.

I thought of Erin, busy fighting her own battles with Hounslow Council on behalf of us all. What would she do? And then it came to me.

Fight. That's what.

'Right,' I said, sitting bolt upright. 'Let's get on the phone to the papers.'

'And say what?' she gasped.

'That we're not moving. We'll bloody barricade ourselves in if necessary. We will not be moved.'

Tracey's face lit up.

'You're on, gal, I'll tell the others.'

Fired up with a new determination, I suddenly felt stronger than ever before. If Hounslow Council wanted a fight, then that's exactly what they were going to get.

CHAPTER 15

Sweet Victory

It was 2 April and the eviction was due for 20 April. There was no time to lose. The house became a frantic hive of activity as we busily wrote and called every newspaper we could think of, and every person who might support us.

Ten days later, we had contacted everyone we thought could help. But I still felt like we were missing something.

'Who was the most important person in the country?' I asked myself.

The Prime Minister, of course.

'Look after the girls. I'm going round to the Big House to use their typewriter,' I yelled to Tracey as I dashed out the house.

'Who you writing to?' she asked.

'The Prime Minister,' I replied.

'Blimey, girl, you're aiming high!' she laughed.

'You know it!' I grinned.

Anne let me use the cubbyhole office and, sitting down, I typed out the Prime Minister's name.

It was 12 April 1976 and the Right Honourable James Callaghan had only been in the top spot for seven days. Well, he could bleedin' well start with dealing with my pressing problem.

Dear Mr Callaghan,

Please help us! We are four ex-battered wives with eleven children between us. We came to live in the Borough of Hounslow three years ago because of our violent husbands.

We are all registered on the housing list in Hounslow, but we are now told that we are to be put into bed and breakfast accommodation by Hounslow for a maximum of fourteen days, after which our respective boroughs will take over the establishment's bill. We have had no connection with our boroughs for the last three years, but Hounslow Council say that because we have been living in 'hostel accommodation', those three years must be disregarded.

Regardless of the circumstances which brought us to Chiswick, the fact remains that we have all been living in Hounslow for the last three years, and Hounslow seem determined to shun their responsibilities by referring us back to our own boroughs under a so-called 'gentleman's agreement'.

We feel that because of Hounslow's fight with Chiswick Women's Aid, they are conducting a personal vendetta against women who have passed through Chiswick Women's Aid and are therefore jeopardizing our children's lives. All we are asking for is to be able to lead a normal, healthy life with our children – surely we qualify for that? Our eviction date is 20th April.

Yours in desperation,
Jennifer Smith

It may have sounded complicated, but it was really quite simple. A 'gentleman's agreement' between boroughs would allow battered women to be returned to the very places from which they had run.

What was so gentlemanly about that?

The times and the law had to change. How long until the government sat up and took notice and started to protect battered wives?[14]

It took me hours to write that letter, but putting down my feelings on paper was cathartic and empowering. What's more, I believed every word I wrote. You couldn't shunt vulnerable women about at will, deliberately placing them back into harm's way.

Back at Marlborough Road, the other women had been busy too and a number of reporters had turned up. We stood shoulder to shoulder on the doorstep, our hands planted on our children's shoulders and posed, grim-faced, as the camera shutters clicked.

'What'll you do if the eviction order goes ahead?' asked a reporter from the *Evening Standard*.

'We'll barricade ourselves in if necessary,' said Tracey. 'We can't go back to where we came from, or what would be the point in leaving there in the first place? All we want is to lead a normal life with our children. Is that too much to ask?'

---

[14] In 1976, The Domestic Violence and Matrimonial Proceedings Act was introduced to protect women and children from domestic violence. The act gave new rights to those at risk of violence through Civil Protection Orders.

'We're not moving from here,' I added. 'Once we leave, we won't have a leg to stand on. Hounslow want us to go back to our own boroughs. This is the last thing we want. I left my home because I was so desperate to get away from my husband.'

We stayed that way on the doorstep, speaking to the press; four angry, defiant women and our eleven children, telling anyone who would listen about our plight.

Erin turned up to lend her support too.

'There is no way Hounslow are going to force these women back into the boroughs which they came from,' she told the press. 'They are established in Hounslow and they and their children cannot be disturbed any more.

'We have no other accommodation for these families and it would be a backward step to take them back into the hostel. They are human beings, not parcels.'

'Exactly,' I agreed. 'My daughter has been going to school in Chiswick. We pay rent here and we have made our lives here. We will fight to the end.'

The resulting publicity put more fire in our bellies.

'Battered wives fight for permanent home,' read the headline in the *Evening Standard* and 'Wives will fight eviction' reported the *Middlesex Chronicle*. Maybe we half hoped the press attention would make Hounslow back down but, speaking in the press, a spokesman said:

'Temporary hostel accommodation does not count as a permanent address. On 20th April, we will accept responsibility for them as homeless families under the agreement between London boroughs. We will be able to offer them some sort of bed and breakfast accommodation

for fourteen days but, after that, they must go back to their own boroughs.'

They weren't backing down. But then neither were we.

A seismic shift was occurring in Britain. Change wasn't just happening in Marlborough Road, Chiswick, but all over Britain that fateful April in 1976. It was out with the old and in with the new.

Carry On star Sid James collapsed and died on stage having suffered a fatal heart attack. Meanwhile, a man called Steve Jobs helped form the Apple Computer Company and a little-known band called the Sex Pistols blazed onto the music scene.

The office of our newly appointed Prime Minister also wrote back to me to say my letter was receiving attention. I showed it to the girls.

'But will it be in time?' said Tracey. 'We've only got seven days now.'

Putting my arm round her and the other women, we had a cuddle.

'We vowed to fight and fight on we will,' I said.

That afternoon we stockpiled tins of food and candles. If we were going to barricade ourselves in, we had to be prepared. That night we cooked a simple dinner and sat together in silence, all of us lost in our own personal nightmare.

No one dared voice our worst fears. What if we were all sent packing back to where we had run from?

Deep down, I felt a great sadness. Whatever else happened, it meant we would be split up and our home demolished to make way for more of the soulless flats that were springing up to cater for the new middle-class inhabitants of this area. Chiswick's streets were changing and its residents didn't want to look out of their windows and see hordes of campaigning battered wives. It was the end of an era.

No more seeing Tracey's cheeky face each morning, no more 'high tea' on the window ledge, no more Saturday night visits to the reggae club in Shepherd's Bush. And, crucially, no more moral support!

I pushed the dark thoughts out of my brain before they took hold. I wanted to confide my fears in Erin, but how could I burden her? She was fighting her own bitter battle for survival. The case against her had been set for last month (March 1976), but had been adjourned.

Talks had been held between her and Hounslow Council officials, but no agreement had been reached. She had now been summoned to appear at Acton Magistrates Court at the end of the month.

Each and every one of us had a battle on our hands. We had done all we could. Now we just had to sit and wait.

The day of the eviction dawned and with it a letter. I ripped it open.

'What's it say?' asked Tracey.

'It's from the bailiffs,' I gasped. 'The eviction date has been delayed by twenty-four hours.'

'Is that a good thing?' she asked.

'I've no idea,' I said, shaking my head. 'But it's another day with a roof over our heads.'

My nerves were in tatters as we called the newspapers and asked them to meet us outside the house.

As we waited, an extraordinary thing happened. Groups of women started to trickle down the road towards us. The trickle soon turned to a human tidal wave. A lump formed in my throat as, one by one, women from the Big House turned up to stand with us and show solidarity and support. Young and old mixed with middle-class and working-class, a defiant human barricade of hormones and happiness.

'Looks like they'll have a fight on their hands if they want to kick you lot out,' grinned Jerry, taking her place next to me.

Her Afro wig alone would take two bailiffs an hour to get through!

'Yeah,' added Sally. 'They'll have to get through us lot first.'

You couldn't have got a more mixed and motley crew. But we all had one thing in common. We weren't victims. We were survivors taking a stand.

And as I stared round this incredible group of pioneering women, I felt honoured to include myself amongst their number.

Soon there was a huge crowd of women standing side by side with us. There was Erin and Anne, alongside both long-termers and new faces. Erin may have been dragged down in her own battle, but on the day of the eviction she was there for us.

She had always said that the power was in the group. She was right.

'Whatever happens, Erin, thank you,' I said. 'For everything.'

Twenty-four hours later, the letterbox snapped open and we all jumped. But it wasn't the dreaded bailiffs. Instead, it was a letter addressed to us.

Holding my breath, I ripped it open and scanned the words on the page.

> *It has been agreed between this borough and the London Borough of Hackney that you will be accommodated in this area initially. Arrangements have been made for you to be nominated by London Borough of Hackney to a GLC property in west London. An offer will be made as soon as possible.*

The letter was signed by the Director of Housing for Hounslow Council. It turned out that Hounslow had referred our case to the Greater London Council, who had agreed to rehouse us away from the boroughs from which we had run.

'Victory,' I screamed, flinging myself into Tracey's out-stretched arms. 'It's a bloody victory.'

We'd done it! We'd actually done it.

Who knows if our campaigning and press attention forced Hounslow to refer us to the GLC and, in doing so, triggered a landmark case for battered wives? I like to think so.

Nowadays, victims of domestic violence are protected by law. Local authorities are required, under the Housing Act 1996, to accept as homeless, women who are fleeing violent homes. This may mean being placed in temporary accommodation and re-homed elsewhere, permanently if necessary. Women shouldn't have to be from the local area to be accepted as homeless and they may be housed away from their immediate area.

In 1976, we fought for that right to safety.

★

Erin had been there for us and so were we for her when she faced the music at Acton Magistrates Court.

Outside, press and court-workers had to pick their way through the sea of placard-wielding women.

'Don't jail Erin Pizzey,' we chanted.

Once inside, Tracey and I slid onto a bench in the public gallery, right in front of one of Erin's biggest supporters, Spike Milligan.

A hush fell over the court as Erin's defence claimed that Chiswick Women's Aid was not a common hostel but an Elizabethan coaching house and there were therefore no regulations as to the numbers who could live there. It was a tactic, of course, but Erin had to play whatever cards she could.

As the long-winded legal arguments wound on, I suddenly became aware of Tracey's shoulders shaking up and down. Her face was nearly purple, she was trying that hard not to laugh.

'That barrister looks like a parrot,' she whispered.

Sure enough, one of the legal team did resemble a parrot with his wig and hooked nose. That was it. Tracey and I were overcome with a serious fit of the giggles. It was too much. The relief of not being sent back to our boroughs, combined with the serious air in court, reduced us both to a giggling mess.

Fearing an explosive outburst, we got up and edged our way past a wide-eyed Spike Milligan.

'Sorry,' apologized Anne to the court from the public gallery. 'They are overcome with emotion.'

Soon enough, the court spilled out and Erin was enveloped by the hordes of clamouring press.

'Success,' grinned a jubilant Anne to me. 'We've won.'

But the relief was short-lived. Hounslow Council quickly lodged an appeal at the High Court. Erin's battle seemed set to run and run. But my own fight was over. It was time to leave, and I knew that would bring up some bittersweet emotions.

A few days later, I stood on the steps of the Big House, clutching my girls in my arms, and said my goodbyes to the women who had saved and then changed my life for ever. I stared at the kitchen where I'd cooked and shared so many meals, at the communal living room where I'd answered the phone to countless frightened women and, finally, the staircase where I'd made my frantic, scrambled escape from Lenny.

I'd arrived here a broken and battered victim. Three years on, Chiswick Women's Aid had put me back together again. Now I was a strong, confident woman capable of giving talks and writing to prime ministers. It had been the very worst and the very best of times.

'Well,' I grinned. 'All in all, it's been a fine old experience. Ta-ta.'

It was time to put a foot out and make my way in the world.

Ten weeks later, on 7 July 1976, and at the beginning of what was to be the hottest summer on record since 1772, I moved into my new home in Lambeth, south-west London. The tar was melting on the pavement and the thermometer hitting an astonishing thirty-two degrees for the fifteenth day on the trot as I lugged what few possessions we had over the threshold.

It was like an oven inside the little flat and, fanning myself, I threw open the kitchen windows that looked out over a grassy communal garden. It was filled with children playing in the sunshine.

'Mum, can I go outside and play, please?' piped up Francesca, now five.

'Yeah,' I replied. 'I don't see why not.'

I watched as she charged outside, shortly followed by 4-year-old Rebecca, running as fast as she could to keep up.

I smiled as I watched them vanish off in search of adventure and new friends. At last! This was what I had wanted for so long; a permanent home and safety and stability for my girls. Finally they had a shot at a normal childhood and a chance to put down roots.

So why did I feel so sad?

I stared forlornly around the flat. It wasn't much, but at least it was my own. Anne had kindly donated some bunk beds from the Big House for the girls, a grant from the Social had given me sufficient to put down some lino on the floor and buy some basic pots and pans and I had a little pre-war 1940s gas oven to cook on. After the way I'd lived for the past ten years, this was luxury!

The girls were enrolled in new schools and in a few days' time I was to start a cleaning job. It wouldn't pay much, but it would put food on the table.

No matter that the kitchen table was so cheap the legs bent when you looked at them. It was my kitchen table, my shot at a normal life.

But something was missing and, deep down, I knew just what – camaraderie, friendship and community. For the first time in years, I wasn't sharing my living space with dozens of other women.

Tracey wasn't in the next room any more. She was six miles away. The only person in my bedroom would be me. Suddenly I was filled with an aching loneliness.

Shaking myself, I started to unpack.

'That wasn't real life, Jenny,' I scolded myself. 'This is. And you can do this. You have to do this. Your fight is over.'

Just then the doorbell rang and a cheery voice called out.

'Hello, darling, only me.'

JoJo, the house mother from Chiswick stood on my doorstep clutching a tatty old ironing board.

'Thought you might like this. It's going spare. Gosh, it's hot out there. Have you time for a cuppa?'

I could have wept and grabbed her in a bear hug. Instead I smiled and lit the flame under the kettle. And in doing so, the realization spread through me like warm, sweet tea. *Of course.* I may have left Chiswick. But Chiswick would never leave me.

In the last week of August, the dry spell was broken and the rains began, washing away my past.

But not quite all of my past . . .

I waited until the girls were at school before picking up a pen and paper to write a long overdue letter.

'Dear Mam and Dad. Sorry I haven't been in touch for a while, but I'm safe . . .'

CHAPTER 16

Life After the Refuge

When I took the girls up to visit Mam and Dad back in Chesterfield, they greeted me as if I had seen them just the week before, not five years previously. There were no difficult questions, no recriminations for not having replied to their letters, and no guilt or anguish placed at my door. They simply opened their arms to me and embraced their long-lost daughter and her babies.

It was the first time I had seen Mam since I took Francesca up to see her when she was just six weeks old, right before Lenny's violence had exploded.

Five years on, and without saying a word, she held out her arms to me. That unconditional love was a shining example of what it means to be a parent and I loved them all the more for it.

The years rolled away when I saw Mam back home in her little kitchen where she belonged. She was still ill and heavily medicated, but when she spotted her granddaughters her eyes lit up like stars.

Her only question came later when we had a good meal in our tummies and the girls were safely tucked up in bed.

'You are safe now, aren't you, love?' she asked.

I nodded and I knew that was enough for her. No more was said. No more was needed.

After that we visited when we could and she wrote weekly, always sending the most beautifully wrapped parcels containing talcum powder, perfumed soaps and old-fashioned full-length underskirts, all wrapped round a crisp ten-pound note.

Tearing open the brown paper, the nostalgic fragrance of lavender was enough to whisk me back twenty years in time.

Those sweet-smelling, cherished parcels carried on arriving, even when Mam got ill with lung cancer, even when she was too weak to visit. I always said the women of my mother's generation were as tough as old boots.

When Mam died, aged sixty-two, in 1983 she'd been mopping the floor just hours before she took her last breath. She knew the end was near and was clearly in agony, but she resolutely refused to go into hospital.

Instead, she stayed in the place she loved more than anything. Her kitchen.

'This is my home and I'm stopping here,' she said.

And with one hand clinging to the draining board and the other tightly gripping the end of a wooden mop handle, she washed every inch of her kitchen floor.

Old habits die hard. When she had finished, she wrung out the mop and placed it back in the scullery.

'I'm going upstairs now, Tom, to lie down,' she said to my dad.

And that's where he found her a couple of hours later. Finally at peace, the voices in her head for ever quietened.

At her funeral, the vicar rambled on about what a good life she'd had and anger pulsed through me. What rubbish! To this day I don't understand why her life was glossed over in the way it was. I have never cried such fierce, angry tears, so hot they stung my cheeks.

I was devastated to think I'd never be able to tell her how much I loved her again, or go shopping with her and do all the silly mother–daughter things you take for granted. I never got the chance to really tell her how sorry I was for the anguish I must have caused her by running away, when I should have been caring for her, not adding to her problems.

I often wonder if our lives would have turned out differently had it not been for Mam's illness. Would I have run away to London, then fallen for Lenny? Who knows? But you can't turn back the hands of time. All you can do is keep moving onwards and upwards. I liked to think that's what I did after we moved to Lambeth.

A year after moving to my new flat, I met a fella and in April 1981 gave birth to a beautiful baby boy, Barry. On reflection, I got into that relationship too soon, but I put on a good front of forgetting my past and being the dutiful housewife.

The single biggest source of pride was seeing my kids happy and well fed. They may have been covered in dirt from playing outside all the time and permanently sporting a grazed knee, but

I made sure they always had smart shoes on their feet and a good home-cooked meal in their belly.

Mam's legacy lived on in my children. As long as they were happy, well-fed and respectful, then I reckoned I was doing her memory proud.

Despite Mam's illness, she had given me an idyllic childhood, and though my kids had had a bumpy start, I was determined to give them happy memories to cherish. I didn't want them to grow up remembering my screams for mercy. I wanted them to remember cheese on toast on their laps in front of their favourite telly programme, me waiting at the school gates and tucking them into bed at night. I wanted so desperately to replace the reverberations of fear and violence with routine and safety.

So that's what I did. Day after day. Month after month. Year after year. I was so caught up in caring for my three kids, in fact, that I didn't want to accept that my relationship was failing.

Women coming from a violent relationship need time before rushing into a new one. Sadly, when I'd left Chiswick, my self-esteem was still so low I thought I needed a man around to take care of me.

Barry's dad was a nice-enough guy, but the relationship wasn't right and after eleven years together we split up.

It was around this time that Chiswick came hurtling back into my life. Erin had been writing to me and I'd kept in touch with Anne too, so I knew that in 1981 Erin had stepped down from the running of the refuge, handing over the reins to Anne – but not before securing the future of the Big House.

Her long, drawn-out battle with Hounslow Council had rumbled on for years, with neither side prepared to back down.

Along the way, though, Erin had managed to attract the support of some very high-profile and influential men in the form of Lord Goodman and David Astor, proprietor of the *Observer*. They were to become powerful allies in her fight.

Together, they had formed a fundraising committee which many influential people, including actress Joanna Lumley, sat on.

With the committee's help, David Astor and Lord Goodman secured public funding from the GLC. The public money brought about a great many changes, including greater Health and Safety, a crackdown on numbers, accounts and staff salaries. It was a far cry from when I had first joined, but at least it secured the future of the refuge.

After stepping down, Erin moved to the Cayman Islands, where she wrote fiction.

But we were all reunited for a Cutting Edge documentary called *Sanctuary*, which was broadcast on Channel 4 in February 1991, twenty years on from the opening of the refuge.

'Twenty years ago, the first refuge in the world for battered wives opened in London, founded by Erin Pizzey. The Chiswick Refuge gave thousands of women a chance to begin a new life without violence. But where are the Chiswick women today?' read the promotional material to publicise the documentary.

Living a quiet life in Lambeth, London, that's where.

I threw open my life for the camera crew once again. For three months, they followed me about, filming me. It was a big step and I'll admit, at first I'd hesitated to expose my life to the cameras. Fifteen years had passed since I'd left Chiswick.

I'd just turned thirty when I moved into my new flat, now I was forty-five. In those years I'd moved on. No one on the estate I lived on even knew about my past life. But I knew in the end I'd do it. How could I not? As long as women were still being beaten, I had to help others. I owed that much to the refuge. Besides, I had nothing to be ashamed of. I'd be more ashamed if I didn't pass the word on that it's not OK to let people abuse you.

But I was still a bag of nerves when *Sanctuary* aired at 9 p.m. one Monday evening.

I needn't have worried.

What a different woman I was to the pale, thin victim shown sleeping on a mattress at the refuge all those years ago in *Scream Quietly or the Neighbours Will Hear*.

In the first ten years, Chiswick saw 12,000 women pass through its doors. I was proud to be one of them. This time I spoke with confidence about my time at the Big House.

'It was the best time of my life,' I told the cameras. 'I could feel like a woman again, appreciate my children and get my self-respect back. Without Chiswick I wouldn't have survived. We were like pioneers for battered wives, treading on virgin grounds, not only for ourselves but for battered wives of the future.'

Never one to do things by halves, I even shared my recent relationship breakdown with Barry's father on camera.

'I jumped at the first relationship,' I said shakily. 'That relationship tried to contain me. I didn't have the capability of thinking for myself. A man was there to do it for me.

'Barry's dad was supportive and kind, but I have no intention of getting together with another man who can feel king of my castle. I should never have picked up on the first relationship after coming out of a violent one. Today I have an inner peace.'

In the documentary Erin also spoke glowingly of her time at the helm.

'The pace of life in the Cayman Islands helped me to recover from the trauma of Chiswick,' she said. 'I miss it. I miss the mothers, but I don't miss the nightmare, the wounds, the bleeding, the terrible state of the children, but innovators need to move on.'

The morning after the documentary aired, I nervously pushed open my front door and headed to the shops. I'd laid my whole life bare for the country to see. But on the way home, an amazing thing happened. A woman I recognised who lived locally approached me and gripped my arm.

'I didn't know you'd been battered, Jen,' she whispered.

Before I could answer, she was crying, tears streaming down her face.

'I've been battered for years,' she admitted. 'I thought you were so brave to speak out, good on ya.'

I stared at her, stunned. This woman lived on my doorstep and was being beaten, and I never knew.

I was filled with a helpless rage.

'You don't have to live like that, darling,' I urged. 'There are places you can go. Go to the police station, they have the numbers you need. Please do it. There is life after.'

She stared hard at me.

'All right, Jen, I'll think about it, thanks.'

My head was still swimming a few days later when a letter dropped on my mat.

To my amazement it was from Sally, the lovely lady I'd given a makeover to when I was living at Marlborough Road.

'It was really great seeing you on television, Jenny,' she wrote. 'I don't know if you remember me, but you made me start to stand up for myself. I'm remarried now with a new baby.

'I don't think you could forget me. I used to come round to your flat and you'd feed me and when I was going on my first date you dolled me up. It's so hard to believe it's fifteen years since I last saw you. I'll never forget what you did for me.'

Now it was my turn to cry.

Her letter was a potent reminder that recovery and freedom from the past is possible. Change is possible. How I prayed that in time my neighbour would find that peace too.

My only sadness was that Mam wasn't alive to see me in the documentary. But Dad was. I'd only really got to know him properly after the death of my mother and, when I visited him, we talked, really talked, about the past.

He even showed me all the newspaper cuttings he kept from when I'd run away and, with a jolt, I realised what I'd put him and Mam through.

'I had to pay for you when you were at that Approved Home you know, you little bugger,' he'd laughed.

But I knew he was proud of what I achieved. He told me so soon after *Sanctuary* came out.

'You did well, love,' he said on the phone from Chesterfield. 'We're all dead proud of you.'

'I love you, Dad,' I told him, before I hung up.

'Gaah, get away,' he scoffed in his usual gruff voice. But before he hung up, he shocked me.

'Aye, I love you too.'

It was the first time he'd said it.

To celebrate the documentary and her birthday, Erin threw a party at the posh London hotel The Savoy and invited me. I took Barry and I felt so proud to have him on my arm.

It was quite the night and made a change from housework, especially when I was introduced to Joanna Lumley, a long-time supporter of Erin and Chiswick Women's Aid.

'You're even more beautiful in person than on the telly,' I blurted out before I had a chance to stop myself.

Barry groaned next to me.

Joanna laughed. 'Thanks,' she grinned.

We talked and I told her my story.

She seemed genuinely moved by the time I'd finished.

'You're a very brave lady,' she said in that wonderful husky voice.

A woman from a glossy magazine came over and said: 'Do you know you look like Meryl Streep?' she said.

'I wish I had her money,' I quipped back.

By the time I left the party, my head was spinning.

'What about that, Jenny,' I laughed to myself as I tucked up in bed.

As I drifted off, I reflected on my journey, from growing up in a small miners' village to a star-studded party at The Savoy, by way of violence, mental illness, breakdowns and murder attempts. Quite a life!

But that life wasn't over yet, as I was soon to discover. The story may be over, but the journey had only just begun.

After *Sanctuary*, I felt at a loss. My beloved father died two years after the documentary came out, aged seventy-seven, in 1993. I'm grateful that he lived to see me happy and settled.

I returned to Chesterfield for his funeral and a little piece of my heart died with that gentle, clever, funny man.

The village of my childhood has changed beyond recognition. The fields have been built over, the bluebell woods ripped up and the little hillbilly shop that sold cigarettes destroyed to make way for modern housing.

The miners' estates that once looked so smart and enticing now looked tatty and slightly sad. The pits where my father and his generation risked their lives daily were all closed, a way of life gone for ever.

Mining was now a long-vanished world.

At his funeral it felt like not just the end of a human life, but the end of an era.

'I love you, Dad,' I whispered as his coffin was lowered underground.

As the brave old miner took his final journey into the earth, a tear slid down my cheek. That courageous man had fought for most of his life – in the war, in the pits and in his toughest battle ever, against his wife's illness. But he had left behind an incredible legacy. I saw his stubborn chin and his razor-sharp brain in my kids and I knew he had much to be proud of.

What did I have to be proud of? I still couldn't answer that question. The kids were fast growing up: Francesca was twenty-two, Rebecca twenty-one and Barry twelve. My babies were all grown up and had ventured out into the big wide world to make lives of their own. But what of me? I couldn't just sit around dwelling on the past.

Once again, the words of all the great women who have featured in my life drifted into my head.

You have so much to give.

Try as I might, I just couldn't shake the belief that I was wasting my talents. I was fifty years old, but I knew it wasn't too late to make something of my life.

So I sat and thought long and hard about all the things I wished I could change.

It always came back to children and their safety. My biggest regret was my girls' start in life. Knowing they witnessed their father's violence and spent three years in a refuge ate away inside me. I should have been able to give them safety and structure, but back then I hadn't been able to. Deep down, I felt sure that Francesca and Rebecca remembered the violence. It may have been filed away within their subconscious, but I feared it was there.

It was then I realised that I might never be able to erase my guilt entirely, but I could help to improve the childhood of other vulnerable kids. Childhood is so precious and every kid deserves a safe place to live.

With that in mind, in 1997, I applied to become a foster carer with an amazing agency called TACT, the UK's largest Fostering and Adoption charity.

I was brutally honest with them about all that I had experienced in my life and they seemed to think that my past might help qualify me to help kids.

And so, after a year's training, I began fostering and finally

– at the age of fifty-one – a truly amazing and thrilling thing happened.

My life began! Fostering wasn't a job to me, it became my vocation. It made sense of everything. With Rebecca as my back-up carer, I began.

Waiting for my first placement was so nerve-wracking, but for the first time in years I felt alive. The call finally came at 1 a.m. in the morning.

'Jenny,' said my link worker. 'Can you collect three little boys from a police station?'

My heart pounding, I called a cab and packed a flask of tea and a warm rug. Rebecca and Barry stayed behind and rallied round to get things ready.

As the neon-lit streets flashed past, I wondered what state the boys would be in. But when I walked into the police station, nothing could have prepared me for the pitiful sight that greeted me.

You would think after all I had witnessed at the refuge, I would be immune somehow to the sight of children's suffering, but something about these three little boys took my breath away.

They were four, three and nineteen months old, but they were nothing but skin and bones, just huge, terrified eyes staring out from dirty, traumatized faces.

'Oh my darlings,' I cried out. 'Let's get you home, shall we?'

'The parents were drug addicts,' explained a police officer, taking me to one side. 'They will need a lot of care,' she warned.

Their clothes hung off them in rags and the stench from their skin told me it had probably been years since they'd had a decent wash, if ever.

I shook my head in despair. How could a human being treat three such lovely little boys like this?

Back at home, Rebecca and I gently bathed them, then fed them Weetabix and warm milk. We got them dressed in whatever clothes we could find and I improvised a nappy for the youngest boy out of a hand towel and a carrier bag.

Three sets of eyes continued to stare out at us, confused and frightened. They didn't utter a word and I quickly realised they were traumatized. Like the children of Chiswick, whatever sights they'd seen would stay with them for ever.

Eventually I noticed the eldest boy's gaze settle on a plant in a pretty blue and white pot.

'What a luverly ting to 'ave in yer 'ouse,' he whispered in a thick Irish accent. He'd never even seen a pot plant! My heart broke all over again.

Over the following weeks, my house came alive as the boys came back to life. To begin with they were wild, running round the shops, hanging on to everything in sight. Bedtimes were the worst. The darkness seemed to bring out their fears.

I spent hours sitting by their bedsides, stroking their heads.

'There are monsters under the bed,' they howled.

'There are no monsters under my bed,' I insisted. 'Because monsters can't live in MY house.'

Slowly but surely, I won them over. It took a long time, but through love, routine and security – not to mention countless bowls of beef soup and dumplings – the boys came to trust me and feel safe (see the back of this book for the recipe). I, more than anyone, knew what a wonderful feeling safety was and seeing their smiles made me feel euphoric.

The rewards of fostering were unimaginable. I knew I was helping, but I was also fulfilling a need inside myself, the need to turn all the trauma of the past into something positive.

It may sound clichéd, but love, patience and understanding are all you need to be a good foster carer. Money and a big house don't make a jot of difference.

By the time the boys left me after two years, to be adopted by a wonderful couple, they were well on their way to happiness and stability. What more could I have wished for?

They were just the beginning. I was blessed to help, and in turn have my life enriched by so many children, many of whom left an indelible mark on my heart. From the children of addicts to asylum seekers, so many vulnerable children called my flat home for a while. I never questioned them on their past or put them under any pressure to talk. I simply gave them the greatest gifts of all, safety and love.

Vitally, I never judged these children and their troubled behaviour either. How could I? Especially after all the things I did when I was a young girl.

Fostering brought such emotionally rich rewards. In 2002, I was asked by TACT if I could take a 14-year-old asylum seeker from Kosovo. The boy's name was Fisnik and he had run from his home and travelled in the back of a lorry for four days. My heart went out to him. I had been his age, if not younger, when I'd travelled for days in the backs of lorries, so I knew that he would be scared, tired and hungry.

That night he slept while I sat up all night at the kitchen table. It takes a teenage runaway to know a teenage runaway and I wanted to talk to him if he decided to do a moonlit flit.

Gradually, he came to trust me. I learnt that in his war-torn country he had only had four years of schooling. Soon a bond sprang up between us and I enrolled him at school. Fisnik went from strength to strength, learning to speak English, getting made head boy, and even graduating with such good grades that he secured a place at university studying Accountancy and Finance. Not only that, but he also had a voice in parliament, speaking up for children in care. Not bad for a boy who turned up in the back of a lorry, unable to speak a single word of English. He no longer lives with me but I consider him one of my biggest success stories.

By the time I retired from fostering in 2010, after thirteen years, I must have cared for seventeen kids and, in turn, conquered all my own demons. I also received two accolades, one for ten years' service and one for Exceptional Foster Carer.

The rewards were endless. I saw countless kids in the state I was in, vulnerable and scared witless and, through nurturing love, I sent them on their way a bit happier and a whole lot safer.

Fostering made sense of everything. I had so much to give and it gave me the opportunity to kick-start my life and heal the wounds of my own past. I don't know any other job that could bring such rewards.

I thought life would be quieter after I retired. Wrong! My kids and grandkids keep me busier than ever.

Francesca is forty-three. She has two beautiful children, Marcus and Susan, who I see all the time. She recently graduated with a degree in Criminology. Could there be a prouder mum on the planet?

Rebecca is forty-two and doing just as well. She emigrated to New Zealand with her lovely Maori husband, Gary, and together they have Christina, Charlotte and Louis. Christina even has a beautiful son called David which means I'm a – gulp – great-grandmother. Rebecca's carried on the good work of fostering and I've had the privilege of travelling to New Zealand four times and seen the difference she's making to all the children in her care, both fostered and her own. She's doing an excellent job and uses all the training she's had from TACT as my back-up carer.

My son Barry, thirty-three, is another blessing. He is a very loving and thoughtful man who is married to a lovely Zambian lady called Jane and, together, they have two beautiful children called Sarah and Louise. I have seven wonderful grandchildren and a great-grandchild.

Today I still feel I failed my children on some level but despite this, they fill me with enormous love and pride, as do all my grandchildren.

So what of the other people who have had such a marked impression on my life?

Sadly, my handsome brothers, Michael and Philip, have passed away, but Howard is still living in Chesterfield. He's my rock and I visit him as often as I can. I know he and all my brothers were just as profoundly affected by Mam's illness.

Also, sadly, my great friend Anne Ashby passed away in January 2005. I went to her funeral and wept tears for the woman whose steely resolve saved my life. She left Chiswick in 1984, but continued to work for women's rights, first as patron of Westminster Women's Aid and then with London Emergency Housing Association. Her work meant she was honoured by the Women of the Year organization.

Erin is alive and living in Greater London where she writes books and articles. I will never forget her tireless work, energy and total dedication in setting up and running Chiswick Women's Aid. It was she who first recognised the huge problem that the rest of society was ignoring and she who did something practical about it by setting up the refuge. She gave me safety first but then confidence, self-esteem and a voice. For that I will forever be truly grateful.

Lovely, 'darling' JoJo has now passed away. I still have her ironing board. She was a true friend and a loyal and warm lady to her core.

As for Lenny? To this day I don't know if he's dead or alive or where he is. The girls and I haven't seen him since the day he stepped on that plane. I just pray he got the help he so desperately needed.

So here I am, aged sixty-eight, still as rough as a bear's arse. I may not have the perm or the bell-bottom flares of my campaigning days, but the fighting instinct remains. Though, admittedly, these days I prefer a quieter life, staying in baking cakes with my grandkids.

That should be enough, except then something remarkable happened. I was in my local supermarket last year when who should I bump into but none other than the beautiful Joanna Lumley. Even more remarkably, she remembered me from Erin's party.

'You should write a book,' she smiled.

'If I do, Joanna, I'll remember you in my credits,' I replied cheekily.

Her words stuck with me, and today that's exactly what I've done. I hope you've enjoyed reading it as much as I've enjoyed writing it. I wrote it because I wanted to put a spotlight on how battered wives were treated in the 1970s and how, thanks to one incredible house, these women were finally given a chance.

It was a dynamic, dangerous, experimental, crazy yet wonderful time in history and I feel proud to have played my small part in it.

When I joined Chiswick in 1973, it was the first women's refuge in the world. In 2012, at the last estimate, there were 1,000 refuge houses in England, providing at least 4,200 separate family spaces in total. On average, 20,000 women reside in refuges each year. (Source: Women's Aid.)

In 1993 the organisation changed its name to Refuge, to reflect its growing national status. The change in name also marked a shift in the organisation's ethos and practice, as it sought to define domestic violence as a product of wider social inequality between men and women. In 2014, there are many charities working tirelessly to end domestic violence against women and children. Now every woman is protected by law and has the right to freedom and safety.

Hackney Council, the borough from which I fled all those years ago, now even has a dedicated page on its website about what to do if you are a victim, your rights and where you can go, along with a free phone number offering non-judgemental advice. There's a button you can press quickly which will allow you to exit the pages and take you to the weather pages, presumably in case the violent partner walks in the room.

All a far cry from the days where I was simply offered pills. It would be inconceivable to send an abuse victim for electric shock therapy in 2014. Yet this happened to me just forty-four years ago in 1970. This is recent history in Britain – our shared history – and yet so few people realise what life was like for battered wives as we were branded back then.

But, despite this and the whole raft of legislation that now protect women and children from violence, one tragic fact remains the same as it was back when I was being abused in the 1970s. Women are *still* on the receiving end of horrific violence.

Everything has changed in attitudes towards domestic violence and yet nothing about the crime itself has changed. We fought so hard and yet women are still being beaten.

In fact, from what I can tell, violence towards women has escalated. An astonishing two women are killed *each week* in England and Wales, by a current or former partner. (Source: Homicide Statistics, 1998–2012.) That's every week!

UK police receive a domestic assistance call every single minute in the UK (Source: Stanko, 2000; Home Office, 2002) and in any one year there are thirteen million separate incidents of physical violence or threats of violence against women from partners or former partners. (Source: Women's Aid.) Added to which, an estimated thirty women attempt suicide every day to escape domestic violence. (Source: Walby, 2004.)

Disgusting, heartbreaking and chilling . . .

Can you imagine? Beaten, stabbed or kicked to death. Those women aren't simply statistics. They have names and heartbroken parents, sisters, brothers, friends and children who will have to live with the knowledge that Daddy killed Mummy for the rest of their lives.

Please don't make the mistake that this is an issue that affects just working-class women. Women from across the board are beaten, from lawyers and judges to doctors and cleaners and labourers. Domestic violence cuts across the classes and doesn't discriminate.

Why can't we stamp violence out once and for all? You can't seem to pick up a newspaper without reading about a criminal trial with domestic violence at its core.

I couldn't say why, but I do know this: the legal system has got it wrong and, until they get it right, it will go on. The hand-wringing has to stop. I wish the powers-that-be would get a backbone and come down *hard* on the perpetrators.

What do I have to do to emphasize how I feel about domestic violence? I still have two scars on my back from where I was burnt and bitten, but ask any domestic violence victim and they will agree it's the mental scars and guilt that lingers long in the memory. Why me, what did I do to deserve it?

Recently I was lucky enough to be allowed briefly into the offices of a women's refuge in the north of England and the experience and memory will stay with me for the rest of my life.

Where once there was chaos and noise, today there is calm, order and a feeling of safety. Kind, softly spoken women bustled about making cups of tea and offering advice. There were no bare floorboards or mattresses covering every available floor space. No women dropping off bags of jumble or husbands hanging about outside.

There was carpet on the floor and toys for the children. Each woman had a room, somewhere to shut herself away from the rest of the world and seek sanctuary, or if they wanted to be sociable, a common room with comfy chairs, a kettle and a biscuit tin. But, more importantly, one aspect remained exactly the same as in my day, beating firmly at the heart of the refuge, and that something is pure magic.

The women staying there had found their safe place and the violence had stopped. Forty years ago, I was blessed to have found my safe place.

It saved my life.

Jenny's Recipe for Soup from the Soul

My three foster boys loved this soup. Bet you know some little ones who will love it just as much. To make, simply fry up some carrot and onion in a big pot. Then add some good-quality chunks of beef on the bone. Next, add stock. I find packet chicken noodle soup makes a tasty stock. Add cubes of pumpkin, yam, green bananas, potato, pimento, a pinch of salt, thyme and a little Scotch bonnet chilli to give it a kick, then let it simmer over a low heat until all the vegetables are cooked and the meat falls off the bone. Serve piping hot with some dumplings on top.

These dumplings are Jamaican, not English, so make them with just plain flour, water and a pinch of salt.

The Children of Chiswick by Jenny's Daughter, Francesca Smith

Looking back, I recall the familiarity of certain faces of those who showed me kindness in Chiswick, particularly Anne Ashby and the nursery workers. I recall my mother and Tracey always laughing – an infectious laughter that lifted an underlying mood that I didn't understand.

My mother's memories of Chiswick are just that, hers, but I understand a lot of her experiences were somehow shared through sensing them as only children do. Watching *Scream Quietly or the Neighbours Will Hear* in the present day, I noticed the abysmal surroundings the women preferred over the homes they fled but, as a child, I found it all quite normal.

I found watching the documentary quite distressing; it stirred up a range of emotions about my childhood that I had long ago come to terms with. I know Mum did her utmost to protect us and shield us from harm. We were always immaculately washed, bathed and dressed as children and we always felt love. In return,

I have always loved and protected her. I do hope the other children came out of Chiswick as relatively unscathed as I feel I did. I was very young, but I do sometimes wonder how the older ones fared in life.

My mother spoke very little of my father growing up and simply described him as a handsome, very well-dressed man who loved her and us after all's said and done. I am not so sure of the latter, but who knows? In the few discussions we did have later in life, I understood my father was a victim of an unfamiliar English way of life and his treatment by the police and authorities. This 'understanding', rather than the simple label of 'wife-beater', later propelled me to attempt to search for my father at great length, but without success. I am left with one picture to wonder at, as far as my real father is concerned.

My mother has always been my backbone and a great source of strength and encouragement and for her I am very thankful. Through the refuge and my mother I was taught about survival, courage and strength. I wouldn't swap my mother for anything. I have never once in my life felt unloved, neglected, gone unwashed or gone hungry and, to this day, I have the utmost respect for my remarkable mother.

At secondary school I was labelled educationally subnormal by the head teacher and I dropped out of school during exams because of the impression it left on me, fearing I would be incapable.

I recall sitting one or two exams and to this day I do not know the results. I later went to work in the NHS. As I set about my working life I began to be suspicious of this definition of me. I learnt names and methods of complex medical work and I was exceptional at my job and proud of my new-found skills. An opportunity arose to train as an investigator and, with my father in mind, I worked in this field for many years. I used these qualifications as a springboard to gain entrance into university to study criminality, the law and society even achieving an additional distinction for outstanding achievement. I am immensely proud to be continuing my studies today in the form of an MSc. I love to learn and feel the journey of education never really stops. Importantly I feel I have dispelled the myth and stigma of being labelled and treated as educationally subnormal through my achievements in further education.

Memories from Anne Ashby's Son, Mark

I always think of Jenny with great affection. In the early days of Chiswick she used to look after my brother, sister and I before my mum Anne came back from a day at the refuge. I remember they had a great many laughs and they remained good friends until the day Mum died.

I remember when Lenny, Jenny's husband, broke into the refuge and all pandemonium broke out. He kicked my dad John in the balls and poor Dad was left black and blue. It was a very intense time.

I remember going up to Jenny's flat round the corner from the refuge. She was into reggae music and West Indian food and had, it seemed, a great love of life.

Jenny went on the European tour with Erin. Anne stayed in London and continued the day-to-day work, which was groundbreaking in its way, and spread the news of what they were doing at the refuge. In return, many people from different countries came to the refuge and took away their best practice, which included having the women very much involved in the running of the place, daily group meetings where any issues could be brought up, and also the inclusion of male workers in the staff.

It was, in retrospect, a very therapeutic model. I know Jenny took a lot away from her experience there, her self-esteem being built up and hope reinstalled in her. It was a dynamic and edgy period with a lot of pain but also happiness. It was a sanctuary, albeit a slightly grubby one, a community of people whose main objective was to help others help themselves.

I remember the drama of the place, families at the end of their tether, explosions of grief and fear, and the terrible damage that had been done both psychologically and physically to these families. To see some of the disturbed children was heartbreaking.

Looking back, we were all affected by those times: staff, family members, visitors to the refuge and, of course, the mothers and children.

In my role as a counsellor I am particularly interested in working with young people and the now adult children that have passed through refuges, because I feel they experienced a unique situation that hasn't been addressed. The levels of trauma and stress these young people go through often make a healthy transition into adulthood more than difficult.

A Memory of Chiswick Women's Aid

By Michael Whyte – director of groundbreaking documentary *Scream Quietly or the Neighbours Will Hear.*

In 1973 I heard an interview with Erin Pizzey on the BBC's one o'clock news and rang her up to see if she might be interested in having a documentary made about the work she and others were doing at Chiswick Women's Aid. She was very polite on the phone and invited me to come and visit.

I had recently graduated from the Royal College of Art and was doing the usual rounds of television and film companies seeking employment and pitching ideas. Something about the interview stayed with me; I didn't have any first-hand experience of domestic violence apart from a few stories about the parents of a kid I knew down the street whilst I was growing up, but these were made comic and laughed off; so I made the call.

The refuge was a small terraced house in Belmont Terrace,

Chiswick, probably due for demolition, but given over to Erin as an interim refuge for battered wives. It was shabby on the outside and just as shabby inside. On my first visit it seemed empty, rather calm and uneventful, not quite what I had expected from the radio interview. Erin, a kind but formidable woman, introduced me to a couple of the women who were staying there and they joined us to discuss their experiences. Erin led or guided the conversation, I guess because she had more confidence in these kinds of meetings. During this time the phone rang, the caller was a husband whose wife had taken shelter; the call was taken calmly with a polite refusal to allow him to speak to his wife, at her request, despite some threats. Apart from that one incident, the evening was not dissimilar to spending time in a squat with all the makeshift arrangements and communal living.

I remember leaving and wondering whether there would be enough material to make a film, and how to make it. Nothing dramatic seemed to be going on in the house other than people making do and, short of dramatizing the violence suffered by these women, it could easily end up as a series of interviews, not much of an improvement on the radio interviews. Why make a film?

Over the next few weeks I would visit the refuge and stay each time for a few hours, spending my time watching, observing and asking questions, also answering any question that the women put to me. I tried to balance the length of my stay so as not to overstay my welcome and at the same time get a sense of the day-to-day living in the house. I was very privileged; the refuge then had a policy of no men in the house, but Erin had made an exception for me. Also, I hadn't realised at the time that all the major TV companies had been pressing Erin to allow them access to the refuge in order to make a film.

For some reason, and only Erin knows the answer to this, Erin trusted me to make the documentary. I didn't offer her editorial control. I didn't even discuss the content with her. I couldn't even promise her that the film would get made, as I hadn't secured any funding and hadn't approached ITV or the BBC with any proposals.

By the time I secured funding, independently financed with the help of Roger Hacker, the film's producer, the refuge had moved from the small terraced house in Belmont Terrace to a large sprawling house on several floors and a large back garden on Chiswick High Road.

The atmosphere in the house was markedly different from the first small refuge for several reasons. Due to Erin's tenacity, commitment and astute handling of the press, more and more people became aware of domestic violence and this in turn led to more and more women seeking refuge. As the only refuge in Britain, it wasn't surprising that the refuge was overflowing with women and their children, escaping from the abuse they had suffered for many years.

I don't think Erin ever turned a woman away. The atmosphere was electric, chaotic, noisy and, at the same time, welcoming. The stairs and landings were full of children playing games, squabbling and reading as women negotiated up and down the stairs, hands full of shopping or small babies, sometimes both, going to and from the communal kitchen or to the room where they had laid out the meagre belongings they had managed to bring with them.

In some of the rooms there would be a small group talking amongst themselves, often just gossip or idle chatter, sometimes offering support and comfort to a newly arrived and distressed woman, helping her to settle in and taking care of her children. In the communal kitchen, which was the hub of the house, endless cups of tea and cigarettes were consumed, young mothers would breastfeed babies, mothers would prepare meals for their children, children would be helping out or demanding food, children would be getting on their mother's nerves, children would be in their own space trying to make sense of the world around them and, in the midst of all this, Erin, solid, calm, supporting without patronising and encouraging the women to trust in themselves, to make decisions, to go to Social Services, giving them all the help they needed and delegating tasks amongst the staff as well as encouraging the women themselves to take control of their lives.

In this she was aided and abetted by Anne Ashby. Both Erin and Anne brought their own family life into the refuge, often their children would be helping out and participating in whatever needed doing. It was a remarkable set-up, controlled chaos, phones ringing, new arrivals and departures, children of all ages all over the house, a lack of privacy, not too bad when the weather was fine and the possibility of a quiet spot in the garden, but when it rained the house became overcrowded to such an extent that probably today it would have been closed down due to Health and Safety regulations.

Despite all of this, I didn't witness any huge arguments, any violence, bitterness or resentment; quite the opposite – I was welcomed warmly by the women and made to feel part of the household. Of course there were moments of tension between the women and moments when fights broke out amongst the children, how could there not? If you can imagine what was going on in their lives, leaving a violent partnership, but often one that was financially secure or at least stable, to arrive at this chaotic, almost anarchic refuge, overcrowded, noisy and without a lot of creature comforts, a refuge yes, but no space to call your own, a bed which was often a mattress laid down on a floor, in an overcrowded room, little space for whatever belongings brought with you and the possibility that your children would be in another room equally full of mattresses and makeshift beds. This wasn't a policy but a necessity; Erin was constantly battling for funds from councils and government to keep up with the increasing demands being put on the refuge.

When I did start filming, I had a crew of three, Nic Knowland the cinematographer, Dave Johns the sound recordist and Penny Eyles, production assistant. They were all very experienced and very supportive of me despite the fact that this was my first professional film. They settled into the house in an unobtrusive way, almost as though they were living there, which in a way we were. We spent a week in total filming from early morning to late in the evening and on one occasion Nic and I came back very late at night to film the sequence of the children sprawled across the mattresses deep in sleep.

At no time did Erin interfere, except to reassure the women, some of whom were nervous of being filmed; those who didn't want to appear we respected their wishes. Erin had made a decision to allow me to make the film and with that trust let me get on with it. In fact, she didn't see the film until I had more or less completed the final cut of the film. She turned up with several of the women from the refuge to view the film for the first time. This was an anxious moment for me, having made all the editorial decisions, along with Tim Lewis, the editor, and being not sure how they would react.

I remember trying to gauge their reaction whilst they were watching the film without much success. Finally, when the lights went up, Erin and the women were very positive and pleased with the result, thank goodness. I'm not sure how I would have reacted if they hadn't been.

Jeremy Isaacs at Thames Television bought the film and it was transmitted on the ITV network in 1974. Isaacs was one of a disappearing breed of television producers who had a vision and commitment to individual and committed film-making.

Over the following eight years I made quite a few documentaries for Thames Television and he was always there to fight any battles I faced over content or censorship. The only battle he had to fight for *Scream Quietly or the Neighbours Will Hear* was to support me in my decision to allow the women to speak for themselves; there was no commentary in the film other than the voices of Erin and the women. The convention at the time was for an 'authoritative voice', usually male, to lead the viewer through the film. The proceeds and profits from the sale of the film went to Chiswick Women's Aid.

Acknowledgements

With thanks to Mark Ashby for information on Chiswick Women's Aid.

Thanks to Channel 4 and Laurie Wiseman of Laurie Wiseman Productions/Primal Pictures, producer on Cutting Edge documentary *Sanctuary* (1991).

To Michael Whyte, director of *Scream Quietly or the Neighbours Will Hear* (1974).

To Gregg Noades for his recollections of growing up in Hackney during the 1970s.

With thanks to Kate Williams for help in research.

Resources

Refuge runs the Freephone 24 Hour National Domestic Violence Helpline in partnership with Women's Aid, 0808 2000 247. For further information about Refuge please visit: www.refuge.org.uk

TACT – Fostering charity: 0808 115 3542

ChildLine – Children's helpline: 0800 1111

NSPCC – National Society Prevention of Cruelty to Children: 0808 800 5000

Shelter – Housing and Homeless charity: 0808 800 4444

MIND – National Association for Mental Health: 0300 123 3393